LANGUAGE!®

The Comprehensive Literacy Curriculum

Jane Fell Greene, Ed.D.

SOPRIS WEST EDUCATIONAL SERVICES
A CAMBIUM LEARNING COMPANY

BOSTON, MA • NEW YORK, NY • LONGMONT, CO

Editorial Director: Nancy Chapel Eberhardt
Word and Phrase Selection: Judy Fell Woods
English Learners: Jennifer Wells Greene
Lesson Development: Sheryl Ferlito, Donna Lutz,
Isabel Wesley, Straightline Editorial Development, Inc.
Text Selection: Sara Buckerfield
LANGUAGE! eReader is a customized version of the
CAST eReader for Windows® (3.0). CAST eReader
©1995-2003, CAST, Inc. and its licensors. All rights reserved.

ISBN 1-59318-375-5

Printed in the United States of America

Published and distributed by

Sopris West™
EDUCATIONAL SERVICES

A Cambium Learning Company

4093 Specialty Place • Longmont, CO 80504 • (303) 651-2829
www.sopriswest.com

115991/2-07

*"For me, dancing is like life, the lessons
of the one are the lessons of the other."*

—Savion Glover (b. 1973)

Table of Contents

This book contains six units.

Each unit builds knowledge in:

- Sounds and Letters
- Spelling and Words
- Vocabulary and Roots
- Grammar and Usage
- Listening and Reading
- Speaking and Writing

Unit 25 Form a Circle

Unit 26 · Create Movement

Unit 28   Enjoy the View

Unit 29 Give a Call

Appendix

Form a Circle

Phonemic Awareness and Phonics

Unit 25 introduces the soft sounds for the letters **c** and **g**. It also introduces an alternate spelling **-dge** for final / *j* /.

Sound-Spelling Patterns for c and g

The letter **c** represents two sounds:

- The hard sound / *k* / as in **cat**, **cot**, and **cut**
- The soft sound / *s* / as in **cent**, **circle**, and **cycle**

When **c** is followed by **e**, **i**, or **y**, it usually sounds like / *s* /. This is called the soft sound for **c**.

The letter **g** represents two sounds:

- The hard sound / *g* / as in **gas**, **got**, and **gum**
- The soft sound / *j* / as in **gem**, **ginger**, and **gym**

When **g** is followed by **e**, **i**, or **y**, it usually sounds like / *j* /. This is called the soft sound for **g**.

Remember:
Before **a**, **o**, or **u**, both **c** and **g** represent hard sounds.
Before **e**, **i**, or **y**, both **c** and **g** represent soft sounds.

Multiple Spellings for / j /

Review: The letters **j** and soft **g** represent the sound / *j* /. Examples: jazz, gentle

The final / *j* / sound is also represented by the sound-spelling pattern **-dge**. Examples: badge, ridge

STEP 2

Word Recognition and Spelling

Prefixes

We can expand words and change meaning by adding **prefixes**. These word parts are added to the beginnings of words. Example: **post** + date = postdate

(See Step 3: Vocabulary and Morphology for links to meaning.)

> **Unit 25 Prefix**
>
> **post-**

Suffixes

We can expand words and change meaning by adding **suffixes**. These word parts are added to the ends of words. Example: reduce + **ible** = reducible

(See Step 3: Vocabulary and Morphology for links to meaning and Step 4: Grammar and Usage for function.)

> **Unit 25 Suffixes**
>
> **-ible, -ive**

Roots

We can build words using **roots**. Roots carry the most important part of a word's meaning. We usually attach a prefix or suffix to make a root into a word. Example: in + **cred** + ible = incredible

(See Step 3: Vocabulary and Morphology for links to meaning.)

> **Unit 25 Roots**
>
> **plic/plex/pli; pon/pound/pos; cred**

Essential Words

> ## Unit 25 Essential Words
>
> | | | |
> |---|---|---|
> | carriage | marriage | shoes |
> | machine | pigeon | surgeon |

Sound-Spelling Pattern for -dge

The sound / j / is represented by **-dge** after a short vowel at the end of a one-syllable word. Examples: badge, edge, ridge, dodge, fudge

The Drop e Rule

Review: The **Drop e Rule** is used with words ending with a final silent **e**.

1. When adding a suffix that begins with a *vowel*, drop the **e** from the base word. Example: trace + ing = **tracing**

2. When adding a suffix that begins with a *consonant*, do not drop the **e** from the base word. Example: grace + ful = **graceful**

Spelling Lists

The Unit 25 spelling lists contain three categories:

1. Words with soft **c** and **g** or with the **-dge** pattern

2. **Essential Words** (in italics)

3. Words with prefixes, roots, and suffixes

Spelling Lists

Lessons 1—5		Lessons 6—10	
bicycle	*imagine*	accident	manager
carriage	*machine*	apologized	parcel
center	*marriage*	complicated	pondered
circle	origin	complex	posted
edge	*pigeon*	exceed	postmarked
energy	*shoes*	illegible	tangible
fudge	*surgeon*	incentive	urge
general		large	

Vocabulary and Morphology

Unit Vocabulary

Sound-spelling correspondences from this unit and previous units make up this unit's vocabulary.

■ What do these words mean?

■ Do some of them mean more than one thing? Which ones?

UNIT Vocabulary

soft c	excellent	process	baggage	suggest
absence	except	produce	cage	teenager
accident	excess	pronounce	change	tragic
advice	exercise	race	cottage	urge
anticipate	face	rejoice	damage	vegetable
balance	fancy	replace	energy	village
bicycle	fence	reproduce	engine	voyage
cent	force	rice	general	
center	grace	romance	generous	**dge for / j /**
ceremony	ice	sacrifice	huge	bridge
chance	medicine	sentence	imagine	budge
circle	mercy	since	large	budget
city	nice	space	manage	edge
civilize	niece	substance	message	fudge
commerce	notice	surface	orange	judge
confidence	office	trace	origin	trudge
dance	parcel	voice	oxygen	
decimal	pencil		page	
difference	piece	**soft g**	passage	
distance	place	age	revenge	
electricity	practice	apologize	stage	
essence	prejudice	arrange	strange	

Word Relationships

Attributes refine meaning and build associations between words. An attribute is a characteristic or quality, such as size, part, color, or function. Examples: circle/round, ice/cold, fudge/sweet

Meaning Parts

Prefixes

Prefixes can add to or change the meanings of words. The Unit 25 prefix has the following meanings.

Unit 25 Prefix	Meanings	Examples
post-	after; behind; following	postdate, postpone, postscript

Suffixes

Suffixes can add to or change the meanings of words. When added to a base word or root, they can change the base word or root to an adjective. The Unit 25 suffixes are adjective suffixes.

Unit 25 Suffixes	Meanings	Examples
-ible	capable of; can do; able to be	expressible, reducible, responsible
-ive	causing; making; characterized by	active, impressive, objective

Roots

A **root** is the basic meaning part of a word. Roots of English words often come from another language, especially Latin. A root usually needs a prefix or suffix to make it into a word.

Example: **cred** + ible = credible (**cred** = to believe, ible = able to be, credible = able to be believed)

Unit 25 Roots	Meanings	Examples
plic	to fold; twist; weave	complicate, explicit, implicate
pli	to fold; twist; weave	pliable, pliant, pliers
plex	to fold; twist; weave	complex, duplex, perplex
pon	to put; place	component, exponent, proponent
pound	to put; place	compound, expound, impound
pos	to put; place	deposit, disposal, positive
cred	to believe	credible, creditor, incredible

Challenge Morphemes

Root	Meanings	Examples
vid	to see	evident, provide, video
vis	to see	invisible, visitor, visor
cede	to move; withdraw	concede, precede, recede
ceed	to move; withdraw	exceed, proceed, proceeding
cess	to move; withdraw	excess, process, recess

STEP 4

Grammar and Usage

Adjectives

Review: **Adjectives** describe nouns. They answer: **Which one? How many? What kind?**

Adjectives

Several classes learned a **rhymed** poem **with a defined** meter.

Which one?   **with a defined** meter (prepositional phrase that acts as an adjective)

How many?   **several** (single word that acts as an adjective)

What kind?   **rhymed** (past participle that acts as an adjective)

Some adjectives are formed when a **suffix** is added to the base or root word. The suffixes **-ible** and **-ive** added to roots or base words can change words into adjectives. Examples: an incredible story, an impressive lesson

Past Participles

Review: **Verbs** are words that describe actions (point, organize, speculate) or a state of being (is, were).

The **past participle** of **regular** verbs is formed by adding **-ed** to the base verb. Example: dance + **ed** = (have) **danced**

Some past participles are **irregular**. Their forms must be memorized.

Irregular Past Participles

begin—(have) **begun**

give—(have) **given**

go—(have) **gone**

See the Appendix, page A36, for a complete list of irregular verbs.

■ Past participles can be in **verb phrases** or can act as **adjectives**.

In a verb phrase, a past participle is used with a form of the helping verb **have** (**have**, **has**, **had**). Examples: have begun, has spoken, had won

When functioning as an adjective, a past participle tells more about a noun. Examples: an unstressed syllable, a broken circle

Phrases and Clauses

Review: A **phrase** is a group of words that functions as a single word. A phrase does not have a subject and predicate. Examples: in each line, about the theme, to recite the poem

A **clause** is a group of words that contains a subject and a predicate.

> **Clauses**
>
> The poet wrote quickly.
>
> The poem rhymes.

An **independent clause** has one subject and one predicate; it represents a complete thought. A **simple sentence** is an independent clause because it contains one subject and one predicate.

Sentence Pattern

Review: **Conjunctions** join words, phrases, or clauses in a sentence. Any sentence part can be joined by a conjunction to create a compound component.

A **compound sentence** has two **independent clauses** joined by the conjunction **and**, **or**, or **but**. Example: Poetry expresses thoughts through exquisite words, **but** it uses words sparingly.

Two independent clauses can also be joined by a **semicolon** to create a compound sentence. The semicolon replaces the conjunction.

> **Compound Sentence With a Semicolon**
>
> The poet's meanings are clear.
>
> I understood the poem.
>
> The poet's meanings are clear; I understood the poem.

Sentence Types

English has four basic sentence types:

- A **declarative** sentence states a fact or opinion. The end punctuation for a declarative sentence is a period.

- An **interrogative** sentence asks a question. The end punctuation for an interrogative sentence is a question mark.

- An **imperative** sentence gives a command. The end punctuation for an imperative sentence is a period.

- An **exclamatory** sentence expresses strong emotion. The end punctuation for an exclamatory sentence is an exclamation point.

Sentence Types

Declarative:	The poem was funny.
Interrogative:	Have you memorized the poem?
Imperative:	Speak more slowly, please.
Exclamatory:	We won!

Confusing Word Pairs

Precede and **proceed** are confused because they sound alike. They can be distinguished by identifying the meanings of their prefixes and roots. **Precede** is a verb that means "to come before in time or order." **Proceed** is a verb that means "to continue, to move on." Examples:

The day's classwork is usually **preceded** by announcements from the office.

After the fire alarm interruption, our class **proceeded** to finish the test.

The word pairs **device** and **devise** and **advice** and **advise** are also often confused. The first word in each pair is a noun with / s / spelled **c**, while the second is a verb with / z / spelled **s**. **Device** means "a plan, procedure, or technique." **Devise** means "to invent or imagine." Examples:

The student invented a **device** for doing homework.

The students will **devise** a plan to complete their work.

Advice means "a recommendation regarding a decision or course of conduct." **Advise** means "to counsel, recommend, or inform." Examples:

The counselor gave **advice** about the test.

The counselor will **advise** students about their schedules.

Listening and Reading Comprehension

Informational Text

■ Some **informational text** is nonfiction material written about a specific topic, event, experience or circumstance. It is often accompanied by visual information in the form of charts, graphs, or illustrations. The visual information provides additional content about the subject matter. "**Stonehenge: Secrets of an Ancient Circle**" and "**Living in a Circle**" use visual information to enhance the text content.

Vocabulary in Context

■ **Context clues** help us understand new vocabulary. Pronoun referents, meaning signals, and visuals, such as charts and graphs, provide meaning links.

Signal Words

■ Different types of sentences can help us think about new information and ideas in different ways. Identifying signal words within sentences can improve comprehension.

See the Appendix, page A20, for a complete list of signal words based on Bloom's Taxonomy.

Literary Genres

 Genres are types or categories of literature. Unit 25 features poetry.

■ **Poetry** is a literature genre that contains some or all of these six elements: thought, imagery, mood, melody, meter, and form. These elements are illustrated through the poetry selections in "**Circle Poems Take Many Forms**," "**Circles in Nature**," and "**The Circle of Life**."

Thought: Thought is the element that contains the poem's message. One component of thought is the **theme**, which is often stated as a universal truth—unlimited by time or space.

Imagery: Imagery refers to the poem's creation of mental pictures, or images, for the reader. Metaphor, simile, and personification are examples of techniques that poets use to create imagery.

Mood: Poems evoke emotions and set an atmosphere or a tone for the reader. This element is called mood.

Melody: Melody is the element created by a poet's use of sound. Alliteration, rhyme, assonance, consonance, and onomatopoeia are examples of devices used to create melody in poetry.

Meter: Patterns of stressed and unstressed syllables in a poem create meter or poetic rhythm.

Form: Form is the element that defines the poem's actual structure. Examples of poetic forms include quatrain, sonnet, blank verse, limerick, ballad, and free (open) verse.

STEP
6

Speaking and Writing

Signal Words

- Different types of sentences require different responses depending on the focus of **signal words**. Identifying signal words within sentences improves the accuracy of responses to oral and written questions.

  See the Appendix, page A20, for a complete list of signal words based on Bloom's Taxonomy.

Paragraph or Composition Organization

- Some paragraphs or compositions compare. A **compare and contrast paragraph** or **composition** tells the readers how two or more things are alike (compare) and how they are different (contrast). The organization helps us to compose the specific similarities and differences, helping to make our writing clear to our readers.

  Transition words signal this organization. Some of the transition words identify how things are alike. Other transition words identify how things are different.

Transition Words for Compare and Contrast	
Compare	**Contrast**
Both are similiar.	They are different.
Both are alike.	They are not the same.
They share these features.	They do not share these features.

More About Words

- **Bonus Words** use the same sound-spelling correspondences that we have studied in this unit and previous units.

- **Idioms** are common phrases that cannot be understood by the meanings of their separate words—only by the entire phrase.

- **Why? Word History** explains the origin of the word **circus**.

UNIT Bonus Words

soft <u>c</u>	device	peace	angel	register
access	dice	percent	cabbage	rigid
acid	displace	policy	challenge	sponge
adjacent	enforce	precede	charge	strategy
bounce	enhance	precise	college	
brace	exceed	price	danger	**<u>dge</u> for /_j_/**
capacity	explicit	prince	detergent	badge
cease	facilitate	principal	emerge	dodge
celebrate	finance	principle	gender	fidget
circumstance	glance	proceed	generate	gadget
circus	hence	reinforce	gentle	hedge
cite	ignorance	reluctance	giant	ledge
civil	implicit	sequence	gym	lodge
coincide	incentive	silence	ideology	nudge
commence	incidence	slice	image	pledge
concentrate	instance	specific	legislate	ridge
concept	intelligence	specify	logic	sludge
convince	lettuce	successor	luggage	smudge
currency	license		magic	wedge
cycle	palace	**soft g**	margin	
decide	participate	analogy	range	

Idioms	
Idiom	**Meaning**
be a piece of cake	be very easy to do
be just the tip of the iceberg	be a very small part of a larger problem
come full circle	after changing a lot, come back to the same opinion or place you were in the beginning
cut off your nose to spite your face	make a situation worse for yourself when you are angry with someone
face the music	accept the unpleasant consequences of your own actions
have egg on your face	be embarrassed or humiliated for something foolish that you did or said
hit the ceiling	lose your temper suddenly; become angry
skate on thin ice	take a big chance; risk danger
straddle the fence	be undecided or uncommitted
wait for the other shoe to drop	wait for an event that seems likely to happen

Why? Word History

Circus—The modern word **circus** gets its name from ancient Roman entertainment. The Latin word *circus*, which comes from the Greek word *kirkos*, meaning "circle, ring," referred to a circular or oval area surrounded by rows of seats for spectators. In the center ring chariot races and gladiatorial combats provided bloody and brutal spectacles.

The first recorded use of **circus** in English is in a work that Chaucer wrote around 1380. He refers to ancient Rome's Circus Maximus. Our modern word **circus** dates back to the late 1700s. Originally, it meant an equestrian spectacle. Later, ropedancers, acrobats, and jugglers joined trick horseback riders in the ring. The arena's circular shape and the riding performances were carried over from the original use of **circus**. But our modern word **circus** has little connection with its brutal Roman namesake of long ago.

STONEHENGE:
SECRETS OF AN ANCIENT CIRCLE

Stonehenge has puzzled people for thousands of years. This circle of large, upright stones in southern England is one of the world's great mysteries. It holds the secrets of an ancient people. Over time, discoveries have been made
5 about how it was built. Why it was built remains a puzzle.

What Do We Know About the Ancient Circle?

One fact that we know about Stonehenge is that it was built over a period of 2,000 years. Scientists believe that its construction had three stages.

Stage One

The building of
10 Stonehenge began around 5,000 years ago. Starting about 3100 BC, a circular ditch was dug. Dirt from the ditch was piled up
15 into a bank, or henge. Within the bank, 56

*Stage One: 3100–2500 BC
Ditch and holes dug.*

holes were dug. These holes may have held wooden posts. The digging was done using deer antler picks. Carbon dating the picks tells us how old they are. This also tells us
20 when the first work began. There may have been a wooden building inside the circle. Not many stones were used in the first stage.

*The location of
Stonehenge in England.*

Stage Two

Stage Two began about 2500 BC. The builders built more wooden structures in the circle. They built an avenue into the circle. They also set up pillars of stone. They used bluestones, named for their color. These are the smaller stones we still see today. They came from South Wales, about 137 miles away. They may have been dragged down to the sea and floated on rafts. They may have then been brought up the River Avon and dragged overland. At last, they were placed in the circle. Each stone weighed about five tons. The ancient builders had no modern tools. How did they move the stones? It was an amazing feat.

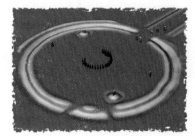

Stage Two: 2500–2100 BC Bluestones set and avenue constructed.

Stage Three

Stage Three began about 2100 BC. During this stage most of the stones we see today were placed. In Stage Three, builders dug up the bluestones. They rearranged them. Next, they brought in even bigger stones. Five sets of two sandstone pillars were set up. Each set of pillars had a stone laid on top of it. How did they get the stones in an upright position? How did they lift the top stones into place? We're not sure. The heaviest stones weighed about 45 tons (*90,000 pounds!*).

Stage Three: 2100–1400 BC Sandstone pillars with top stones set.

An Ancient Calendar?

Stonehenge is built aligned to the midsummer sunrise. This happens on June 21. Each year on that date, the sunrise aligns along the avenue into the circle. Did ancient people use this circle to mark the years? Did they build the circle to celebrate that day? We don't know.

Every year, thousands visit the ancient circle. The curious come. Tourists come. Scientists come. They come to study the circle. But the ancient circle remains a mystery. And the answers to the mystery may remain forever within the circle.

Circle *Poems* Take Many Forms

A poem begins with a lump in the throat, a home-sickness or a love-sickness. It is a reaching-out toward expression; an effort to find fulfillment. A complete poem is one where the emotion has found its thought and the thought
5 *has found the words.*
　　　　　　　　　　　—Robert Frost, 20th century poet

What Is Poetry?

Poetry is a special kind of literature. A poem uses words **sparingly** and imaginatively. Most poems are meant to be read out loud because the language of poetry combines the qualities of speech and song.

10 　　Poetry often includes six major elements: thought, form, imagery, melody, meter, and mood. In this unit, we will be learning about two elements: thought and form. The thought is the sum of the poet's ideas. One element of a poem's thought is its theme. A poem's theme may be stated as a
15 universal truth, a truth that is not limited by time and space.

Poems come in many different forms as well. Let's look at two major forms of poetry: closed form and open form, or free verse. Closed form poetry is written in specific

sparingly
in a limited manner

patterns, often with regular rhythm, line lengths, and line
20 groupings called stanzas. Open form poetry does not use
regular rhythmic patterns, has varying line lengths, and has
no set line groupings or stanzas.

Closed Form

Our first experience of poetry is often nursery rhymes
and songs, so we usually think that poetry rhymes.
25 Rhyming poetry is one kind of poetry; it repeats the
same or similar sounds of words in a defined pattern. For
example, in the poem below, the word "out" rhymes with
"flout." Read the poem out loud. What other two words
rhyme in the poem?

30 **O**utwitted
—by Edwin Markham
He drew a circle that shut me out—
Heretic, a rebel, a thing to flout.
But Love and I had the wit to win:
35 **We drew a circle that took him in!**

flout
to mock; make fun of

What are the thought and theme of this poem? What
makes "Outwitted" a closed form poem?

Haiku—A Closed Form

The haiku poetry form originated in Japan. A haiku
40 consists of three lines with 5, 7, and 5 syllables respectively.
Because there is a limit to the number of syllables in each
line and the number of lines, it is considered a closed form.
Even though haiku poems are very short, they are intended
to convey profound emotion and insight. Read the
45 poems out loud. Count the number of syllables in each line.

convey
to express; carry

profound
intellectually deep;
insightful

From
Haiku: This **O**ther World
—by Richard Wright

#745

50
    In the summer lake,
The moon gives a long shiver,
    Then swells round again.

#716

gaping

opening wide   55
    With mouth gaping wide,
Swallowing strings of wild geese,—
    Hungry autumn moon.

A haiku is often about an individual experience with the environment that transcends everyday experience. Read the haiku poems out loud again. What are the thoughts or
60 themes being expressed in these haiku poems?

Open Form or Free Verse

Another form of poetry is called free verse or open form. Free verse does not have regular rhyme. Free verse uses the natural rhythm of language to emphasize the thought and theme. Free verse is a form preferred by many
65 modern and contemporary poets.

Read the following poem out loud. Describe the poem's thought and theme.

The Life Of a Man Is a Circle
—by Black Elk, Lakota Sioux

70 The life of a man is a circle
From childhood to childhood,
And so it is in everything
Where power moves.

Our teepees were round like the nests
75 Of birds, and these were always set
In a circle, the nation's hoop,
A nest of many nests,
Where the Great Spirit meant for us
to hatch our children.

Concrete Form—An Open Form

80 Concrete poetry is a unique kind of poetry. The concrete poem uses a visual image to create its meaning. Concrete poems often have few words. The way the 85 words are arranged on the page is as important to the meaning of the poem as what the 90 words say. Read the following poem out loud. What is the thought or theme of the poem when it is 95 read out loud?

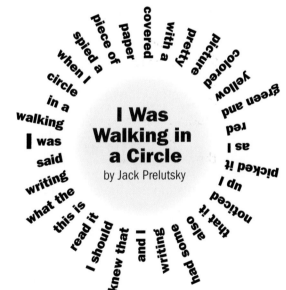

I Was Walking in a Circle
by Jack Prelutsky

I was walking in a circle when I spied a piece of paper covered with a pretty colored picture yellow green and red as I picked it up I noticed that it also had some writing and I knew that I should read it this is what the writing said I was

Hearing a concrete poem read out loud may not give the listener the whole experience or appreciation of the poem. A reader must see the poem on the page to understand the poem. Read the poem again. What is the 100 theme or thought of the poem when it is typed in a circle on the page? What makes this poem an open form poem?

"Outwitted," from *The Man With the Hoe and Other Poems* by Edwin Markham

"The Life of a Man Is a Circle," from *Black Elk Speaks: Being the Life Story of a Holy Man of the Oglala Sioux* by John G. Niehardt

"#716" and "#745," from *Haiku: The Other World* by Richard Wright

"I Was Walking in a Circle," from *A Pizza the Size of the Sun* by Jack Prelutsky

Answer It

1. Summarize the poem "The Life of a Man Is a Circle."

2. Hypothesize what types of things the author is talking about when he refers to "everything/Where power moves" in "The Life of a Man Is a Circle."

3. Contrast the form of "Outwitted" with the form of "The Life of a Man Is a Circle."

4. Compare the forms of the two Richard Wright haikus, "#745" and "#716."

5. All the poems involve circles. How can you distinguish the elements of thought and form in these poems?

Circles In NATURE

Experimental Poetry

Another open form is experimental poetry. This form "experiments" or tries something new with language and form. Experimental poetry has lots of **variations**, but experimental poems have one thing in common. They

5   try not to sound or look like closed form poetry. Read the poem below. What do you think is experimental about this poem?

variations

types; kinds

who knows if the moon's
by E.E. Cummings[1]

who knows if the moon's
10 a balloon, coming out of a **keen** city
in the sky—filled with pretty people?
(and if you and i should

get into it, if they
should take me and take you into their balloon,
15 why then
we'd go up higher with all the pretty people

than houses and steeples and clouds:
go sailing
away and away sailing into a keen
20 city which nobody's ever visited, where

always
    it's
        Spring) and   everyone's
in love and flowers pick themselves

keen
splendid; fine

25 The modern poet E.E. Cummings (1894–1962) was
famous for writing experimental poetry. Why do you think
that Cummings refers to himself as "i" instead of "I" in
the poem?

Barbara Juster Esbensen's poem "circles" combines open
30 form (free verse) and concrete form. It is another example
of experimental poetry. What main thoughts does the poet
share in this poem? Does the way the words appear on the
page **enhance** the meaning of this poem?

enhance
to improve; add to

[1]You may see this poet's name typed in the following ways: e.e. cummings or e e cummings.
However, scholars now believe that his preference was E.E. Cummings.

circles

by Barbara Juster Esbensen

35   Did you see? Did you
                          see
        the rainbow-scaled fish
             arch into the air
             and fall?

40   Did you see
          those perfect circles?
    Those hoops of water and light?
         They fit together   one
             inside another

45   Wider and wider
                they grow
                    out
            and
        out
50   and   out
            from the quick splash
                to the shore

Circles
set in wood— **concentric**
55 a round calendar
Its widening rings grow slowly
out

        and out

                and   out
60 from the old tree's
    earliest day
    to the shore of
    now

concentric
having a common
center

                                    A circle
65   is the shape of
                           safety where wolf
                                      shadows
                           prowl in the far north
                                         where
70   musk oxen stand — spokes
                           of a dark muscular
                                         wheel

                           Their **massive** heads
                     point in every direction
75   a watchful compass-rose
                              set in the snow

Deep in the forest
curled in its grassy
bed
80   the fawn
lies
dappled with circles
lies
hidden under
85   medallions of sunlight
and woodland gloom
almost invisible

                     Think of a circle   think
                                 of our planet
90   Earth
                                 solid globe
                     spinning   holding us
                                       holding
                 oceans and forests and drifting
95   deserts
                     in the blackness of space

Think of the sun
our blazing disk   our
daystar
100 and the planet spinning from
day into night and
return
Think of all that light
washing over us
105 flowing into starlit dark—
a whirling cycle of days
and nights

A circle
is the shape of sleep
110 In hollow places
deep under winter snow
small animals dream Their toes
are tucked up
their tails curl down
115 and around

Heavy circular bears
breathe
the slow sleep of cold
nights and days

120 Sleep draws a soft line around you
curled and folded
in the **arc** of an arm
holding the nighttime book

arc
a curved line

At the foot of the bed
125 the orange and white cat
has wound herself tight
and the circles of the moon coming in
fit her shape exactly

Echoes for the eye!

Deep in the forest curled in its
grassy bed the fawn lies dappled with
circles lies hidden under medallions of
sunlight and woodland gloom
almost invisible

"who knows if the moon's," from *E.E. Cummings*
Complete Poems 1904–1962 by E.E. Cummings
"circles," from *Echoes for the Eye: Poems to Celebrate*
Patterns in Nature by Barbara Juster Esbensen

Answer It

1. Compare and contrast the theme of the poem "who knows if the moon's" with the theme of "circles."

2. Identify the use of repetition in the poem "circles" and explain what this repetition adds to the poem.

3. Paraphrase what the narrator imagines happening in the poem "who knows if the moon's."

4. Describe the "experimental" aspects of each poem.

5. Identify which poem in the selection you like best and explain why you like it.

LIVING IN A CIRCLE

If you close your eyes and think of a room—any room—
what shape do you see? If you answered, four flat walls, a
flat ceiling, a flat floor, and eight corners with right angles,
then you're still thinking inside the box. Consider, instead,
5 living inside a circle.

Buckminster Fuller was one of the most famous
futurists and global thinkers of the 20th century. He was an
inventor, architect, engineer, and mathematician. He spent
his life thinking outside the box. He dedicated himself
10 to finding solutions for some of humankind's biggest
problems, such as disease, hunger, and homelessness. Fuller
is best known for creating an efficient and inexpensive
shelter. This structure is the geodesic dome.

A geodesic dome is a half-sphere. Its outer shell is
15 composed of a complex network of triangles. The triangles
create a self-bracing framework. The weight of the dome
is **distributed** evenly throughout the series of triangles,
making it much stronger than a box-shaped or rectangular-
shaped structure.

20 For these reasons, a geodesic dome stands up extremely
well in strong winds. If a wind blows against a rectangular
structure, it will exert its force against the **vertical** face of
the wall. There is a risk that the wind could knock it down.
However, if a wind blows against the curved side of a dome,
25 the air will slide up and over the structure. A domed roof is
also good in heavy snow because the snow will slide off of

Buckminster Fuller promoted the geodesic dome as a strong and energy-efficient structure.

distributed
spread out

vertical
upright; straight up and down

it rather than pile up. Scientists in the Arctic and Antarctic often use dome structures to protect their scientific equipment from wind and snow.

30   Besides strength, the dome has many other advantages. A half-sphere encloses the most amount of space with the least amount of material. This means that the shelter requires less building materials than square or rectangular shelters. Since domes have less surface area to lose heat

35 from, they're also very **energy efficient** . A dome acts like a giant reflector. It concentrates interior heat and prevents radiant heat loss. Buckminster Fuller believed in the principle of "doing more with less." Dome shelters meet this requirement.

40   The geodesic dome is one of the lightest, strongest, most cost-effective structures ever devised. There are now over 300,000 domes in the world, including the Epcot Center at Disney World in Florida. But this structural design isn't really that new. In fact, for

45 centuries, people around the world have created and lived in circular housing.

On this continent, many of the Native American tribes lived in dwellings based on the circle. The Mandan Indians, who settled in what is now western North Dakota in the

50 1600s, made round houses. First they dug out a floor. Next they built a big fire pit in the center. Wooden poles and willow rods were placed around the outside of the lodge. These were covered with heavy sod. Grass grew on the soil roofs, providing more waterproofing and structural

55 strength. From the outside, the homes looked like hilly mounds. They were arranged around a **central** ceremonial plaza. Sometimes the Mandans built walls or ditches around the villages.

Tipis, used by Plains Indian tribes such as the Sioux

60 and Cheyenne, were also based on a circular plan. They used the idea that a triangle is much stronger than a rectangle. The Plains Indians followed the buffalo herds. They depended on the buffalo for just about everything they used in their daily lives, including food, medicine,

65 clothing, and robes. Because they moved **frequently**, the

energy efficient

designed to con-serve energy

central

in the center; in the middle of

frequently

often

Plains Indians needed portable homes. Tipis, which were covered with tanned and stitched buffalo hides, were very easy to put together and take down. They were relatively light for carrying to the next camp. The women in the tribe
70 were often the ones to take down, pack, and set up the tipis in a new location. From the outside, the tipi looked like a big cone. On the inside, the tipi consisted of a circular room with a pointed ceiling. The door, a hide that flapped open, always faced the east. This allowed the first rays of
75 morning sunlight to enter. The central hearth fire was placed near the center, but closer to the door, allowing for more headroom and family space in the back of the tipi.

The Navajo people, who live in the southwestern United States, build round, earth-covered houses called hogans.
80 Most Navajos now live in rectangular houses. Hogans are used for ceremonial and spiritual purposes. A traditional hogan is constructed of logs, bark, and packed earth in a round dome-roofed shape, according to instructions found in the Navajo creation story. The sections of the
85 hogan correspond to the structures of the universe. For instance, the earthen floor represents Mother Earth and the round roof symbolizes Father Sky. Like the tipis of the Plains Indians, the doors of hogans face the east in order to catch the first rays of dawn. Inside the hogan, clockwise
90 movement represents harmonious choices. Blessings and ceremonies are always conducted in a clockwise direction.

Tipis, used by Plains Indian tribes, were based on a circular plan.

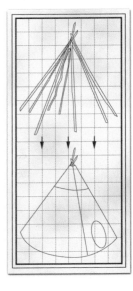

Far to the north, in the Arctic, Inuit hunters also build domed shelters. These dwellings are constructed of ice. They are called igloos. Igloos have long, low tunnel entries that
95 must be traveled on hands and knees. This entry design keeps the icy wind from blowing into the house. The round interior of the igloo is sometimes draped with reindeer skins; the air space between the ice and skins creates good insulation. Furs are laid out on the circular floor for sleeping.

100 In central Asia, Mongolian nomads have used domed shelters since the 12th or 13th centuries. These herders need to move from pasture
105 to pasture so that their sheep, yaks, horses, camels, and goats have enough grass to graze on and water to drink. For shelter, these nomads carry a
110 round, portable tent called a *ger*. Members of a Mongolian nomad family can take a *ger* apart in less than an hour. The

Mongolian nomads use a round, portable tent called a ger.

pieces of their home can then be loaded up on the backs
115 of camels, or into a small truck, and carted off to the next pasture. In a *ger*, the door always faces south, rather than east like in tipis and hogans. The wind in Mongolia usually blows from the north, so by placing the door to the south, the family is protected from the wind when they enter and
120 leave the *ger*.

Even in the warm climate of the Caribbean, domed shelters have been built for their energy efficiency and ability to withstand strong winds. The Taino people, who were native to the islands throughout the Greater Antilles,
125 including Cuba, Jamaica, Haiti, the Dominican Republic, and Puerto Rico, built round houses called *bohíos*. These were constructed using wooden frames. They were roofed with palm fronds or straw. The floors were earthen. Because of the round shape, *bohíos* were strong enough to
130 resist hurricanes.

This old but excellent idea of living in circular spaces continues to evolve. RCA Dome in Indianapolis, Indiana holds 60,000 fans. The roof of this giant dome covers eight acres and weighs more than 200 tons. The inside of
135 the roof is made of a canvas-like material. The exterior is made of Teflon-coated fiberglass. What holds up this massive roof? The RCA Dome is an example of pneumatic architecture: structures supported by pressurized air. The roof is held on to the building by 16 cables and supported
140 by 20 electric fans. The air blown by the fans creates the pressure supporting this immense structure. **Proponents** of pneumatic domes say they are perfect for concerts, fairs, and emergency shelters because they are so easy to put up and take down.

145   Humans haven't yet constructed housing on other planets, but extraterrestrial architecture may be a science of the future. For reasons already explained by Buckminster Fuller and demonstrated by native people the world over, circular or spherical dwellings may be the space
150 architecture of choice. After all, such structures can be designed to be strong, wind resistant, highly portable, and energy efficient. Thinking—and living—outside the box in the future may be the smartest thing to do.

Proponents

supporters

Think About It

1. List advantages of the geodesic dome structure.

2. Contrast how a geodesic dome and a rectangular-shaped building withstand bad weather.

3. Explain Fuller's goal of "doing more with less."

4. Compare the portable, circular structures used by some Plains Indian tribes and Mongolian nomads to the portable, circular structures that are used today.

5. Assess the meaning of the phrase "thinking outside of the box."

6. Suppose a temporary school must be built while a permanent school is renovated. Using information from "Living in a Circle," plan how the temporary building could be cost effective and make use of natural benefits.

THE CIRCLE OF Life

As a young man, William Shakespeare became a famous playwright.

WHO WAS WILLIAM SHAKESPEARE?

William Shakespeare is one of the greatest writers in the history of the English language. His works have been translated into hundreds of languages, and his plays have been performed around the world for more than 500 years.

5   William Shakespeare was baptized on April 26, 1564 in his hometown of Stratford-upon-Avon. His exact birthday is unknown, but it is celebrated on April 23.

Shakespeare, like most boys of his age, probably went to one of Stratford's junior schools, where he would have

10   learned to read and write. From the age of about 7, he would have attended the King's New School, where the **emphasis** would have been on learning Latin, still the international language of Europe in the 1500s.

As a young man, he left Stratford and went to

15   London, where he became a famous playwright. In 1594, Shakespeare became a founding member, actor, playwright, and shareholder of the Lord Chamberlain's Men. This company put on many plays, including plays by Shakespeare such as *Richard III, Hamlet, Othello,* and *King*

20   *Lear.* Later the company was renamed The King's Men. They performed at court for James I, the king of England, more often than any other company.

Sometime after 1611, Shakespeare retired to Stratford. On April 23, he died at age 52 and was buried there.

25   Shakespeare is credited with writing 37 plays and 154 poems.

emphasis

stress; special importance

The following poem, "The Seven Ages of Man," is a dramatic monologue from one of William Shakespeare's plays, *As You Like It*. Its topic has to do with the circle of life. Many **segments** from Shakespeare's plays have become famous in

30 their own right. This poem has been translated into many languages and studied by students all over the world.

segments

sections; separate pieces

The Seven Ages of Man
by William Shakespeare

    All the world's a stage,
And all the men and women merely players:

35 They have their exits and their entrances;
And one man in his time plays many parts,
His acts being seven ages. At first the infant,
Mewling and puking in the nurse's arms.
Then the whining schoolboy, with his satchel,

40 And shining morning face, creeping like snail
Unwillingly to school. And then the lover,
Sighing like furnace, with a woeful ballad
Made to his mistress' eyebrow. Then a soldier,
Full of strange oaths, and bearded like the **pard**,

45 Jealous in honour, sudden and quick in quarrel,
Seeking the bubble reputation
Even in the cannon's mouth. And then the justice,
In fair round belly with good **capon** lined,
With eyes severe and beard of formal cut,

50 Full of wise **saws** and modern instances;
And so he plays his part. The sixth age shifts
Into the lean and slippered **pantaloon**,
With **spectacles** on nose and pouch on side;
His youthful **hose**, well saved, a world too wide

55 For his shrunk **shank**; and his big manly voice,
Turning again toward childish **treble**, pipes
And whistles in his sound. Last scene of all,
That ends this strange eventful history,
Is **second childishness** and mere **oblivion**,

60 **Sans** teeth, sans eyes, sans taste, sans everything.

"The Seven Ages of Man" is a dramatic monologue. A dramatic monologue is a long speech that a character in a play or a poem makes to others, such as other characters, the audience, or the reader. Here, the character, Jacques, in the play *As You Like It* is expressing his opinion about life to other characters on the stage. Jacques is known to be a melancholic, which means he is often sad and gloomy.

The Circle of Life 35

"The Seven Ages of Man" Vocabulary

mewling	crying weakly, whimpering
pard	a leopard or other large cat
capon	a chicken
saws	sayings
pantaloon	a foolish older man
spectacles	eyeglasses
hose	stockings
shank	a human leg
treble	a high, shrill sound
second childishness	a state of mental decline in old age
oblivion	total forgetfulness
sans	without

THE ELEMENTS OF POETRY

incorporates
includes, contains

Poetry **incorporates** six major elements: thought, imagery, mood, melody, meter, and form. In this selection, we focus on the study of three elements: thought, meter, and form.

Thought and Theme. A major element of poetry is thought. The thought is related to the subject of the poem. In this poem, Shakespeare describes the circle of life. The poem identifies seven distinct stages through which a long human life progresses: infant, schoolchild, lover, soldier, **justice**, pantaloon, and elderly person. Infants are helpless beings. As children become young adults, they become stronger and more independent. As people age, they **gain** in wisdom. In oldest age, human strength **diminishes**, and the circle completes itself.

justice
a judge

gain
to acquire; increase

diminishes
decreases; lessens

In a great work of literature, the theme is true of all people, across all time. This theme is also unlimited in space; it is true for people all over the world. When a literature selection's major theme is unlimited by time or space, its theme is universal. This poem has a universal theme, because it is true for all humans, across time, and in all places.

95   **Meter.** Meter refers to a regular number of stressed and unstressed syllables in each line.

We identify a poem's rhythmic pattern by examining poetic feet.

A poetic foot is a line segment that consists of
100 one stressed syllable in combination with one or more unstressed syllables. For example:

And **all**´ the **men**´ and **wo**´men **mere**´ly **play**´ers

105 Here, the second syllable in the line is stressed. Thereafter, every other syllable continues to be stressed. To divide the line into poetic feet, or segments, divide so that each foot has one stressed syllable. The division would look like this:

And *all*´ | the *men*´ | and *wo*´ | men *mere*´ | ly *play*´ | ers

The metric pattern is: two syllables in a foot, with stress
110 on the second of the two syllables. A poetic foot that has two syllables, with the stress on the second of the two syllables, is called an *iamb*. The poem's rhythm, then, is *iambic*.

To describe both the meter and the rhythm—the part of meter that refers to stressed syllables—we would say
115 that this poem is written in iambic pentameter.

Form. Shakespeare wrote his plays in a poetic form called blank verse. Blank verse is unrhymed iambic pentameter. This is one of the most common metrical patterns in English. Blank verse is a poetic form that has
120 been used by classic poets for many centuries.

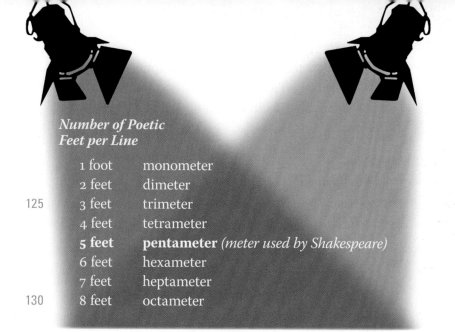

Number of Poetic Feet per Line	
1 foot	monometer
2 feet	dimeter
3 feet	trimeter
4 feet	tetrameter
5 feet	**pentameter** *(meter used by Shakespeare)*
6 feet	hexameter
7 feet	heptameter
8 feet	octameter

125

130

"The Seven Ages of Man" reprinted from *As You Like It*, Act II, scene vii by William Shakespeare

Think About It

1. Summarize the events in William Shakespeare's life.

2. Tell why the vocabulary list included after "The Seven Ages of Man" speech is likely to be helpful to a modern reader.

3. Paraphrase the thought of the speech, "The Seven Ages of Man."

4. Decide what you think Jacques' attitude is toward human life and the parts we play, taking into account that Jacques is a sad and gloomy character.

5. Consider how you might revise Jacques' descriptions of the phases of life to represent the opposite of his opinion.

6. Choose a line or lines from the speech, "The Seven Ages of Man." Rewrite the line or lines. Divide each line into poetic feet, or segments. Underline the syllables that are stressed.

Create Movement

STEP

1

Phonemic Awareness and Phonics

Unit 26 introduces the two sounds for **oo**: / ŏŏ / as in **book** and / ōō / as in **moo**. It also introduces three additional sound-spelling correspondences for / ōō /.

Sound-Spelling Patterns for oo

The letters **oo** represent two sounds:

- ■ / ŏŏ / as in **took**
- ■ / ōō / as in **moo**

Here are three additional sound-spelling correspondences for / ōō /:

- ■ **ue** as in **blue**
- ■ **ui** as in **suit**
- ■ **ou** as in **soup**

Go to the **Vowel Chart** on page A3. Find these vowel sounds on the chart:

Find / ŏŏ /. Find the cue word **took**.

Find / ōō /. Find the cue words **moo**, **blue**, **suit**, and **soup**.

Word Recognition and Spelling

Prefixes

We can expand words and change meaning by adding **prefixes**.
These word parts are added to the beginnings of words.
Example: **ob** + serve = observe

(See Step 3: Vocabulary and Morphology for links to meaning.)

> **Unit 26 Prefix**
> **ob-**

Suffixes

We can expand words and change meaning by adding **suffixes**.
These word parts are added to the ends of words.
Example: symbol + **ic** = symbolic

(See Step 3: Vocabulary and Morphology for links to meaning and
Step 4: Grammar and Usage for function.)

> **Unit 26 Suffixes**
> **-ic, -ity**

Roots

We can build words using **roots**. Roots carry the most important
part of a word's meaning. We usually attach a prefix or suffix to
make a root into a word. Example: con + **tain** = contain

(See Step 3: Vocabulary and Morphology for links to meaning.)

> **Unit 26 Roots**
> **cept/cap/ceit; ten/tin/tain**

Essential Words

Unit 26 Essential Words

four	move	movie
lose	movement	prove

Spelling Lists

The Unit 26 spelling lists contain three categories:

1. Words with **oo** for / $\breve{oo}$ / and / $\overline{oo}$ /; words with **ou**, **ui**, and **ue** for / $\overline{oo}$ / and / $y\overline{oo}$ /

2. **Essential Words** (in italics)

3. Words with prefixes, roots, and suffixes

Spelling Lists

Lessons 1–5		Lessons 6–10	
argue	*movement*	afternoon	tenants
choose	*movie*	continue	textbooks
four	*prove*	group	took
fruit	rescue	historic	tour
juice	soup	lookout	unacceptable
loose	stood	maintenance	value
lose	wool	obsolete	woodland
move		quality	

Vocabulary and Morphology

Unit Vocabulary

Sound-spelling correspondences from this unit and previous units make up this unit's vocabulary.

- What do these words mean?
- Do some of them mean more than one thing? Which ones?

UNIT Vocabulary

oo for / o͝o /	wood	hoot	soon	pursue
book	woodland	igloo	spool	rescue
brook	woof	kangaroo	spoon	true
childhood	wool	loop	stool	value
cook		loose	tattoo	
cookie	**oo for / ō͞o /**	moo	too	**ui for / ō͞o /**
crook	afternoon	moon	tool	fruit
crooked	baboon	moose	tooth	juice
foot	balloon	mushroom	toothbrush	suit
football	bathroom	noodle	toothpaste	suitcase
good	bloom	noon	toothpick	
goodbye	boo	poodle	troop	**ou for / ō͞o /**
hood	boom	pool	zoo	contour
hoof	boot	proof		group
hook	booth	raccoon	**ue for / ō͞o /**	route
look	broom	roof	argue	soup
lookout	cartoon	room	avenue	tour
notebook	choose	root	blue	tournament
shook	cool	scoop	clue	wound
stood	food	shampoo	continue	you
textbook	fool	shoot	due	youth
took	goose	smooth	glue	

Word Relationships

Antonyms are words that have opposite meanings.
Example: true/false

Synonyms are words that have the same or similar meanings.
Example: look/observe

Meaning Parts

Prefixes

Prefixes can add to or change the meanings of words. The Unit 26 prefix has the following meanings.

Unit 26 Prefix	Meanings	Examples
ob-	down; against; facing; to	oblige, observe, obsolete

Review: A prefix often assimilates to the base word or root to which it is attached. In **assimilation**, the last letter of the prefix changes or sounds more similar to the first letter of the base or root. This change makes pronunciation easier. The meaning of the prefix does not change when it is assimilated.
Examples: **ob** + **fer** = **offer**; **ob** + **pose** = **oppose**

Suffixes

Suffixes can add to or change the meanings of words. When added to a base word or root, they can change the base word or root to a noun or an adjective.

Unit 26 Suffixes	Meanings	Examples
-ity	state or quality of	finality, legality, rigidity
-ic	of; pertaining to; characterized by	economic, historic, symbolic

Roots

Roots form the basic meaning part of a word. Roots of English words often come from another language, especially Latin. A root usually needs a prefix or suffix to make it into a word.

Example: con + **tain** = contain (con = with; tain = to hold; contain = to hold something within)

Unit 26 Roots	Meanings	Examples
cept	to take; hold; catch	except, intercept, percept
cap	to take; hold; catch	capable, captivate, captor
ceit	to take; hold; catch	conceit, deceit, deceitful
ten	to hold	content, retentive, tenure
tin	to hold	continue, discontinue, pertinent
tain	to hold	contain, detain, retain

Challenge Morphemes

Root	Meanings	Examples
vert	to turn	divert, invert, revert
vers	to turn	converse, reverse, universe

Grammar and Usage

Adverbs

Review: **Adverbs** are words that describe verbs, adjectives, or other adverbs. They answer the questions: **How? When? Where? Why?** or **Under what conditions?** They can be:

- Single words. Examples: **daily**, **suddenly**
- Prepositional phrases that function as adverbs. Example: **to Mango Street** is a prepositional phrase that answers the question **Where?** It is a prepositional phrase in *form*, but *functions* as an adverb.

Conjunctions

Review: **Conjunctions** join words, phrases, or clauses in a sentence. **And**, **or**, and **but** are **coordinating conjunctions**.

Subordinating conjunctions establish the relationship between a dependent clause and the rest of the sentence.

> **Subordinating Conjunctions in Unit 26**
> although, because, if, unless, while

Participles

Review: The **present participle** is formed by adding **-ing** to the base verb. Example: look + **ing** = looking

The **past participle** of a regular verb is formed by adding **-ed** to the base verb. Example: obtain + **ed** = (have) obtained. Some past participles are irregular; their forms must be memorized.

See the Appendix, page A36, for a complete list of irregular verbs.

- Participles can be in verb phrases or can act as adjectives.

    In a verb phrase, a present participle is used with a form of the helping verb **be** (**am, is, are**). Examples: is arguing, are gluing

    In a verb phrase, a past participle is used with a form of the helping verb **have** (**have, has, had**). Example: has chosen

    In an adjective phrase, present and past participles tell more about a noun. Examples: a moving van, a mistaken identity

Phrases

Review: A **phrase** is a group of words that functions as a single word. A phrase does not have a subject and predicate.
Examples: an enormous tsunami, with a loud crash

A **participial phrase** begins with a participle and is followed by a word (or group of words) that modifies it or receives its action. A participial phrase functions as an adjective because it modifies a noun or pronoun. It can come before or after the word it modifies.

> **Participial Phrases**
>
> The tsunami, **crashing on the shore**, caused devastation.
>
> **Crashing on the shore**, the tsunami caused devastation.
>
> The participial phrase **crashing on the shore** modifies the noun **tsunami**.

Clauses

Review: A **clause** is a group of words that contains a subject and a predicate. An **independent clause** has one subject and one predicate; it represents a complete thought. A **dependent clause** cannot stand by itself. It combines with an independent clause to create meaning.

Some dependent clauses function as adverbs. An **adverbial clause**:

- Answers the questions: **How? When? Where? Why?** or **Under what condition?** It expands the predicate part of the sentence.
- Usually begins with a subordinating conjunction.
- Can occur at the beginning or end of a sentence.

> **Adverbial Clause**
>
> I lived in the house on Mango Street **while I dreamed of a new one**.
>
> The clause **while I dreamed of a new one** answers the question **when** about the action verb **lived**. It begins with the subordinating conjunction **while**.

Sentence Pattern

Adverbial clauses can help vary sentence structure. They can come at the beginning or end of a sentence. A comma is placed after the adverbial clause at the beginning of the sentence.

> **Sentences With Adverbial Clauses**
>
> **If you walk down Mango Street**, you can see the little red house.
>
> You can see the little red house **if you walk down Mango Street**.

Sentence Types

Review: English has four basic sentence types:

- A **declarative** sentence states a fact or opinion. The end punctuation is a period. Example: Their house was on Mango Street.
- An **interrogative sentence** asks a question. The end punctuation is a question mark. Example: Do you play chess?
- An **imperative sentence** gives a command. The end punctuation is a period. Example: Watch your step.
- An **exclamatory sentence** expresses strong emotion. The end punctuation is an exclamation point. Example: Get out!

Punctuation

Review: The **colon** has several uses. One use of the colon is to follow the greeting in a business letter.

The colon also introduces a list following an independent clause.

> **Colon Introducing a List**
>
> Waverly played chess against many different opponents: men, students, and competitors.

Confusing Word Pairs

Lie is a verb that means "to recline." It can never take a direct object. **Lay** is a verb that means "to put or place." It must take a direct object. These words are often confused because the past tense form of **lie** is **lay**. Examples:

The children **lie** on their backs in bed.

The girls **lay** the chess pieces on the table.

Gone and **went** are also often confused. **Gone** is the past participle of **go,** while **went** is the past tense of **go**. When **gone** is used as a past participle, it must have the helping verb **have** to complete it.

Waverly had **gone** to meet her mother.

Waverly **went** to many chess competitions.

STEP 5

Listening and Reading Comprehension

Informational Text

■ Some **informational text** is nonfiction material about a specific topic, event, experience, or circumstance. It is often accompanied by visual information in the form of charts, graphs, or illustrations. The visual information provides additional content about the subject matter. "**Tsunamis**" uses visual information to enhance the text content.

Vocabulary in Context

■ **Context clues** help us understand new vocabulary. Pronoun referents, meaning signals, and visuals, such as charts and graphs, provide meaning links.

Signal Words

■ Different types of sentences can help us think about new information and ideas in different ways. Identifying **signal words** within sentences can improve comprehension.

See the Appendix, page A20, for a complete list of signal words based on Bloom's Taxonomy.

Literary Genres

■ **Genres** are types or categories of literature. Unit 26 features fiction and autobiography.

■ **Fiction** is a literary genre that includes imaginary stories. Fiction is sometimes based on real people, places, or events. "**The House on Mango Street**" and "**Rules of the Game**" are examples of fiction.

■ **Autobiography** is a special type of biography. In an autobiography, writers tell of their own lives, rather than someone else's. The selection, "**Savion Glover: The Man Can Move**," is autobiographical.

Plot Analysis

- **Plot** refers to the sequence of events in a narrative or drama. The plot guides the author in composing the work. It guides the reader through the story.

- **Characters and setting**, found in the introduction, set the foundation for a story. The characters, which can be people, animals, or things, interact in the story. The setting is the story's time and place. Together these two components make up the introduction in the first element of plot development.

- To understand how a plot develops, we must first identify a story's main **problem** and its **solution**. Without a problem, or conflict, there would be no story—everything would remain the same.

- After we become proficient in identifying a story's main problem and solution, we will learn more about plot development and apply it in our writing.

- Plot development usually consists of five elements:

  Introduction (setting and characters);

  Conflict (rising action);

  Climax (turning point);

  Resolution (falling action);

  Conclusion (the situation at the end of the story, with a look to the future).

STEP

6 Speaking and Writing

Signal Words

■ Different types of sentences require different responses depending on the focus of signal words. Identifying **signal words** within sentences improves the accuracy of responses to oral and written questions.

See the Appendix, page A20, for a complete list of signal words based on Bloom's Taxonomy.

Paragraph or Composition Organization

■ Some paragraphs or compositions compare. A **compare and contrast paragraph** or **composition** tells the readers how two or more things are alike (compare), and how they are different (contrast). The organization helps us to compose the specific similarities and differences, helping to make our writing clear to our readers.

Transition words signal this organization. Some of the transition words and phrases identify how things are alike. Other transition words identify how things are different. Selecting the specific word to use in a composition also helps to make our writing clear to our readers.

Transition Words for Compare and Contrast

Compare	Contrast
Both are similiar.	They are different.
Both are alike.	They are not the same.
They share these features.	They do not share these features.

More About Words

- **Bonus Words** use the same sound-spelling correspondences that we have studied in this unit and previous units.

- **Idioms** are common phrases that cannot be understood by the meanings of their separate words—only by the entire phrase.

- **Why? Word History** explains the origin of the word **etymology**.

UNIT Bonus Words

oo for / ŏŏ /
bankbook
bookends
bookkeeper
booklet
bookmark
bookstore
checkbook
cookbook
cookery
falsehood
fishhook
foothill
goody-goody
guidebook
hoodwink
woodcutter
woodpecker

oo for / ōō /
bamboo
bamboozle
bassoon
blooper
boomerang
boost
bootstrap
bridegroom
brood
broomstick
caboose
carpool
childproof
coolant
coop
croon
darkroom
doom
drool
droop
eyetooth
fireproof
foolery
foolhardy
foolproof
gloom
gooseberry
gooseneck
groove
lagoon
loophole
mongoose
paratroop
pontoon
proofread
roommate
roost
spoof
spook
stoop
tablespoon
taboo
teaspoon
toot
tycoon
zookeeper

ue for / ōō /
bluebell
bluebird
blueblood
blueprint
ensue
overdue
residue
subdue
undue

ui for / ōō /
bruise
cruise
grapefruit
recruit

ou for / ōō /
acoustic
ampoule
boutique
cougar
coupon
courier
croup
detour
goulash
grouper
louver
mousse
nougat
recoup
subgroup
toucan
tourney
tourniquet
troupe
velour

Idioms	
Idiom	**Meaning**
be off the hook	be released from blame or obligation
be on the move	be busily moving about; active; making progress; advancing
be out of the woods	be safe from trouble or danger
be penny wise and pound foolish	be careful in small matters, but careless about important things
cook your goose	ruin your chances
have a sweet tooth	like sweet foods
hit the books	study; prepare carefully for class
hit the roof	lose your temper; become violently angry
look a gift horse in the mouth	be critical or suspicious of something you have received as a gift or for free
shoot the breeze	talk idly; have a trivial conversation

Word History

Etymology—The true meaning of a word is revealed through its history—its etymology. The science of word history is called **etymology**. But where did the word **etymology** come from?

In fact, the word **etymology** comes from ancient Greek. Words in Ancient Greek were made up of combining forms. Many of the scientific and technological terms of modern English come from Greek. **Etymology** is an example of a borrowing from Greek. The first combining form, **etumon**, means "true sense of a word." It is combined with the second combining form, **logy**, which means "study of." Together, the combined forms reveal the meaning of the scientific term, **etymology**.

Tsunamis

An aerial photo shows damage caused by a tsunami in Banda Aceh, Indonesia, 2005.

On December 26, 2004, there was a huge 9.0 earthquake. It happened under the Indian Ocean. Soon after, a tsunami slammed into the coastlines of South Asia. It hit India and Africa. This deadly wave couldn't be
5 stopped. Some people saw what was happening. They knew a tsunami was coming. They saved lives. Sadly, thousands of people also died.

What is a tsunami? A tsunami is a giant wave. A wave is movement. It moves energy through water. Have you
10 thought that a wave is water moving forward? This is not the case. In fact, the water itself does not move forward. Only the energy moves. Imagine a seagull. The seagull is sitting on a wave. The wave rolls toward the beach. The seagull doesn't move forward. It just bobs up and down.
15 What would happen if the water itself were moving? The seagull would move forward with it. Most ordinary waves are driven by wind. The wind blows across the water's surface. Tsunamis, however, are not ordinary waves. They begin with energy. It comes from the ocean floor.
20 Earthquakes are the most common cause. But landslides and volcanic eruptions can also cause tsunamis.

The earth's crust is divided into several large pieces. These are called plates. Plates make up the continents. They make up the seafloor. Sometimes, the edges of the
25 plates rub against one another. Sometimes, the edge of one plate pushes down. It can push under the edge of another plate. This movement is slow. Usually, it's a few centimeters a year. Sometimes, there is a much faster, bigger shift. An earthquake results. Suddenly, one ocean
30 crust plate pushes under another. When this happens, the upper crust springs up. It can displace vast amounts of water. A massive wave is born.

The wave's energy can travel at the speed of a jet. But the movement happens below the surface. In the deep sea,

35 it's hardly noticeable. Then the wave nears the shore. The shoreline is much more shallow. The wave gains height. Some come in as giant waves. Others come in as a series of strong floods.

Scientists are finding better ways to predict these deadly
40 waves. Stations in the Pacific record earthquake activity. They measure changes in sea level. They detect changes in water pressure. These changes can indicate a tsunami. If one is spotted, a warning goes out. There is not a warning system in the Indian Ocean. Now we know one is needed.

45 We can also learn more about these deadly waves. A schoolgirl was on the beach in Thailand. She saw the ocean going out before the wave hit. She had studied tsunamis in school. She warned others and saved them. Her knowledge saved lives.

50 We cannot avoid disasters such as tsunamis. We can build more warning systems. We can learn about tsunamis. We can be better prepared when the next one comes.

What Causes a Tsunami?

2 The force of the earthquake pushes up a large amount of water. Big waves are created.

1 Two plates of the earth's crust grind against each other and cause an earthquake.

3 The waves spread in all directions. The waves get higher and higher as they hit shallow water near the shore.

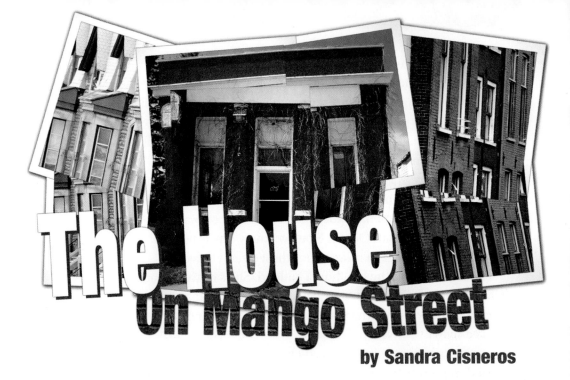

The House on Mango Street

by Sandra Cisneros

You remember periods in your own childhood, periods that affected you in different ways. As you read these segments from Sandra Cisneros' The House on Mango Street, think about the storyteller's childhood experiences,

5 *and see if you can relate to any of them. Have you ever had to move? What's it like to move into a new neighborhood? How does moving into a new neighborhood translate to moving into a new passage of your life?*

The House on Mango Street

We didn't always live on Mango Street. Before that we
10 lived on Loomis on the third floor, and before that we lived on Keeler. Before Keeler it was Paulina, and before that I can't remember. But what I remember most is moving a lot. Each time it seemed there'd be one more of us. By the time we got to Mango Street we were six—Mama, Papa, Carlos,
15 Kiki, my sister Nenny and me.

The house on Mango Street is ours, and we don't have to pay rent to anybody, or share the yard with the people downstairs, or be careful not to make too much noise, and there isn't a landlord banging on the ceiling with a broom.
20 But even so, it's not the house we'd thought we'd get.

We had to leave the flat on Loomis quick. The water pipes broke and the landlord wouldn't fix them because the house was too old. We had to leave fast. We were using the washroom next door and carrying water over in empty milk gallons. That's why Mama and Papa looked for a house, and that's why we moved into the house on Mango Street, far away, on the other side of town.

They always told us that one day we would move into a house, a real house that would be ours for always so we wouldn't have to move each year. And our house would have running water and pipes that worked. And inside it would have real stairs, not hallway stairs, but stairs inside like the houses on TV. And we'd have a basement and at least three washrooms so when we took a bath we wouldn't have to tell everybody. Our house would be white with trees around it, a great big yard and grass growing without a fence. This was the house Papa talked about when he held a lottery ticket and this was the house Mama dreamed up in the stories she told us before we went to bed.

But the house on Mango Street is not the way they told it at all. It's small and red with tight steps in front and windows so small you'd think they were holding their breath. Bricks are crumbling in places, and the front door is so swollen you have to push hard to get in. There is no front yard, only four little elms the city planted by the curb. Out back is a small garage for the car we don't own yet and a small yard that looks smaller between the two buildings on either side. There are stairs in our house, but they're ordinary hallway stairs, and the house has only one washroom. Everybody has to share a bedroom—Mama and Papa, Carlos and Kiki, me and Nenny.

Once when we were living on Loomis, a nun from my school passed by and saw me playing out front. The laundromat downstairs had been boarded up because it had been robbed two days before and the owner had painted on the wood YES WE'RE OPEN so as not to lose business.

Where do you live? she asked.

There, I said pointing up to the third floor.

You live *there*?

60   *There.* I had to look to where she pointed—the third floor, the paint peeling, wooden bars Papa had nailed on the windows so we wouldn't fall out. You live *there*? The way she said it made me feel like nothing. *There.* I lived *there.* I nodded.

65   I knew then I had to have a house. A real house. One I could point to. But this isn't it. The house on Mango Street isn't it. For the time being, Mama says. **Temporary**, says Papa. But I know how those things go.

Temporary

for a limited time; short-term

Boys & Girls

    The boys and the girls live in separate worlds. The boys
70 in their universe and we in ours. My brothers for example. They've got plenty to say to me and Nenny inside the house. But outside they can't be seen talking to girls. Carlos and Kiki are each other's best friend . . . not ours.

    Nenny is too young to be my friend. She's just my sister
75 and that was not my fault. You don't pick your sisters, you just get them and sometimes they come like Nenny.

    She can't play with those Vargas kids or she'll turn out just like them. And since she comes right after me, she is my responsibility.

80   Someday I will have a best friend all my own. One I can tell my secrets to. One who will understand my jokes

without my having to explain them. Until then I am a red balloon, a balloon tied to an anchor.

Laughter

Nenny and I don't look like sisters . . . not right away.
85 Not the way you can tell with Rachel and Lucy who have the same fat popsicle lips like everybody else in their family. But me and Nenny, we are more alike than you would know. Our laughter for example. Not the shy ice cream bells' giggle of Rachel and Lucy's family, but all of a sudden
90 and surprised like a pile of dishes breaking. And other things I can't explain.

One day we were passing a house that looked, in my mind, like houses I had seen in Mexico. I don't know why. There was nothing about the house that looked exactly like
95 the houses I remembered. I'm not even sure why I thought it, but it seemed to feel right.

Look at that house, I said, it looks like Mexico.

Rachel and Lucy look at me like I'm crazy, but before they can let out a laugh, Nenny says: Yes, that's Mexico all
100 right. That's what I was thinking exactly.

Meme Ortiz

Meme Ortiz moved into Cathy's house after her family moved away. His name isn't really Meme. His name is Juan. But when we asked him what his name was he said Meme, and that's what everybody calls him except his mother.
105 Meme has a dog with gray eyes, a sheepdog with two names, one in English and one in Spanish. The dog is big, like a man dressed in a dog suit, and runs the same way its owner does, clumsy and wild and with the limbs flopping all over the place like untied shoes.
110 Cathy's father built the house Meme moved into. It is wooden. Inside the floors slant. Some rooms uphill. Some down. And there are no closets. Out front there are twenty-one steps, all **lopsided** and jutting like crooked teeth (made that way on purpose, Cathy said, so the rain will
115 slide off), and when Meme's mama calls from the doorway,

lopsided
sagging; leaning to one side

Meme goes scrambling up the twenty-one wooden stairs
with the dog with two names scrambling after him.

Around the back is a yard, mostly dirt, and a greasy
bunch of boards that used to be a garage. But what you
120 remember most is this tree, huge, with fat arms and mighty
families of squirrels in the higher branches. All around, the
neighborhood of roofs, black-tarred and A-framed, and in
their gutters, the balls that never came back down to earth.
Down at the base of the tree, the dog with two names
125 barks into the empty air, and there at the end of the block,
looking smaller still, our house with its feet tucked under
like a cat.

This is the tree we chose for the First Annual Tarzan
Jumping Contest. Meme won. And broke both arms.

Bums in the Attic

130   I want a house on a hill like the ones with the gardens
where Papa works. We go on Sundays, Papa's day off. I
used to go. I don't anymore. You don't like to go out with
us, Papa says. Getting too old? Getting too stuck-up, says
Nenny. I don't tell them I am **ashamed** —all of us staring
135 out the window like the hungry. I am tired of looking at
what we can't have. When we win the lottery . . . Mama
begins, and then I stop listening.

People who live on hills sleep so close to the stars they
forget those of us who live too much on earth. They don't

ashamed
embarrassed

look down at all except to be content to live on hills. They
have nothing to do with last week's garbage or fear of rats.
Night comes. Nothing wakes them but the wind.

One day I'll own my own house, but I won't forget who
I am or where I came from. Passing bums will ask, Can I
come in? I'll offer them the **attic**, ask them to stay, because
I know how it is to be without a house.

Some days after dinner, guests and I will sit in front of a
fire. Floorboards will squeak upstairs. The attic grumble.

Rats? they'll ask.

Bums, I'll say, and I'll be happy.

> **attic**
> a space under the roof of a house

A Smart Cookie

I could've been somebody, you know? my mother says
and sighs. She has lived in this city her whole life. She can
speak two languages. She can sing an opera. She knows
how to fix a TV. But she doesn't know which subway train
to take to get downtown. I hold her hand very tight while
we wait for the right train to arrive.

She used to draw when she had time. Now she draws
with a needle and thread, little knotted rosebuds, tulips
made of silk thread. Someday she would like to go to the
ballet. Someday she would like to see a play. She borrows
opera records from the public library and sings with velvety
lungs powerful as morning glories.

Today while cooking oatmeal she is Madame Butterfly
until she sighs and points the wooden spoon at me. I
could've been somebody, you know? Esperanza, you go to
school. Study hard. That Madame Butterfly was a fool. She
stirs the oatmeal. Look at my *comadres*. She means Izaura
whose husband left and Yolanda whose husband is dead.
Got to take care all your own, she says shaking her head.

Then out of nowhere:

Shame is a bad thing, you know. It keeps you down. You
want to know why I quit school? Because I didn't have nice
clothes. No clothes, but I had brains.

Yup, she says disgusted, stirring again. I was a smart
cookie then.

Alicia & I Talking on Edna's Steps

I like Alicia because once she gave me a little leather purse with the word GUADALAJARA stitched on it, which is home for Alicia, and one day she will go back there. But today she is listening to my sadness because I don't have
180 a house.

You live right here, 4006 Mango, Alicia says and points to the house I am ashamed of.

No, this isn't my house I say and shake my head as if shaking could undo the year I've lived here. I don't belong.
185 I don't ever want to come from here. You have a home, Alicia, and one day you'll go there, to a town you remember, but me I never had a house, not even a photograph . . . only one I dream of.

No, Alicia says. Like it or not you are Mango Street, and
190 one day you'll come back too.

Not me. Not until somebody makes it better.

Who's going to do it? The mayor?

And the thought of the mayor coming to Mango Street makes me laugh out loud.
195   Who's going to do it? Not the mayor.

A House of My Own

Not a flat. Not an apartment in back. Not a man's house. Not a daddy's. A house all my own. With my **porch** and my pillow, my pretty purple petunias. My books and my stories. My two shoes waiting beside the bed. Nobody
200 to shake a stick at. Nobody's garbage to pick up after.

Only a house quiet as snow, a space for myself to go, clean as paper before the poem.

Mango Says Goodbye Sometimes

I like to tell stories. I tell them inside my head. I tell
205 them after the mailman says, Here's your mail. Here's your mail he said.

I make a story for my life, for each step my brown shoe takes. I say, "And so she trudged up the wooden stairs, her sad brown shoes taking her to the house she never liked."

porch

a covered structure outside the entrance to a house

210 I like to tell stories. I am going to tell you a story about a girl who didn't want to belong.

We didn't always live on Mango Street. Before that we lived on Loomis on the third floor, and before that we lived on Keeler. Before Keeler it was Paulina, but what I 215 remember most is Mango Street, sad red house, the house I belong but do not belong to.

I put it down on paper and then the ghost does not **ache** so much. I write it down and Mango says goodbye sometimes. She does not hold me with both arms. She sets 220 me free.

ache
a dull, lasting pain

One day I will pack my bags of books and paper. One day I will say goodbye to Mango. I am too strong for her to keep me here forever. One day I will go away.

Friends and neighbors will say, What happened to that 225 Esperanza? Where did she go with all those books and paper? Why did she march so far away?

They will not know I have gone away to come back. For the ones I left behind. For the ones who cannot out.

From *The House on Mango Street* by Sandra Cisneros

Answer It

1. Make a generalization about Esperanza's relationship with her sister Nenny.

2. In "Meme Ortiz," the narrator describes her house as looking like a cat with "its feet tucked under." Describe the image that is created by that comparision.

3. In "Alicia and I Talking on Edna's Steps," Alicia says to Esperanza, "Like it or not, you are Mango Street, and one day you'll come back, too." Paraphrase Alicia's words.

4. In "Mango Says Goodbye Sometimes," the narrator announces, "I am going to tell you a story about a girl who didn't want to belong." Explain the meaning of that line.

5. Summarize how writing helps Esperanza feel better about where she comes from.

RULES OF THE GAME

by Amy Tan

American author,
Amy Tan.

Like Sandra Cisneros' The House on Mango Street, Amy Tan's "Rules of the Game," an excerpt from The Joy Luck Club, deals with childhood memories that involve movement.

In addition to being highly respected for their writing
5 *abilities, both writers are famous for their focus and keen insights into their own cultures. Sandra Cisneros writes about Latino culture; Amy Tan writes about Chinese Americans.*

As you read these selections, think about what the word "movement" means in each selection. What did it mean in
10 *The House on Mango Street? Does "movement" have more than one layer of meaning?*

I was six when my mother taught me the art of invisible strength. It was a strategy for winning arguments, respect from others, and eventually, though neither of us knew it at
15 the time, chess games.

"Bite back your tongue," scolded my mother when I cried loudly, yanking her hand toward the store that sold bags of salted plums. At home, she said, "Wise guy, he not go against wind. In Chinese we say, Come from South,
20 blow with wind—poom!—North will follow. Strongest wind cannot be seen."

The next week I bit back my tongue as we entered the store with the forbidden candies. When my mother

finished her shopping, she quietly plucked a small bag of
25 plums from the rack and put it on the counter with the rest
of the items.

My mother imparted her daily truths so she could help
my older brothers and me rise above our circumstances.
We lived in San Francisco's Chinatown. Like most of the
30 other Chinese children who played in the back alleys of
restaurants and curio shops, I didn't think we were poor.
My bowl was always full, three five-course meals every day,
beginning with a soup full of mysterious things I didn't
want to know the names of.
35 We lived on Waverly Place, in a warm, clean, two-
bedroom flat that sat above a small Chinese bakery
specializing in steamed pastries and dim sum. In the early
morning, when the alley was still quiet, I could smell
fragrant red beans as they were cooked down to a pasty
40 sweetness. By daybreak, our flat was heavy with the odor
of fried sesame balls and sweet curried chicken crescents.
From my bed, I would listen as my father got ready for
work, then lock the door behind him, one-two-three clicks.
At the end of our two-block alley was a small sandlot
45 playground with swings and slides well-shined down the
middle with use. The play area was bordered by wood-slat
benches where old-country people sat cracking roasted

watermelon seeds with their golden teeth and scattering
the husks to an impatient gathering of gurgling pigeons.
50 The best playground, however, was the dark alley itself.
It was crammed with daily mysteries and adventures. My
brothers and I would peer into the medicinal herb shop,
watching old Li dole out onto a stiff sheet of white paper
the right amount of insect shells, saffron-colored seeds, and
55 pungent leaves for his ailing customers. It was said that he
once cured a woman dying of an ancestral curse that had
eluded the best of American doctors. Next to the pharmacy
was a printer who specialized in gold-embossed wedding
invitations and festive red banners.
60   Farther down the street was Ping Yuen Fish Market.
The front window displayed a tank crowded with doomed
fish and turtles struggling to gain footing on the slimy
green-tiled sides. A hand-written sign informed tourists,
"Within this store, is all for food, not for pet." Inside, the
65 butchers with their bloodstained white smocks deftly
gutted the fish while customers cried out their orders and
shouted, "Give me your freshest," to which the butchers
always protested, "All are freshest." On less crowded
market days, we would inspect the crates of live frogs and
70 crabs which we were warned not to poke, boxes of dried
cuttlefish, and row upon row of iced prawns, squid, and
slippery fish. The sanddabs made me shiver each time;
their eyes lay on one flattened side and reminded me of
my mother's story of a careless girl who ran into a crowded
75 street and was crushed by a cab. "Was smash flat," reported
my mother.
      At the corner of the alley was Hong Sing's, a four-table
café with a recessed stairwell in front that led to a door
marked "Tradesmen." My brothers and I believed the bad
80 people emerged from this door at night. Tourists never
went to Hong Sing's, since the menu was printed only in
Chinese. A Caucasian man with a big camera once posed
me and my playmates in front of the restaurant. He had
us move to the side of the picture window so the photo
85 would capture the roasted duck with its head dangling
from a juice-covered rope. After he took the picture, I told

him he should go into Hong Sing's and eat dinner. When
he smiled and asked me what they served, I shouted, "Guts
and duck's feet and octopus gizzards!" Then I ran off with
90 my friends, shrieking with laughter as we scampered across
the alley and hid in the entryway grotto of the China Gem
Company, my heart pounding with hope that he would
chase us.

My mother named me after the street we lived on:
95 Waverly Place Jong, my official name for important
American documents. But my family called me Meimei,
"Little Sister." I was the youngest, the only daughter. Each
morning before school, my mother would twist and yank on
my thick black hair until she had formed two tightly wound
100 pigtails. One day, as she struggled to weave a hard-toothed
comb through my disobedient hair, I had a sly thought.

I asked her, "Ma, what is Chinese torture?" My mother
shook her head. A bobby pin was wedged between her lips.
She wetted her palm and smoothed the hair above my ear,
105 then pushed the pin in so that it nicked sharply against
my scalp.

"Who say this word?" she asked without a trace of
knowing how wicked I was being. I shrugged my shoulders
and said, "Some boy in my class said Chinese people do
110 Chinese torture."

"Chinese people do many things," she said simply. "Chinese people do business, do medicine, do painting. Not lazy like American people. We do torture. Best torture."

115 My older brother Vincent was the one who actually got the chess set. We had gone to the annual Christmas party held at the First Chinese Baptist Church at the end of the alley. The missionary ladies had put together a Santa bag of gifts donated by members of another church. None of the gifts had names on them. There were separate sacks for 120 boys and girls of different ages.

One of the Chinese parishioners had donned a Santa Claus costume with a stiff paper beard with cotton balls glued to it. I think the only children who thought he was the real thing were too young to know that Santa Claus 125 was not Chinese. When my turn came up, the Santa man asked me how old I was. I thought it was a trick question; I was seven according to the American formula and eight by the Chinese calendar. I said I was born on March 17, 1951. That seemed to satisfy him. He then solemnly asked me if I 130 had been a very, very good girl this year and did I obey my parents. I knew the only answer to that. I nodded back with equal solemnity.

Having watched the other children opening their gifts, I already knew that the big gifts were not necessarily the 135 nicest ones. One girl my age got a large coloring book of

biblical characters, while a less greedy girl who selected a smaller box received a glass vial of lavender toilet water. The sound of the box was also important. A ten-year-old boy had chosen a box that jangled when he shook it. It was
140 a tin globe of the world with a slit for inserting money. He must have thought it was full of dimes and nickels, because when he saw that it had just ten pennies, his face fell with such undisguised disappointment that his mother slapped the side of his head and led him out of the church hall,
145 apologizing to the crowd for her son who had such bad manners he couldn't appreciate such a fine gift.

As I peered into the sack, I quickly fingered the remaining presents, testing their weight, imagining what they contained. I chose a heavy, compact one that was
150 wrapped in shiny silver foil and a red satin ribbon. It was a twelve-pack of Life Savers and I spent the rest of the party arranging and rearranging the candy tubes in the order of my favorites. My brother Winston chose wisely as well. His present turned out to be a box of intricate plastic parts; the
155 instructions on the box proclaimed that when they were properly assembled he would have an authentic miniature replica of a World War II submarine.

Vincent got the chess set, which would have been a very decent present to get at a church Christmas party,
160 except it was obviously used and, as we discovered later, it was missing a black pawn and a white knight. My mother graciously thanked the unknown **benefactor**, saying, "Too good. Cost too much." At which point, an old lady with fine white, wispy hair nodded toward our family and said with a
165 whistling whisper, "Merry, merry Christmas."

When we got home, my mother told Vincent to throw the chess set away. "She not want it. We not want it," she said, tossing her head stiffly to the side with a tight, proud smile. My brothers had deaf ears. They were already
170 lining up the chess pieces and reading from the dog-eared instruction book.

I watched Vincent and Winston play during Christmas week. The chess board seemed to hold elaborate secrets

benefactor

a donor; person who gives something to another

waiting to be untangled. The chessmen were more
175 powerful than Old Li's magic herbs that cured ancestral
curses. And my brothers wore such serious faces that I was
sure something was at stake that was greater than avoiding
the tradesmen's door to Hong Sing's.

"Let me! Let me!" I begged between games when one
180 brother or the other would sit back with a deep sigh of
relief and victory, the other annoyed, unable to let go of the
outcome. Vincent at first refused to let me play, but when I
offered my Life Savers as replacements for the buttons that
filled in for the missing pieces, he relented. He chose the
185 flavors: wild cherry for the black pawn and peppermint for
the white knight. Winner could eat both.

As our mother sprinkled flour and rolled out small
doughy circles for the steamed dumplings that would
be our dinner that night, Vincent explained the rules,
190 pointing to each piece. "You have sixteen pieces and so
do I. One king and queen, two bishops, two knights,
two castles, and eight pawns. The pawns can only move
forward one step, except on the first move. Then they
can move two. But they can only take men by moving
195 crossways like this, except in the beginning, when you can
move ahead and take another pawn."

"Why?" I asked as I moved my pawn. "Why can't they
move more steps?"

"Because they're pawns," he said.
200   "But why do they go crossways to take other men. Why
aren't there any women and children?"

"Why is the sky blue? Why must you always ask stupid
questions?" asked Vincent. "This is a game. These are the
rules. I didn't make them up. See. Here. In the book." He
205 jabbed a page with a pawn in his hand. "Pawn. P-A-W-N.
Pawn. Read it yourself."

My mother patted the flour off her hands. "Let me see
book," she said quietly. She scanned the pages quickly, not
reading the foreign English symbols, seeming to search
210 deliberately for nothing in particular.

"This American rules," she concluded at last. "Every
time people come out from foreign country, must know

rules. You not know, judge say, Too bad, go back. They not telling you why so you can use their way go forward. They say, Don't know why, you find out yourself. But they knowing all the time. Better you take it, find out why yourself." She tossed her head back with a satisfied smile.

I found out about all the whys later. I read the rules and looked up all the big words in a dictionary. I borrowed books from the Chinatown library. I studied each chess piece, trying to absorb the power it contained.

I learned about opening moves and why it's important to control the center early on; the shortest distance between two points is straight down the middle. I learned about the middle game and why **tactics** between two **adversaries** are like clashing ideas; the one who plays better has the clearest plans for both attacking and getting out of traps. I learned why it is essential in the endgame to have foresight, a mathematical understanding of all possible moves, and patience; all weaknesses and advantages become evident to a strong adversary and are obscured to a tiring opponent. I discovered that for the whole game one must gather invisible strengths and see the endgame before the game begins.

I also found out why I should never reveal "why" to others. A little knowledge withheld is a great advantage one should store for future use. That is the power of chess. It is a game of secrets in which one must show and never tell.

I loved the secrets I found within the sixty-four black and white squares. I carefully drew a handmade chessboard and pinned it to the wall next to my bed, where at night I would stare for hours at imaginary battles. Soon I no longer lost any games or Life Savers, but I lost my adversaries. Winston and Vincent decided they were more interested in roaming the streets after school in their Hopalong Cassidy cowboy hats.

On a cold spring afternoon, while walking home from school, I detoured through the playground at the end of our alley. I saw a group of old men, two seated across a folding table playing a game of chess, others smoking pipes, eating

tactics

plans; strategies

adversaries

opponents; foes

peanuts, and watching. I ran home and grabbed Vincent's chess set, which was bound in a cardboard box with rubber bands. I also carefully selected two prized rolls of Life Savers. I came back to the park and approached a man who
255 was observing the game.

"Want to play?" I asked him. His face widened with surprise and he grinned as he looked at the box under my arm.

"Little sister, been a long time since I play with dolls,"
260 he said, smiling benevolently. I quickly put the box down next to him on the bench and displayed my **retort**.

retort

a quick reply or answer

Lau Po, as he allowed me to call him, turned out to be a much better player than my brothers. I lost many games and many Life Savers. But over the weeks, with each
265 diminishing roll of candies, I added new secrets. Lau Po gave me the names. The Double Attack from the East and West Shores. Throwing Stones on the Drowning Man. The Sudden Meeting of the Clan. The Surprise from the Sleeping Guard. The Humble Servant Who Kills the King.
270 Sand in the Eyes of Advancing Forces. A Double Killing Without Blood.

There were also the fine points of chess etiquette. Keep captured men in neat rows, as well-tended prisoners. Never announce "Check" with vanity, lest someone with an
275 unseen sword slit your throat. Never hurl pieces into the

sandbox after you have lost a game, because then you must find them again, by yourself, after apologizing to all around you. By the end of the summer, Lau Po had taught me all he knew, and I had become a better chess player.

280   A small weekend crowd of Chinese people and tourists would gather as I played and defeated my opponents one by one. My mother would join the crowds during these outdoor exhibition games. She sat proudly on the bench, telling my admirers with proper Chinese **humility**, "Is luck."

humility
meekness; modesty

285   A man who watched me play in the park suggested that my mother allow me to play in local chess tournaments. My mother smiled graciously, an answer that meant nothing. I desperately wanted to go, but I bit back my tongue. I knew she would not let me play among strangers. So as we

290 walked home I said in a small voice that I didn't want to play in the local tournament. They would have American rules. If I lost, I would bring shame on my family.

    "Is shame you fall down nobody push you," said my mother.

295   During my first tournament, my mother sat with me in the front row as I waited for my turn. I frequently bounced my legs to unstick them from the cold metal seat of the folding chair. When my name was called, I leapt up. My mother unwrapped something in her lap. It was her *chang*,

300 a small tablet of red jade which held the sun's fire. "Is luck," she whispered, and tucked it into my dress pocket. I turned to my opponent, a fifteen-year-old boy from Oakland. He looked at me, wrinkling his nose.

    As I began to play, the boy disappeared, the color ran

305 out of the room, and I saw only my white pieces and his black ones waiting on the other side. A light wind began blowing past my ears. It whispered secrets only I could hear.

    "Blow from the South," it murmured. "The wind leaves no trail." I saw a clear path, the traps to avoid. The crowd

310 rustled. "Shhh! Shhh!" said the corners of the room. The wind blew stronger. "Throw sand from the East to distract him." The knight came forward ready for the sacrifice. The wind hissed, louder and louder. "Blow, blow, blow. He

cannot see. He is blind now. Make him lean away from the
315 wind so he is easier to knock down."

"Check," I said, as the wind roared with laughter. The
wind died down to little puffs, my own breath.

My mother placed my first trophy next to a new plastic
chess set that the neighborhood Tao society had given to
320 me. As she wiped each piece with a soft cloth, she said,
"Next time win more, lose less."

"Ma, it's not how many pieces you lose," I said.
"Sometimes you need to lose pieces to get ahead."

"Better to lose less, see if you really need."

325 At the next tournament, I won again, but it was my
mother who wore the **triumphant** grin.

triumphant

victorious;
conquering

"Lose eight piece this time. Last time was eleven. What
I tell you? Better off lose less!" I was annoyed, but I couldn't
say anything.

330 I attended more tournaments, each one farther away
from home. I won all games, in all divisions. The Chinese
bakery downstairs from our flat displayed my growing
collection of trophies in its window, amidst the dust-
covered cakes that were never picked up. The day after
335 I won an important regional tournament, the window
encased a fresh sheet cake with whipped-cream frosting
and red script saying, "Congratulations, Waverly Jong,
Chinatown Chess Champion." Soon after that, a flower
shop, headstone engraver, and funeral parlor offered to
340 sponsor me in national tournaments. That's when my
mother decided I no longer had to do the dishes. Winston
and Vincent had to do my chores.

"Why does she get to play and we do all the work,"
complained Vincent.

345 "Is new American rules," said my mother. "Meimei play,
squeeze all her brains out for win chess. You play, worth
squeeze towel."

By my ninth birthday, I was a national chess champion.
I was still some 429 points away from grand-master status,
350 but I was touted as the Great American Hope, a child
prodigy and a girl to boot. They ran a photo of me in *Life*

magazine next to a quote in which Bobby Fischer said, "There will never be a woman grand master." "Your move, Bobby," said the caption.

355   The day they took the magazine picture I wore neatly plaited braids clipped with plastic barrettes trimmed with rhinestones. I was playing in a large high school auditorium that echoed with phlegmy coughs and the squeaky rubber knobs of chair legs sliding across freshly
360 waxed wooden floors. Seated across from me was an American man, about the same age of Lau Po, maybe fifty. I remember that his sweaty brow seemed to weep at my every move. He wore a dark, malodorous suit. One of his pockets was stuffed with a great white kerchief on which
365 he wiped his palm before sweeping his hand over the chosen chess piece with great flourish.

    In my crisp pink-and-white dress with scratchy lace at the neck, one of two my mother had sewn for these special occasions, I would clasp my hands under my chin,
370 the delicate points of my elbows poised lightly on the table in the manner my mother had shown me for posing for the press. I would swing my patent leather shoes back and forth like an impatient child riding on a school bus. Then I would pause, suck in my lips, twirl my chosen piece in
375 midair as if undecided, and then firmly plant it in its new threatening place, with a triumphant smile thrown back at my opponent for good measure.

    I no longer played in the alley of Waverly Place. I never visited the playground where the pigeons and old men
380 gathered. I went to school, then directly home to learn new chess secrets, cleverly concealed advantages, more escape routes.

    But I found it difficult to concentrate at home. My mother had a habit of standing over me while I plotted out
385 my games. I think she thought of herself as my protective ally. Her lips would be sealed tight, and after each move I made, a soft "Hmmmmph" would escape from her nose.

    "Ma, I can't practice when you stand there like that," I said one day. She retreated to the kitchen and made loud

390 noises with the pots and pans. When the crashing stopped, I could see out of the corner of my eye that she was standing in the doorway. "Hmmmph!" Only this one sound came out of her tight throat.

My parents made many concessions to allow me to
395 practice. One time I complained that the bedroom I shared was so noisy that I couldn't think. Thereafter, my brothers slept in a bed in the living room facing the street. I said I couldn't finish my rice; my head didn't work right when my stomach was too full. I left the table with half-finished
400 bowls and nobody complained. But there was one duty I couldn't avoid. I had to accompany my mother on Saturday market days when I had no tournament to play. My mother would proudly walk with me, visiting many shops, buying very little. "This my daughter Wave-ly Jong," she said to
405 whoever looked her way.

One day, after we left a shop I said under my breath, "I wish you wouldn't do that, telling everybody I'm your daughter." My mother stopped walking. Crowds of people with heavy bags pushed past us on the sidewalk, bumping
410 into first one shoulder, then another.

"Aiii-ya. So shame be with mother?" She grasped my hand even tighter as she glared at me.

I looked down. "It's not that, it's just so obvious. It's just so embarrassing."

415 "Embarrass you be my daughter?" Her voice was cracking with anger.

"That's not what I meant. That's not what I said."

"What you say?"

I knew it was a mistake to say anything more, but I
420 heard my voice speaking. "Why do you have to use me to show off? If you want to show off, then why don't you learn to play chess."

My mother's eyes turned into dangerous black slits. She had no words for me, just sharp silence.

425 I felt the wind rushing around my hot ears. I jerked my hand out of my mother's tight grasp and spun around, knocking into an old woman. Her bag of groceries spilled to the ground.

"Aii-ya! Stupid girl!" my mother and the woman cried.
430 Oranges and tin cans careened down the sidewalk. As
my mother stopped to help the old woman pick up the
escaping food, I took off.

I raced down the street, dashing between people, not
looking back as my mother screamed shrilly, "Meimei!
435 Meimei!" I fled down an alley, past dark curtained shops
and merchants washing the grime off their windows. I sped
into the sunlight, into a large street crowded with tourists
examining trinkets and souvenirs. I ducked into another
dark alley, down another street, up another alley. I ran until
440 it hurt and I realized I had nowhere to go, that I was not
running from anything. The alleys contained no escape
routes.

My breath came out like angry smoke. It was cold. I sat
down on an upturned plastic pail next to a stack of empty
445 boxes, cupping my chin with my hands, thinking hard. I
imagined my mother, first walking briskly down one street
or another looking for me, then giving up and returning
home to await my arrival. After two hours, I stood up on
creaking legs and slowly walked home.

450 The alley was quiet and I could see the yellow lights
shining from our flat like two tiger's eyes in the night. I
climbed the sixteen steps to the door, advancing quickly up
each so as not to make any warning sounds. I turned the
knob; the door was locked. I heard a chair moving, quick
455 steps, the locks turning—click! click! click!—and then the
door opened.

"About time you got home," said Vincent. "Boy, are you
in trouble."

He slid back to the dinner table. On a platter were the
460 remains of a large fish, its fleshy head still connected to
bones swimming upstream in vain escape. Standing there
waiting for my punishment, I heard my mother speak in a
dry voice.

"We not concerning this girl. This girl not have
465 concerning for us."

Nobody looked at me. Bone chopsticks clinked against
the insides of bowls being emptied into hungry mouths.

I walked into my room, closed the door, and lay down on my bed. The room was dark, the ceiling filled with
470 shadows from the dinnertime lights of neighboring flats.

In my head, I saw a chessboard with sixty-four black and white squares. Opposite me was my opponent, two angry black slits. She wore a triumphant smile. "Strongest wind cannot be seen," she said.

475 Her black men advanced across the plane, slowly marching to each successive level as a single unit. My white pieces screamed as they scurried and fell off the board one by one. As her men drew closer to my edge, I felt myself growing light. I rose up into the air and flew out the
480 window. Higher and higher, above the alley, over the tops of tiled roofs, where I was gathered up by the wind and pushed up toward the night sky until everything below me disappeared and I was alone.

I closed my eyes and pondered my next move.

"The Rules of the Game," from *The Joy Luck Club* by Amy Tan

Answer It

1. Describe the narrator of "Rules of the Game."

2. Infer why Winston and Vincent stopped playing chess with Waverly.

3. Summarize how Waverly came to be a champion chess player.

4. Compare how Waverly's relationship with her mother is like a chess game. Give an example.

5. At the end of the story, Waverly ponders her next move. Plan what you think her next move should be to make up with her mother.

Savion Glover
THE MAN CAN MOVE

Savion Glover reinvigorates the tap scene in America.

Throughout human history, the joy of movement has been expressed in the art form of dance. From Russia's ballet to Japan's Kabuki and from the Irish jig to the Hawaiian hula, dance is celebrated across
5 cultures and continents. America has contributed its share of dance styles to the global stage.

Many of these dance traditions and styles came to America with the immigrants. Music and dance styles were blended together in the dance halls and in the clubs.
10 America's diverse cultures combined and shared the dance movements of their homelands. New rhythms appeared. New dances emerged.

In the 1920s, tap dancing evolved on the heels of the jazz music craze. Tap blended the drumming and rhythm
15 of West Africa with the syncopations of the Caribbean and a handful of dance styles from the Irish, the French, the English, and the Dutch. Tap's popularity raged during the 1920s and 1930s, then waned over the next several decades. Enter Savion Glover. Just in his early thirties,
20 this tap phenom is thought to be one of the most talented tap dancers of all time. As seen in the following *New York Times* review, Glover has not only reinvigorated the tap scene, but his **innovative** style is pushing the boundaries of tap dancing into new musical territory.

innovative
original; ahead of the times

Bring In da Bach, Bring In da Mendelssohn
Savion Glover wants to conquer the classics with tap.
By Sylviane Gold

languid
listless; lacking
energy

prominence
renown; fame

25 THE most admired feet in showbiz are clad in big—very big—tan work shoes, and the famous dreads are hidden under the hood of a black sweatshirt. Slouched on a metal folding chair in a rented studio to talk about his new show, Savion Glover has the look of a wary, **languid**

30 teenager, not a 31-year-old dynamo whose walloping tap dance revivified an American art form and opened it to the hip-hop generation.

But as he explains why he's returning to the Joyce Theater, not with an encore of last winter's hugely

35 successful song-and-dance turn, "Improvography," but with "Classical Savion," an entirely new show set to classical music, a burst of soft, filigreed tapping erupts from the floor. "I've been listening to classical music since my mom introduced us to it," he says. "So it's nothing new," rat-a-tat,

40 rat-a-tat, rat-a-rat-a-tat-tat.

I look down, startled that those clodhopper shoes are producing such a precise and delicate rustle. But it's too late. His feet are still again. Someone else's foot-tapping might seem rude or impatient. But for Mr. Glover, it's

45 punctuation, a part of his speech, and he goes on, almost unaware, listing the handful of tappers who have tackled classical compositions. "My approach is a fresh energy, an attempt to conquer this music through the dance," he says.

There aren't too many arenas left for Mr. Glover to

50 conquer. From the time he first came to **prominence**, at 12, in the Broadway musical "The Tap Dance Kid," he has "gone to the wood," as he calls it, on television, in the movies, at jazz concerts, even at the White House. He won a Tony for "Bring In da Noise, Bring In da Funk," and is

55 recognized around the world as tap's foremost innovator. But he is well aware that bringing noise and funk to four violins, two violas, two cellos, a bass, and a harpsichord entails certain risks. "From my generation, I don't know

too many dudes who are listening to or would
60 know about classical music," he says. "Maybe if
they heard, 'O.K., this guy's performing,' they're
going to come and see it and hear this other music.
But this may be a point that maybe my generation
won't understand until, I don't know—next year, or
65 five years from now, or whenever. But I feel this is
something that needs to be done."

His accomplice in "Classical Savion," which will also
include at least one segment with his usual combo, is the
conductor and arranger Robert Sadin, who has collaborated
70 with jazz greats and classical singers. Mr. Glover and Mr.
Sadin first worked together at a Carnegie Hall celebration
for tenor saxophonist Wayne Shorter, a concert that was by
many reports the highlight of the 2003 JVC Jazz Festival.
He and Mr. Glover began "kicking ideas around," Mr. Sadin
75 said by telephone, looking for appropriate music. So far,
Vivaldi, Bach, Bartok, and Mendelssohn have made the cut.

After about a year of work, some three weeks from
opening night, Mr. Glover says that nothing is quite settled.
"The more he keeps giving me music that sounds good, the
80 more I'm not going to be able to choose what I want," Mr.
Glover says. He is looking for "hard-core classical," he says,
music with "an edgy subtleness."

"I don't want to go out like a chump, you know?" he says.
"I want to come out strong and powerful." He's not worried

Savion says
his **left heel**
works as his **bass drum**
when he taps.

85 that time is running short—improvising is second nature to him. And the show isn't entirely unformed; it has something of a concept. "It's about this solo dancer needing this music," Mr. Glover says with a little tattoo of foot beats. "Needing to challenge this music, you know? How dare there not be a
90 tap dancer around when this music is being played?"

As we talk, Mr. Glover frequently leans forward and asks me to repeat a question. "Say it again?" he asks. I begin to wonder if a lifetime of hard-driving, amplified tap dance has affected his hearing. Then he accidentally,
95 imperceptibly pushes a button in his pocket, and John Coltrane comes pouring into the room. The sweatshirt hood has been covering not just his hair but his earphones. He is, he says, usually plugged in. "I always try to keep something going," he says. It means there's always dancing
100 going on in his head.

"I just put on John Coltrane every morning, and my day begins," he explains. "It can be with the phone. It can be going to get some records. It can be going to see my mom. That's all practice to me. I talk on the phone, it allows room
105 for ideas to come in. I guess I practice so much in my mind that I'll see it. If I see it's done, it's done. I don't necessarily go to the wood until I find myself on the wood. Then I'm able to say, 'O.K., what is that I was doing?'"

As for keeping in touch with the wood in a regular way,
110 as most dancers must, he says he doesn't. "Man, I haven't gone into a studio for practorial purposes in years. It'll just be, you know, if I'm standing around, waiting for a train or something. I might get an idea and start **fidgeting**."

fidgeting

moving in a nervous fashion

"Improvography," which opened at the Joyce in
115 December 2003, prompted Gene Seymour, *Newsday*'s jazz critic, to ask, "Could Savion Glover be the most important artist in jazz right now?" No one would dream of framing the same question in tap terms; the answer is too obvious. So I ask Mr. Glover why he's still pushing at the form, given
120 that a pre-eminent place in tap history is already **assured**.

assured

guaranteed; certain

"If what you say is true," he responds, "then I guess I'm on my own time right now. I'm doing this stuff for myself." Rat-a-tat, rat-a-tat. "That's a blessing."

In the words of Savion:
On his technique:

I know my feet, all about them. It's like my feet are the
125 drums, and my shoes are the sticks. So if I'm hearing a bass
sound in my head, where is that bass? Well, I have different
tones . My left heel is stronger, for some reason, than my
right; it's my bass drum. My right heel is like the floor tom-
tom. I can get a snare out of my right toe, a whip sound,
130 not putting it down on the floor hard, but kind of whipping
the floor with it. I get the sounds of a top tom-tom from
the balls of my feet. The hi-hat is a sneaky one. I do it with
a slight toe lift, either foot, so like a drummer, I can slip it
in there anytime. And if I want cymbals, crash crash, that's
135 landing flat, both feet, full strength on the floor, full weight
on both feet. That's the cymbals.

So I've got a whole drum set down there. And knowing
where all those sounds are, knowing where I'm trying to
get them from, that's how I go about creating the step.

On his style:

140   I listen to all kinds of music—jazz, classical, rock,
rhythm and blues, gospel, calypso. My mom played it all in
the house when we were growing up. And then among my
brothers and me it was hip-hop and reggae. . . . I dance to
jazz and old stuff and whatever, but mostly it's going to be
145 hip-hop, something with a funky bass line.

I still hear criticism sometimes, cats saying, "Oh, now
Savion's doing hip-hop dance." As if it's some kind of
special dance. But that's not how I see it. In fact, let's get it
straight. It's not hip-hop tap. It's not rap tap. It's hoofing.
150 It's tap dancing.

On his legacy:

I feel like it is my duty to carry on this art form. Just
from knowing cats like [Jimmy] Slyde, knowing what they
stand for, knowing they didn't get the proper recognition.
I mean, I hear all the compliments, and it's lovely to me
155 when people say I'm the best, but I'm looking at what those

tones
sounds

cats are doing, what Gregory's [Hines] doing in his fifties, what Slyde's doing in his seventies, and I'm, like, Whoa, that amazes me. I know deep inside that as a tap dancer I have a lot of room to grow.

160   Because dancing is it for me. It. Just it. There's no person, no food or drink, no movie part going to change my mind about that. I mean, in my mind I'm a tap dancer. How many people can say that? How many people can say what they are? It's one thing to say, "Okay, I'm a celebrity

165 now, I'm going to get me a TV show." Nothing wrong with that, understand, but I'm a tap dancer first.

     And if I have anything to do with it, tap is going to keep growing. It's going to have its proper place at last. I want tap to be like a baseball game, a football game,

170 people coming to see us at Yankee Stadium. I want tap to be on TV. I want tap to be in the movies. I want tap to be massive. Worldwide. Word up.

"Bring In da Bach, Bring In da Mendelssohn," by Sylviane Gold. Copyright 2005 by *The New York Times Co.* Reprinted with permission.
"In the words of Savion" *Savion! My Life in Tap*
by Savion Glover and Bruce Weber

Think About It

1. Locate and read the word the author of the review uses to describe the sound of Glover's tapping feet. Assess why the author chose to use this word.

2. Explain the metaphor that Glover uses to describe how he translates the music he hears into movement.

3. Contrast Glover's two tap shows, "Improvography" and "Classical Savion."

4. Distinguish three different people's opinions about Savion Glover.

5. Analyze the meaning of the review's title, "Bring in da Bach, Bring In da Mendelssohn" in "Savion Glover: The Man Can Move."

6. Suppose you had the opportunity to put on an innovative art, dance, or music show. Plan what styles you would incorporate in your show to impress your audience.

THE WOMEN'S SUFFRAGE MOVEMENT

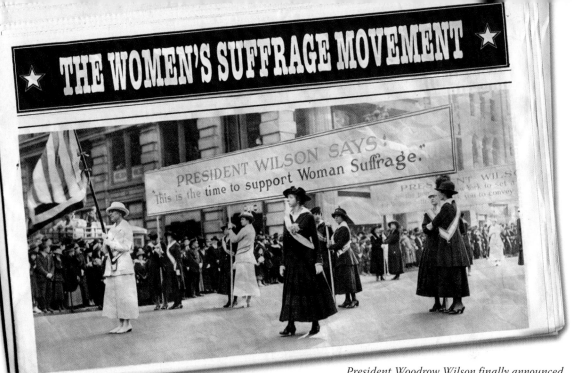

President Woodrow Wilson finally announced his support for women's right to vote in 1918.

The year was 1840. Americans were hotly debating the **morality** of slavery. Elizabeth Cady Stanton and Lucretia Mott were two women who thought it was wrong. They sailed across the Atlantic to attend the World Anti-Slavery
5 Convention in London. Both women were passionate **abolitionists**. They were eager to participate in this international gathering. In fact, Mott, a Quaker minister, was an official delegate to the convention.

As it turned out, Stanton and Mott were bitterly
10 disappointed. They knew that it was considered unseemly for women to speak in public, or for that matter, to hold strong ideas about issues outside the home. Still, they didn't expect to be barred from speaking at a gathering of forward-thinking abolitionists. But that's exactly what
15 happened. After debate among the men at the convention, it was voted that the women would not be able to participate. Angered at their exclusion, Stanton and Mott resolved to hold a women's rights conference when they returned to the United States. In that moment, one of the
20 most important movements in American history was born: the movement for women's **suffrage**.

morality
standards; ideas about right and wrong

abolitionists
reformers who wanted to end slavery

suffrage
the right or privilege of voting

Susan B. Anthony and Elizabeth Cady Stanton founded the National Women's Suffrage Association in 1869.

A social movement is an organized effort by supporters of a common goal over a period of time. Specific conditions, events, and people shape social movements. In the
25 nineteenth century, many women found their lives too restrictive. These conditions included being barred from speaking in public. Women were excluded from schools, colleges, and most jobs. Women who did work earned much less than men. If they were married, all their wages
30 and property belonged to their husbands. Even women's children were owned solely by their husbands. Women could not vote. They could not be elected to public office. They could not serve on juries. Mott and Stanton intended to change all this.

35 In July of 1848, Mott and Stanton held their conference in Seneca Falls, New York. The meeting drew 240 attendees, including Frederick Douglass, the ex-slave abolitionist, and 39 other men. Elizabeth Cady Stanton gave a rousing speech. She presented her Declaration of Sentiments. This document
40 is modeled on the Declaration of Independence, including the words, "We hold these truths to be self-evident: that all men and women are created equal. . . ." The Declaration of Sentiments listed the rights of which women had been **deprived**. It also included a set of Resolutions demanding
45 many of these rights. The Resolutions were approved by

deprived
denied; kept from having

the Seneca Falls conference attendees, except for one—the right to vote. Even Lucretia Mott believed that asking for the vote was too extreme. In the end, the resolution demanding suffrage did pass, but by only a narrow margin.

50 Even so, the right to vote became the centerpiece of the women's movement after the convention at Seneca Falls. Only by having voting muscle, many women in the movement believed, would it be possible to gain the other rights spelled out in the Declaration of Sentiments.

55 The women from Seneca Falls went right to work. One friend of Elizabeth Cady Stanton's, Amelia Bloomer, began the first women's rights newspaper. It was called *The Lily*. Bloomer is also well known for introducing a new style in women's clothing: loose, billowy pants worn under a long 60 tunic. The trousers became known as bloomers. They outraged some people who thought only men should wear pants. In fact, the bloomers got so much attention, some suffragists chose not to wear them. They believed that the pants distracted too much from the real issue, which was 65 winning the vote.

Amelia Bloomer was also responsible for one of the most important events in the history of women's suffrage. She introduced Elizabeth Cady Stanton to Susan B. Anthony. The two became fast friends. They also became unstoppable 70 partners in the campaign for women's votes. At times the opposition was fierce. While traveling the lecture circuit together, they were attacked by mobs. They were pelted with vegetables, rotten eggs, and clods of mud. They were jeered so loudly their words were often drowned out. But nothing 75 stopped these women from championing their cause.

During the Civil War, however, many suffragists did put their efforts on hold. They expected that after the war, women as well as **emancipated** slaves would be **enfranchised** . Over time, this issue deeply divided 80 the women's suffrage movement. Lucy Stone and her husband, Henry Blackwell, believed that enfranchisement of African Americans would be defeated if tied to women's suffrage. Women, they argued, should wait until after African American men won the vote. Therefore, Stone

emancipated
freed; liberated

enfranchised
provided with rights, especially the right to vote

85 and Blackwell supported the 15th Amendment to the
Constitution. This would assure African American men
their voting rights. Stone and Blackwell believed that
women's suffrage should be won on a state-by-state,
rather than national, level. They established the American
90 Woman's Suffrage Association (AWSA) in 1869.

Stanton and Anthony differed in their opinion. They
did not support the 15th Amendment because it did not
enfranchise women. While they were strongly in favor
of voting rights for African Americans, they believed
95 it was important to hold out for an amendment to the
Constitution that included women, too. They formed the
National Woman's Suffrage Association (NWSA) in 1869.

Both sides in the movement used a variety of tactics
and strategies for winning supporters to the cause of
100 women's suffrage. In Rochester, New York, in November
of 1872, Susan B. Anthony convinced the authorities at her
polling place to allow her to vote. Two weeks later, she was
arrested. She was fined for having voted illegally. At her
arraignment, Anthony refused to deposit bail when it had
105 been set. She went to jail so that she could challenge the
proceeding under federal *habeas corpus*. Her trial attracted
nationwide publicity.

The conflict between the AWSA and NWSA may
have slowed the progress toward women's suffrage. The
110 two groups eventually made peace when a large group
of younger feminists joined the movement. In fact, both
Elizabeth Cady Stanton's daughter, Harriot Stanton Blatch,
and Lucy Stone's daughter, Alice Stone Blackwell, became
leaders. Blackwell was instrumental in bringing the two
115 opposing sides together. In 1890, the AWSA and NWSA
merged to become the National American Woman Suffrage
Association (NAWSA).

Carrie Chapman Catt, who believed in working
for women's suffrage on all fronts, became president of
120 NAWSA in 1900. She led campaigns on both the state
and national levels. Large demonstrations in New York
and Washington drew thousands of men and women
who marched through the streets in support of women's

suffrage. By 1910, women had the right to vote in five states:
125 Colorado, Idaho, Utah, Washington, and Wyoming.

A woman named Alice Paul led the final push for an amendment to the Constitution. During the winter of 1917, she and her followers were unrelenting in their demand that President Woodrow Wilson support the cause. They
130 picketed the White House for months, holding signs that read, "Mr. President, how long must women wait for liberty?" On April 6, 1917, the United States entered World War I. The suffragists became more aggressive. They asked how the President could fight a war for democracy when
135 his own country denied voting rights to half its citizens.

The women were eventually arrested for obstructing traffic. When they still didn't stop picketing, they were put in jail. Yet each time they got out of jail, they returned to the White House to picket. Finally, Alice Paul was
140 sentenced to seven months in jail. She was put in solitary confinement. When she went on a hunger strike, the doctors force-fed her, but still she refused to give up her cause. As it turned out, the jail terms and forced feedings drew the attention of the press. The newspaper stories

By 1910, women had the right to vote in only five states: Colorado, Idaho, Utah, Washington, and Wyoming.

Two young women march in a protest for suffrage in 1912.

145 helped win the hearts and minds of many American people. After only five weeks of her sentence, Paul was released from jail.

President Woodrow Wilson could no longer ignore the pleas of Paul and other suffragists. On January 9, 1918, he
150 announced that he would support the Susan B. Anthony Amendment, which would give the right to vote to all American women. The House of Representatives passed the amendment the next day, and the Senate followed suit a year and half later. It took another year for the necessary
155 36 states to ratify the amendment. On August 26, 1920, the 19th Amendment to the Constitution became law.

A social movement began in 1848. It was a movement that included many voices and differing points of view, but all were leading toward suffrage for women. It was
160 a movement that was finally successful, 70 years later. American women at last had the right to vote.

Crowds fill a street in Washington, D.C. during a suffrage parade in 1913.

Think About It

1. Define in your own words what the women's suffrage movement was.

2. List ways in which the lives of American women were restricted in the nineteenth century.

3. Categorize the two conflicting views about what would be the most effective way to conduct the women's suffrage movement.

4. Summarize the different strategies that women suffragists used to win support for their movement.

5. Review the first two paragraphs of the selection. Make an inference about why Elizabeth Cady Stanton and Lucretia Mott were angered by their exclusion from the World Anti-Slavery Convention.

6. The women's suffrage movement in the United States took 70 years to succeed. Discuss reasons why movements for women's rights that have occurred in other countries might take a long or short amount of time to succeed.

Explore Social Forces

STEP 1

Phonemic Awareness and Phonics

Unit 27 introduces more vowel digraphs and sound-spelling correspondences for connectives and Romance loan words.

Vowel Digraphs

Review: A syllable with a vowel digraph is a **vowel digraph syllable**.

- In some syllables, the vowel phoneme is spelled with two vowel letters.
- The vowel sound for the vowel digraph is usually long.
- The vowel digraphs in this unit occur infrequently in English:
  ei for / ē / as in **either** and for / ā / as in **vein**
  ey for / ā / as in **they**
  ui for / ī / as in **guide**
  ou for / ō / as in **soul**

The Sound / *sh* /

The sound / *sh* / is usually represented by the letters **sh**. Examples: sharp, wish

The sound-spelling patterns **ci**, **si**, **ti**, and **xi** can also represent the sound / *sh* /. This usually occurs when the letter **i** is used as a **connective** between a base word or root and a suffix. Examples: social, dimension, spatial, anxious

The sound-spelling pattern **si** can also represent the sound / *zh* /. Example: vision

Loan Words From Romance Languages

Some sound-spelling associations in **Romance loan words** are below. See page 97 for more about these words.
  i for / ē / as in **radio**
  a for / ŏ / as in **father**
  e for / ā / as in **allegro**

Word Recognition and Spelling

Prefixes

We can expand words and change meaning by adding **prefixes**. These word parts are added to the beginnings of words. Example: **ad** + just = adjust

(See Step 3: Vocabulary and Morphology for links to meaning.)

> **Unit 27 Prefixes**
> **ad-, sub-**

Suffixes

We can expand words and change meaning by adding suffixes. These word parts are added to the ends of words. Example: bag + **age** = baggage

(See Step 3: Vocabulary and Morphology for links to meaning and Step 4: Grammar and Usage for function.)

> **Unit 27 Suffixes**
> **-tion, -sion, -age**

Roots

We can build words using roots. Roots carry the most important part of the word's meaning. We usually attach a prefix or suffix to make a root into a word. Example: sub + **mis** + sion = submission

> **Unit 27 Roots**
> **sist/sta/stit; mis/mit**

Essential Words

> **Unit 27 Essential Words**
>
> | | | |
> |---|---|---|
> | billion | opinion | religion |
> | million | region | union |

Spelling Lists

The Unit 27 spelling lists contain four categories:

1. Words with vowel digraphs: **ei**, **ey**, **ui**, **ou**

2. Words with / *sh* / spelled **ci**, **si**, **ti**, or **xi**, and / *zh* / spelled **si**

3. **Essential Words** (in italics)

4. Words with prefixes, roots, and suffixes

Spelling Lists

Lessons 1—5

anxious	*opinion*
billion	receive
dimension	*region*
either	*religion*
guide	social
million	*union*
nation	veil
obey	

Lessons 6—10

admission	permission
confusion	police
convention	storage
decision	subcontractor
erosion	subsoil
fathers	surveyed
luggage	vacationers
media	

Vocabulary and Morphology

Unit Vocabulary

Sound-spelling correspondences from this unit and previous units make up this unit's vocabulary.

- What do these words mean?
- Do some of them mean more than one thing? Which ones?

UNIT Vocabulary

ei for / ē /
conceive
deceive
either
perceive
receive
seize

ei for / ā /
rein
reindeer
veil
vein

ey for / ā /
grey
obey
prey
survey
they

ui for / ī /
disguise
guidance
guide
guideline
guise

ou for / ō /
boulder
poultry
shoulder
soul

ci
appreciate
artificial
associate
commercial
conscious
crucial
delicious
diagnostician
efficient
electrician
especial
judicial
mathematician
musician
official
politician
precious
racial
social
special
sufficient
suspicious
unconscious

si
amnesia
anesthesia
dimension
fantasia
magnesia

ti
differentiate
essential
impatient
infectious
initial
initiate
international
lotion
nation
notion
partial
patient
potential
practitioner
presidential
rational
residential
substantial

xi
anxious
complexion
flexion
noxious
obnoxious

Romance Loan Words
i for / ē /
amino
chili

encyclopedia
gasoline
macaroni
magazine
marine
media
medium
menial
patriotic
piano
pizza
police
radio
routine
spaghetti
studio
superior
taxi
unique
via

a for / ŏ /
drama
father
llama
plaza

e/et for / ā /
allegro
croquet
gourmet
valet

Word Relationships

Synonyms are words that have the same or similar meanings.
Example: artificial/fake

Meaning Parts

Prefixes

Prefixes can add to or change the meanings of words. The Unit 27 prefixes have the following meanings.

Unit 27 Prefixes	Meanings	Examples
ad-	toward; to; near; in	addict, adjust, adverse
sub-	under; beneath; below	subcontract, submerge, subway

Review: A prefix often assimilates to the base word or root to which it is attached. In **assimilation**, the last letter of the prefix changes or sounds more similar to the first letter of the base or root. This change makes pronunciation easier. The meaning of the prefix does not change when it is assimilated.
Examples: **ad + tract = attract; ad + cent = accent**
     sub + ceed = succeed; sub + port = support

Suffixes

Suffixes can add to or change the meanings of words. When added to a base word or root, they can change the base word or root to a noun.

Unit 27 Suffixes	Meanings	Examples
-tion	act of; state of; result of	action, condensation, education
-sion	act of; state of; result of	collision, depression, permission
-age	collection; mass; relationship	baggage, foliage, parentage

Roots

Roots form the basic meaning part of a word. Roots of English words often come from another language, especially Latin. A root usually needs a prefix or suffix to make it into a word.

Example: ad + **mit** = admit (ad = to; mit = to send; admit = to send to)

Unit 27 Roots	Meanings	Examples
sist	to stand; put in place	assist, consist, insist
sta	to stand; put in place	constant, obstacle, station
stit	to stand; put in place	constitution, destitute, substitute
mis	to send; let go	admission, dismiss, promise
mit	to send; let go	admit, commit, permit

Challenge Morphemes

Roots	Meanings	Examples
flect	to bend; curve	deflect, inflect, reflect
flex	to bend; curve	flexibility, flexor, reflex
gen	birth; kind; origin	gender, generous, gene

Loan Words From Romance Languages

Throughout history, English has borrowed large numbers of words from other languages. Because English is spoken all over the world and people from all over the world live in English-speaking countries, borrowings continue today.

What do we know about borrowed words, also called **loan words**? Most of our common, everyday words are old Anglo-Saxon words. But about 60% of English vocabulary comes from Latin. Latin is no longer spoken, but several Romance languages descended from Latin. Most of these languages are still widely spoken. They include Catalan, French, Italian, Occitan, Portuguese, Romanian, and Spanish.

Grammar and Usage

Adverbs

Review: **Adverbs** are words that describe verbs, adjectives, and other adverbs. They answer the questions: **How? When? Where? Why?** or **Under what conditions?** They can be:

- Single words. Examples: **weekly, anxiously**
- Prepositional phrases that function as adverbs. For example, **in debtor's prison** is a prepositional phrase that answers the question **Where?** It is a prepositional phrase in *form*, but it *functions* as an adverb.

Conjunctions

Review: **Conjunctions** join words, phrases, or clauses in a sentence. **And, or,** and **but** are coordinating conjunctions.

Subordinating conjunctions establish the relationship between a dependent clause and the rest of the sentence.

> **Subordinating Conjunctions in Unit 27**
>
> as, how, since, than, until, when, where, why

Participles

Review: The **present participle** is formed by adding **-ing** to the base verb. Example: ride + **ing** = riding

The **past participle** of regular verbs is formed by adding **-ed** to the base verb. Example: fit + **ed** = (have) fitted. Some past participles are irregular; their forms must be memorized.

See the Appendix, page A36, for a complete list of irregular verbs.

- Participles can be in verb phrases or can act as adjectives.

  In a verb phrase, a present participle is used with a form of the helping verb **be** (**am, is, are**). Example: is listening

  In a verb phrase, a past participle is used with a form of the helping verb **have** (**have, has, had**). Example: had ridden

  In an adjective phrase, present and past participles tell more about a noun. Examples: a blowing wind, a forbidden move

Phrases

Review: A **phrase** is a group of words that functions as a single word. It does not have a subject and predicate. Example: with Mr. Micawber

A **participial phrase** begins with a participle and is followed by a word (or group of words) that modifies it or receives its action. A participial phrase functions as an adjective because it modifies a noun or pronoun. It can come before or after the word it modifies. Example: **Watching the people go by**, David stood on the bridge.
       David stood on the bridge, **watching the people go by**.

Clauses

Review: A **clause** is a group of words that contains a subject and a predicate. An **independent clause** has one subject and one predicate; it represents a complete thought. A **dependent clause** cannot stand alone. It combines with an independent clause to create meaning.

Some dependent clauses function as adverbs. An **adverbial clause**:

- Answers the questions: **How? When? Where? Why?** or **Under what condition?** An adverbial clause beginning with **than** shows comparison. It expands the predicate of the sentence.
- Usually begins with a subordinating conjunction.
- Can occur at the beginning or end of a sentence.

> **Adverbial Clause**
>
> David asked Mr. Micawber **how he was going to find his new lodging**.
>
> The clause **how he was going to find his new lodging** answers the question **how**. It begins with the subordinating conjunction **how**.

Sentence Pattern

Adverbial clauses can help vary sentence structure. They can come at the beginning or end of a sentence. A comma is placed after the adverbial clause at the beginning of the sentence.

> **Sentences With Adverbial Clauses**
>
> **When he heard about Mr. Micawber's debt,** David worried.
>
> David worried **when he heard about Mr. Micawber's debt**.

Punctuation

Review: The **colon** has several functions. It follows the greeting in a business letter and introduces a list following an independent clause.

The colon also separates the hour from minutes when writing time.

> **Colon Separating Hours and Minutes**
>
> 11:30 a.m. (*read:* eleven-thirty a.m.)
>
> 6:15 p.m. (*read:* six-fifteen p.m.)

Confusing Word Pairs

Then and **than** are confused because they sound and look alike. **Then** is an adverb that indicates time, order of events, or a summary of what was said. (**Then** tells when.) **Than** can function as a preposition or a conjunction. It is used to link two parts of a comparison. When **than** introduces an adverbial clause, it is acting as a subordinating conjunction. (**Than** compares.) Examples:

First, David washed the bottles. **Then**, he had to dry them.

David's life in London was much harder **than** the life he lived with his mother.

Like and **as** are also often confused. **Like** is a preposition meaning "similar to." It can introduce a prepositional phrase, but not a clause. **As** usually functions as a subordinating conjunction to introduce an adverbial clause. Examples:

David was lucky to have a caring friend **like** Peggotty.

David treated Mr. Micawber **as** he would any older person.

STEP 5

Listening and Reading Comprehension

Informational Text

■ Some **informational text** is nonfiction written about a specific topic, event, experience, or circumstance. It is often accompanied by visual information in the form of charts, graphs, or illustrations. The visual information provides additional content about the subject matter. "**Wolf Society**" uses visual information to enhance the text content.

Vocabulary in Context

■ **Context clues** help us understand new vocabulary. Pronoun referents, meaning signals, and visuals, such as charts and graphs, provide meaning links.

Signal Words

■ Different types of sentences can help us think about new information and ideas in different ways. Identifying signal words within sentences can improve comprehension.

See the Appendix, page A20, for a complete list of signal words based on Bloom's Taxonomy.

Literary Terms and Devices

📖 **Genres** are types or categories of literature. Unit 27 features fiction and narrative.

■ **Fiction** is a literary genre that includes imaginary stories. Some fiction is based on real people, places, and events. "**David Copperfield**" is an example of fiction based on the life of the author, Charles Dickens.

■ A **narrative** is a story told by a narrator, or storyteller. A narrative has characters, a setting, events, conflict, a climax, and a resolution. A narrative told from the "first person point of view" means that the story is told from the perspective of the storyteller. In "**David Copperfield**," the main character, David, tells the story of his life.

Plot Analysis

- **Plot** is the sequence of events in a narrative or drama. The author develops the plot to create the story. The plot guides the reader through the story.

- **Characters** and **setting** are introduced early in the story. They create the necessary background information for a reader. The characters, which can be people, animals, or things, interact in a story. The setting is the story's time and place. Characters and setting comprise the introduction—the first element of plot development.

- To understand how a plot develops, we must first identify a story's main **problem** and its **solution**. Without a problem, or conflict, there would be no story—everything would remain the same.

- After we become proficient in identifying a story's main problem and solution, we will learn more about plot development and apply it in our writing.

- Plot development usually consists of five elements:

  Introduction (characters and setting);

  Conflict (rising action);

  Climax (turning point);

  Resolution (falling action);

  Conclusion (the situation at the end of the story, with a look to the future).

STEP

6

Speaking and Writing

Signal Words

■ Different types of sentences require different responses, depending on the focus of **signal words**. Identifying signal words within sentences improves the accuracy of responses to oral and written questions.

■ See the Appendix, page A20, for a complete list of signal words based on Bloom's Taxonomy.

Composition Organization

■ Some compositions tell a story. This type of writing is called a **narrative**. A narrative is a story that relates a series of events. Some narratives are true; others are fictitious.

■ A narrative has the same elements as a story:

Conflict: The major problem faced by the main characters. The conflict starts with an initiating event. The conflict is also called rising action because the conflict in a story usually keeps rising until the characters reach a turning point.

Climax: A sequential point in narrative literature. It is the turning point in a story, the point at which tension drops and the falling action begins.

Resolution: This is the part of the story after the turning point. It is also called falling action.

Conclusion: This is how the story ends.

■ Narratives use **transition phrases** to introduce events, create rising action, or signal a climax in the story.

> **Transition Phrases for Narratives**
>
> It all started when . . .
>
> Things were going well until . . .
>
> Gradually, I began to suspect that . . .
>
> Suddenly, I . . .

More About Words

- **Bonus Words** use the same sound-spelling correspondences that we have studied in this unit and previous units.

- **Idioms** are common phrases that cannot be understood by the meanings of their separate words—only by the entire phrase.

- **Why? Word History** explains how **loan words** have given English a dual vocabulary system.

UNIT Bonus Words

ei for / ē /
neither
protein

ei for / ā /
lei
skein
surveillance
unveil

ey for / ā /
convey
hey
parley
whey

ui for / ī /
beguile
guile
misguide

ou for / ō /
mould
smoulder

ci
beneficial
capricious
conscience
facial
ferocious
glacier

inefficient
insufficient
omniscient
pernicious
proficient
provincial
spacious
subconscious
superficial
suspicion
vicious

si
artesian
dyspepsia

ti
circumstantial
confidential
consequential
deferential
dementia
differential
fictitious
inertia
negotiate
nutritious
ostentatious
preferential
pretentious

quotient
repetitious
sequential
spatial
substantiate
superstitious
torrential

xi
fluxion
overanxious
transfixion

Romance Loan Words
i for / ē /
amiable
antique
aquarium
atrium
audio
barbarian
broccoli
confetti
debris
exterior
geranium
graffiti
gymnasium
liter

malaria
median
mezzanine
patio
posterior
radius
ravine
regime
serial
stadium
submarine
trio

a for / ŏ /
armada
bravo
desperado
enchilada
piñata
salsa
taco

e/et for / ā /
beret
cabaret
chalet
sauté
soufflé
suede

Idioms	
Idiom	**Meaning**
be head and shoulders above the rest	be much better than other similar people or things
be one in a million	be a very special person because of good qualities
break the mould	be new and different
draw a veil over	hide or avoid something unpleasant
have a chip on your shoulder	have a belligerent attitude or grievance
keep body and soul together	be barely able to pay for things that you need to survive
point you in the direction of something	suggest that you do or buy a particular thing
prey on your mind	worry constantly about something
put your shoulder to the wheel	work hard at something; make a concentrated effort
seize the day	take advantage of present opportunities

 **Word History**

Loan Words—Why does English have two words for farm animals, when other languages have only one? In Modern English, for example, we have cow/beef, calf/veal, pig/pork, and sheep/mutton.

After the Normans conquered England in 1066, they became the aristocracy and the English became the peasants. The Normans continued to speak their language—Old French (which had evolved from Latin). In medieval England, the language absorbed many words from Old French.

The Norman French aristocracy kept their Old French words for meat served at the table (*boeuf, veau, porc, mouton*). These words are still used in Modern English: beef, veal, pork, mutton. The English peasants kept their Anglo-Saxon names for barnyard animals: cow, calf, pig, sheep. As a result of this dual vocabulary system, Modern English has many **loan words** that came into English via Old French.

WOLF Society

Imagine that you are watching a pack of wild wolves. At first, some of their actions might seem strange. Why do some wolves growl like bullies? Why do others keep their tails between their legs and whine? Why does the pack
5 seem to pick on one wolf? The answers to these questions are complex. Wolf packs have rules. These rules govern the behavior of each pack member.

In a wolf society, each member has its own social standing, or rank. Every wolf pack has two leaders. One is
10 male. One is female. These are called the alpha pair. They decide where the pack goes. They decide when the pack hunts. They usually are the only wolves in the pack allowed to have pups. Alpha wolves keep their ears and tails raised. This shows their rank. They bare their teeth. They growl.
15 This threatens the lesser wolves.

Beneath the alpha pair are beta wolves. To show their lower rank, beta wolves often keep their tails hanging down. They keep their ears flat. If a beta wolf approaches an alpha wolf, it puts its tail between its legs. This signals
20 that it knows who is the boss.

At the bottom of the social structure is the omega wolf. The omega wolf is often mistreated by the rest of the pack. Omega wolves are not allowed to get close to the rest of the pack. They must eat last, after the others have had their
25 fill. Omega wolves keep their tails between their legs most of the time. This signals their low rank. An omega wolf might by nature be shy. It might be sick, or just unlucky. The omega's situation in the pack may seem cruel. But the omega is still part of a strong family unit. Without its pack,
30 the omega would probably not survive. Survival is very difficult for a lone wolf.

The wolves in a pack work together as a family unit. They hunt together. They play together. They protect their territory together. Wolf packs as a group raise the young of
35 the alpha pair. Members of the pack bring the mother food. This allows her to stay with her pups.

When the wolf pups are old enough, they begin to play hunting and fighting games. During this time, they form their own social rankings. The stronger, faster pups
40 become dominant. The weaker ones become submissive. Many times the stronger, older wolf pups leave the group. They form their own pack. They may become alpha wolves. If an alpha wolf dies or becomes too weak to lead, then the strongest beta wolf may take its place.
45 Wolves act in certain ways depending on their rank within a pack. These behaviors guarantee their place in the pack and their survival in the wild.

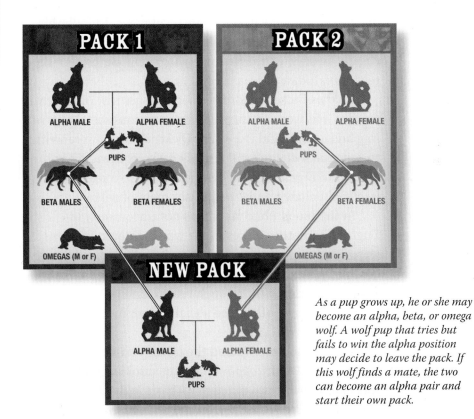

As a pup grows up, he or she may become an alpha, beta, or omega wolf. A wolf pup that tries but fails to win the alpha position may decide to leave the pack. If this wolf finds a mate, the two can become an alpha pair and start their own pack.

DAVID COPPERFIELD

by Charles Dickens

Who Was Charles Dickens?

Charles Dickens (1812–1870) remains one of the most beloved storytellers in the English language. Initially, his stories appeared in newspapers, as serials, and people eagerly awaited chapters—much as people watch serials on
5 television today.

Charles Dickens wrote stories about social issues.

Charles Dickens addressed social issues that other writers avoided. His work set the stage for enormous social reform in England and around the world. Dickens' stories were written to promote social reform in many different areas. This
10 chapter of *David Copperfield* addresses two major social issues: child labor and the imprisonment of debtors.

In the 1800s, child labor was not uncommon in England and other places in the world. Debtors' prisons were full of people who were there simply because they
15 couldn't pay their bills. Eventually, both of these social issues were addressed through reform laws. The stories of Charles Dickens influenced social reform in England and around the world.

Those who have studied the life of Charles Dickens also
20 realize that *David Copperfield* is an autobiographical novel. It is fiction, but it has much of its basis in fact. The novel's story is told in the first person. It includes characters based on people in Dickens' life. In the chapter that follows, David

Copperfield meets Mr. Micawber, an optimistic man with
25 a large family, who is constantly plagued by debt collectors.
The second social issue of this book—that of imprisoning
people who were in debt—begins here. Interestingly,
authorities agree that the character of Mr. Micawber is
based on Charles Dickens' father. A tragic experience
30 occurred when Charles was 12 years old. His father was
imprisoned for debt, and Charles was sent to work in a
factory to support the family. This is essential in knowing
and understanding the passionate urgency of Dickens'
efforts toward social reform through his writing.

Summary of *David Copperfield*: Chapters 1–10

35   *In the first ten chapters, the reader learns that David*
Copperfield's father died before he was born. An only child,
David lived with his mother and Peggotty, a housemaid
who cared for both David and his mother. David's mother
married a cruel man named Mr. Murdstone, who moved
40 *with his sister into the Copperfield's home. Together, they*
stamped out all the joy in the home. When Chapter 11
opens, David is ten years old. His mother has just died, and
the Murdstones have fired Peggotty. They have removed
David from school and sent him off to London, to work
45 *in their factory, cleaning bottles. Here, he first meets Mr.*
Micawber, with whom he will live for a time.

Chapter 11: I Begin Life on my Own Account, and Don't Like it
Excerpt 1

    Murdstone and Grinby's warehouse was at the waterside.
It was down in Blackfriars. Modern improvements have
altered the place; but it was the last house at the bottom of
50 a narrow street, curving down hill to the river, with some
stairs at the end, where people took boat. It was a crazy old
house with a wharf of its own, abutting on the water when
the tide was in, and on the mud when the tide was out, and
literally overrun with rats. Its panelled rooms, **discoloured**
55 with the dirt and smoke of a hundred years, I dare say; its
decaying floors and staircase; the squeaking and scuffling
of the old grey rats down in the cellars; and the dirt and

discoloured
changed or spoiled
in color; stained

rottenness of the place; are things, not of many years ago, in my mind, but of the present instant. They are all before

60 me, just as they were in the evil hour when I went among them for the first time, with my trembling hand in Mr. Quinion's. . . .

There were three or four of us, counting me. My working place was established in a corner of the warehouse,

65 where Mr. Quinion could see me, when he chose to stand up on the bottom rail of his stool in the counting-house, and look at me through a window above the desk. Hither, on the first morning of my so **auspiciously** beginning life on my own account, the oldest of the regular boys

70 was summoned to show me my business. His name was Mick Walker, and he wore a ragged apron and a paper cap. He informed me that his father was a bargeman, and walked, in a black velvet head-dress, in the Lord Mayor's Show. He also informed me that our principal associate

75 would be another boy whom he introduced by the—to me —extraordinary name of Mealy Potatoes. . . .

No words can express the secret **agony** of my soul as I sunk into this companionship. The deep remembrance of the sense I had, of being utterly without hope now; of

80 the shame I felt in my position; of the misery it was to my

auspiciously

favorably

agony

a great pain

David Copperfield spent his days washing bottles. In the 1800s, child labor was common in England.

young heart to believe that day by day what I had learned, and thought, and delighted in, and raised my fancy and my emulation up by, would pass away from me, little by little, never to be brought back any more; cannot be written.

85 As often as Mick Walker went away in the course of that forenoon, I mingled my tears with the water in which I was washing the bottles; and sobbed as if there were a flaw in my own breast, and it were in danger of bursting.

The counting-house clock was at half past twelve, and
90 there was general preparation for going to dinner, when Mr. Quinion tapped at the counting-house window, and beckoned to me to go in. I went in, and found there a stoutish, middle-aged person, in a brown surtout[1] and black tights and shoes, with no more hair upon his head (which
95 was a large one, and very shining) than there is upon an egg, and with a very extensive face, which he turned full upon me. His clothes were **shabby**, but he had an imposing shirt-collar on. He carried a jaunty sort of a stick, with a large pair of rusty tassels to it; and a quizzing-glass[2]
100 hung outside his coat,—for ornament, I afterwards found, as he very seldom looked through it, and couldn't see anything when he did.

"This," said Mr. Quinion, in allusion to myself, "is he."

"This," said the stranger, with a certain condescending
105 roll in his voice, and a certain indescribable air of doing something **genteel**, which impressed me very much, "is Master Copperfield. I hope I see you well, sir?"

I said I was very well, and hoped he was. I was sufficiently ill at ease, Heaven knows; but it was not in my
110 nature to complain much at that time of my life, so I said I was very well, and hoped he was.

"I am," said the stranger, "thank Heaven, quite well. I have received a letter from Mr. Murdstone, in which he mentions that he would desire me to receive into an
115 apartment in the rear of my house, which is at present unoccupied—and is, in short, to be let as a—in short," said the stranger, with a smile and in a burst of confidence, "as

> **shabby**
> worn; threadbare

> **genteel**
> politeness tradition- ally associated with wealth and education

---

[1] surtout—a man's overcoat
[2] quizzing-glass—a single eyeglass used to examine people or objects

a bedroom—the young beginner whom I have now the pleasure to—" and the stranger waved his hand, and settled
120 his chin in his shirt-collar.

"This is Mr. Micawber," said Mr. Quinion to me.

"Ahem!" said the stranger, "that is my name."

"Mr. Micawber," said Mr. Quinion, "is known to Mr. Murdstone. He takes orders for us on commission, when
125 he can get any. He has been written to by Mr. Murdstone, on the subject of your lodgings³, and he will receive you as a lodger."

"My address," said Mr. Micawber, "is Windsor Terrace, City Road. I—in short," said Mr. Micawber, with the same
130 genteel air, and in another burst of confidence—"I live there." I made him a bow.

"Under the impression," said Mr. Micawber, "that your peregrinations in this metropolis have not as yet been extensive, and that you might have some difficulty
135 in penetrating the arcana of the Modern Babylon in the direction of the City Road,—in short," said Mr. Micawber, in another burst of confidence, "that you might lose yourself—I shall be happy to call this evening, and install you in the knowledge of the nearest way."
140   I thanked him with all my heart, for it was friendly in him to offer to take that trouble.

"At what hour," said Mr. Micawber, "shall I—"

"At about eight," said Mr. Quinion.

"At about eight," said Mr. Micawber. "I beg to wish you
145 good day, Mr. Quinion. I will intrude no longer."

So he put on his hat, and went out with his cane under his arm: very upright, and humming a tune when he was clear of the counting-house. . . .

At the appointed time in the evening, Mr. Micawber
150 reappeared. I washed my hands and face, to do the greater honour to his gentility, and we walked to our house, as I suppose I must now call it, together; Mr. Micawber impressing the name of streets, and the shapes of corner houses upon me, as we went along, that I might find my
155 way back, easily, in the morning. . . .

---

³ lodgings—furnished rooms for rent in a person's home

David Copperfield became friends with Mr. and Mrs. Micawber, who were deeply in debt.

My room was at the top of the house, at the back: a close chamber; stencilled all over with an ornament, which my young imagination represented as a blue muffin; and very scantily furnished.

160 "I never thought," said Mrs. Micawber, when she came up, twin and all, to show me the apartment, and sat down to take breath, "before I was married, when I lived with papa and mama, that I should ever find it necessary to take a lodger. But Mr. Micawber being in difficulties, all

165 considerations of private feeling must give way."

I said: "Yes, ma'am.". . .

"If Mr. Micawber's creditors will not give him time," said Mrs. Micawber, "they must take the consequences; and the sooner they bring it to an issue the better. Blood

170 cannot be obtained from a stone, neither can anything on account be obtained at present (not to mention law expenses) from Mr. Micawber.". . .

The only visitors I ever saw, or heard of, were creditors. They used to come at all hours, and some of them were

175 quite ferocious. One dirty-faced man, I think he was a boot-maker, used to edge himself into the passage as early as seven o'clock in the morning, and call up the stairs to Mr. Micawber—"Come! You ain't out yet, you know. Pay us, will you? Don't hide, you know; that's mean. I wouldn't

180 be mean if I was you. Pay us, will you? You just pay us, d'ye hear? Come!" Receiving no answer to these taunts, he

Creditors were the only visitors at the Micawbers'.

would mount in his wrath to the words "swindlers" and "robbers"; and these being ineffectual too, would sometimes go to the extremity of crossing the street, and roaring up 185 at the windows of the second floor, where he knew Mr. Micawber was. At these times, Mr. Micawber would be transported with grief and **mortification**, even to the length (as I was once made aware by a scream from his wife) of making motions at himself with a razor; but within 190 half-an-hour afterwards, he would polish up his shoes with extraordinary pains, and go out, humming a tune with a greater air of gentility than ever. Mrs. Micawber was quite as elastic. I have known her to be thrown into fainting fits by the king's taxes at three o'clock, and to eat lamb chops, 195 breaded, and drink warm ale (paid for with two tea-spoons that had gone to the pawnbroker's) at four. . . .

mortification

shame; embarrassment

Answer It

1. Summarize the events that have happened so far in David's life.

2. Make a generalization about Murdstone and Grinby's warehouse.

3. Paraphrase David's description of his feelings about his new life, lines 77–88.

4. Describe Mr. Micawber's manner of speaking.

5. Make an inference about why the only visitors to Mr. Micawber's house were creditors.

Excerpt 2

In this house, and with this family, I passed my leisure time. My own exclusive breakfast of a penny loaf[1] and a pennyworth of milk, I provided myself. I kept another small loaf, and a modicum of cheese, on a particular shelf
5 of a particular cupboard, to make my supper on when I came back at night. This made a hole in the six or seven shillings[2], I know well; and I was out at the warehouse all day, and had to support myself on that money all the week. From Monday morning until Saturday night, I had no
10 advice, no counsel, no encouragement, no **consolation**, no assistance, no support, of any kind, from anyone, that I can call to mind, as I hope to go to heaven!

I was so young and childish, and so little qualified—how could I be otherwise?—to undertake the whole charge of my
15 own existence, that often, in going to Murdstone and Grinby's, of a morning, I could not resist the stale pastry put out for sale at half-price at the pastrycooks' doors, and spent in that the money I should have kept for my dinner. Then, I went without my dinner, or bought a roll or a slice of pudding. . . .
20 We had half-an-hour, I think, for tea. When I had money enough, I used to get half-a-pint of ready-made coffee and a slice of bread and butter. When I had none, I used to look at a venison shop in Fleet Street; or I have strolled, at such a time, as far as Covent Garden Market,
25 and stared at the pineapples. I was fond of wandering about the Adelphi, because it was a mysterious place, with those dark arches. I see myself emerging one evening from some of these arches, on a little public-house close to the river, with an open space before it, where some coal-heavers
30 were dancing; to look at whom I sat down upon a bench. I wonder what they thought of me! . . .

consolation
comfort; reassurance

[1] penny loaf—a small loaf of bread bought for a penny
[2] shillings—coins in Great Britain worth one twentieth of a pound

I know I do not exaggerate, unconsciously and unintentionally, the scantiness of my resources or the difficulties of my life. I know that if a shilling were given
35 me by Mr. Quinion at any time, I spent it in a dinner or a tea. I know that I worked, from morning until night, with common men and boys, a shabby child. I know that I lounged about the streets, insufficiently and unsatisfactorily fed. I know that, but for the mercy of God, I might easily
40 have been, for any care that was taken of me, a little robber or a little vagabond. . . .

My rescue from this kind of existence I considered quite hopeless, and abandoned, as such, altogether. I am solemnly convinced that I never for one hour was
45 **reconciled** to it, or was otherwise than miserably unhappy; but I **bore** it; and even to Peggotty, partly for the love of her and partly for shame, never in any letter (though many passed between us) revealed the truth.

Mr. Micawber's difficulties were an addition to the
50 distressed state of my mind. In my forlorn state I became quite attached to the family, and used to walk about, busy with Mrs. Micawber's calculations of ways and means, and heavy with the weight of Mr. Micawber's debts. On a Saturday night, which was my grand treat—partly because
55 it was a great thing to walk home with six or seven shillings in my pocket, looking into the shops and thinking what such a sum would buy, and partly because I went home early—Mrs. Micawber would make the most heart-rending confidences to me; also on a Sunday morning, when I
60 mixed the portion of tea or coffee I had bought over-night, in a little shaving-pot, and sat late at my breakfast. It was nothing at all unusual for Mr. Micawber to sob violently at the beginning of one of these Saturday night conversations, and sing about jack's delight being his lovely Nan, towards
65 the end of it. I have known him come home to supper with a flood of tears, and a declaration that nothing was now left but a jail; and go to bed making a calculation of the expense of putting bow-windows[3] to the house, "in case

reconciled

prepared to accept; adjusted to something difficult

bore

endured with tolerance and patience

[3] bow-windows—windows that stick out from a wall and form a curve

anything turned up," which was his favourite expression.
70 And Mrs. Micawber was just the same.

A curious equality of friendship, originating, I suppose, in our respective circumstances, sprung up between me and these people, notwithstanding the ludicrous **disparity** in our years. But I never allowed myself to be prevailed
75 upon to accept any invitation to eat and drink with them out of their stock (knowing that they got on badly with the butcher and baker, and had often not too much for themselves), until Mrs. Micawber took me into her entire confidence. This she did one evening as follows:
80 "Master Copperfield," said Mrs. Micawber, "I make no stranger of you, and therefore do not hesitate to say that Mr. Micawber's difficulties are coming to a crisis."

It made me very miserable to hear it, and I looked at Mrs. Micawber's red eyes with the utmost sympathy.
85 "With the exception of the heel of a Dutch cheese— which is not adapted to the wants of a young family"—said Mrs. Micawber, "there is really not a scrap of anything in the larder. I was accustomed to speak of the larder when I lived with papa and mama, and I use the word almost
90 unconsciously. What I mean to express is, that there is nothing to eat in the house."

"Dear me!" I said, in great concern.

I had two or three shillings of my week's money in my pocket—from which I presume that it must have been on
95 a Wednesday night when we held this conversation—and I hastily produced them, and with heartfelt emotion begged Mrs. Micawber to accept of them as a loan. But that lady, kissing me, and making me put them back in my pocket, replied that she couldn't think of it. . . .
100 At last Mr. Micawber's difficulties came to a crisis, and he was arrested early one morning, and carried over to the King's Bench Prison in the Borough. He told me, as he went out of the house, that the God of day had now gone down upon him—and I really thought his heart was broken and
105 mine too. But I heard, afterwards, that he was seen to play a lively game at skittles, before noon.

> **disparity**
> a difference;
> inequality

Mrs. Micawber wouldn't accept David Copperfield's shillings as a loan.

On the first Sunday after he was taken there, I was to go and see him, and have dinner with him. I was to ask my way to such a place, and just short of that place I should
110 see such another place, and just short of that I should see a yard, which I was to cross, and keep straight on until I saw a turnkey[4]. All this I did; and when at last I did see a turnkey (poor little fellow that I was!), and thought how, when Roderick Random was in a debtors' prison, there was a
115 man there with nothing on him but an old rug, the turnkey swam before my dimmed eyes and my beating heart.

Mr. Micawber was waiting for me within the gate, and we went up to his room (top story but one), and cried very much. He solemnly conjured me, I remember, to
120 take warning by his fate; and to observe that if a man had twenty pounds a-year for his income, and spent nineteen pounds nineteen shillings and sixpence, he would be happy, but that if he spent twenty pounds one he would be miserable. After which he borrowed a shilling of me
125 for porter, gave me a written order on Mrs. Micawber for the amount, and put away his pocket-handkerchief, and cheered up. . . .

At last Mrs. Micawber resolved to move into the prison, where Mr. Micawber had now secured a room to

4 turnkey—a person who keeps the keys to a prison; a jailer

130 himself. So I took the key of the house to the landlord,
who was very glad to get it; and the beds were sent over
to the King's Bench, except mine, for which a little room
was hired outside the walls in the neighbourhood of
that Institution, very much to my satisfaction, since the
135 Micawbers and I had become too used to one another,
in our troubles, to part. The Orfling was likewise
accommodated with an inexpensive lodging in the same
neighbourhood. Mine was a quiet back-garret[5] with
a sloping roof, commanding a pleasant prospect of a
140 timberyard; and when I took possession of it, with the
reflection that Mr. Micawber's troubles had come to a
crisis at last, I thought it quite a paradise.

    All this time I was working at Murdstone and Grinby's
in the same common way, and with the same common
145 companions, and with the same sense of unmerited
degradation as at first. But I never, happily for me no
doubt, made a single acquaintance, or spoke to any of the
many boys whom I saw daily in going to the warehouse, in
coming from it, and in prowling about the streets at meal-
150 times. I led the same secretly unhappy life; but I led it in the
same lonely, **self-reliant** manner. The only changes I am
conscious of are, firstly, that I had grown more shabby, and
secondly, that I was now relieved of much of the weight of
Mr. and Mrs. Micawber's cares; for some relatives or friends
155 had engaged to help them at their present pass, and they
lived more comfortably in the prison than they had lived
for a long while out of it. I used to breakfast with them now,
in virtue of some arrangement, of which I have forgotten
the details. I forget, too, at what hour the gates were opened
160 in the morning, admitting of my going in; but I know that I
was often up at six o'clock, and that my favourite lounging-
place in the interval was old London Bridge, where I was
wont to sit in one of the stone recesses, watching the people
going by, or to look over the balustrades at the sun shining
165 in the water, and lighting up the golden flame on the top of
the Monument. . . .

self-reliant
independent;
able to take care
of oneself

[5] back-garret—an attic to the rear of the house

By way of going in for anything that might be on the cards, I call to mind that Mr. Micawber, about this time, composed a petition to the House of Commons, praying
170 for an alteration in the law of imprisonment for debt. I set down this remembrance here, because it is an instance to myself of the manner in which I fitted my old books to my altered life, and made stories for myself, out of the streets, and out of men and women; and how some main points in
175 the character I shall unconsciously develop, I suppose, in writing my life, were gradually forming all this while.

There was a club in the prison, in which Mr. Micawber, as a gentleman, was a great authority. Mr. Micawber had stated his idea of this petition to the club, and the
180 club had strongly approved of the same. Wherefore Mr. Micawber (who was a thoroughly good-natured man, and as active a creature about everything but his own affairs as ever existed, and never so happy as when he was busy about something that could never be of any profit to him)
185 set to work at the petition, invented it, engrossed it on an immense sheet of paper, spread it out on a table, and appointed a time for all the club, and all within the walls if they chose, to come up to his room and sign it.

When I heard of this approaching ceremony, I was
190 so anxious to see them all come in, one after another, though I knew the greater part of them already, and they me, that I got an hour's leave of absence from Murdstone and Grinby's, and established myself in a corner for that purpose. As many of the principal members of the club
195 as could be got into the small room without filling it, supported Mr. Micawber in front of the petition, while my old friend Captain Hopkins (who had washed himself, to do honour to so solemn an occasion) stationed himself close to it, to read it to all who were unacquainted with its
200 contents. The door was then thrown open, and the general population began to come in, in a long file: several waiting outside, while one entered, affixed his signature, and went out. To everybody in succession, Captain Hopkins said: "Have you read it?"—"No."—"Would you like to hear it
205 read?" If he weakly showed the least disposition to hear

it, Captain Hopkins, in a loud sonorous voice, gave him every word of it. The Captain would have read it twenty thousand times, if twenty thousand people would have heard him, one by one. I remember a certain luscious roll
210 he gave to such phrases as "The people's representatives in Parliament assembled," "Your petitioners therefore humbly approach your honourable house," "His gracious Majesty's unfortunate subjects," as if the words were something real in his mouth, and delicious to taste; Mr.
215 Micawber, meanwhile, listening with a little of an author's vanity, and contemplating (not severely) the spikes on the opposite wall. . . .

When my thoughts go back, now, to that slow agony of my youth, I wonder how much of the histories I invented
220 for such people hangs like a mist of fancy over well-remembered facts! When I tread the old ground, I do not wonder that I seem to see and pity, going on before me, an innocent romantic boy, making his imaginative world out of such strange experiences and **sordid** things!

sordid
wretched; shameful

David Copperfield *is an autobiographical novel, meaning it is based on Dickens' life.*

Charles Dickens wrote 15 outstanding novels and many works in other genres.

Answer It

1. Recall that the target word is "social" and that social issues are problems in a society. Identify two social issues that Charles Dickens writes about in *David Copperfield.* Then tell why Dickens wrote about these issues.

2. Identify a flaw, or negative trait, in Mr. Micawber's character.

3. Illustrate in a few sentences what David's daily life was like when he was living with Mr. and Mrs. Micawber.

4. Discuss how David's life changed after the Micawbers went to prison.

5. Judge whether or not you think that Mr. Micawber's plan to write a petition is a good one.

YOUTH ACTIVISTS
WORK FOR SOCIAL CHANGE

Do you think that young people have no say in what happens in the world? Think again. Read these inspiring stories of students who confronted a problem and didn't give up until they had found a positive solution.

5 **NIKO AND THEO MILONOPOULOS, FOUNDERS OF KIDZ VOICE–LA**

Kids shouldn't . . . have to sleep in bathtubs because they're afraid of being shot.

—Niko Milonopoulos, youth activist who worked on a
10   ban on ammunition sales in Los Angeles

For many kids, gun violence is the reason why their parents won't let them watch certain TV shows. But in 1997, events in their Los Angeles neighborhood forced Niko and Theo Milonopoulos to face some hard facts. Two
15 horrendous gun crimes shattered the ten-year-old twins' illusion of safety. In January, a gunman killed TV star Bill Cosby's son, Ennis, when the young man was changing a flat tire on his car. And in February, bank robbers wielding automatic weapons sprayed a shopping district with bullets,
20 wounding police officers and bystanders. Both crime scenes were close to the twins' school.

Theo recalled, "You could not go anywhere without fear of being shot. At first we thought we couldn't do anything about it. Then we thought somebody else would. But

Lax

careless; lenient

25 nobody did." Indignant that community leaders failed to act, the brothers took matters into their own hands.

First they did their homework. They found that in L.A., gun violence killed 150 kids per year. **Lax** laws made it far too easy to buy firearms. Since there were "so many

30 guns out there," Niko explained, he and Theo decided that "trying to ban guns wouldn't be effective."

The twins' research also revealed that local gun shops sold bullets for as little as 25 cents apiece. So, the boys devised an alternate strategy. Instead of pushing for stricter

35 gun controls, they channeled their energy into making ammunition as difficult as possible to obtain.

To achieve their aim, Niko and Theo formed a nonprofit social activist group called Kidz Voice–LA. Kids ran every aspect of the organization. Its first task

40 was circulating a petition that called for a citywide ban on ammunition sales. When they had collected 7,000 kids' signatures, members presented their petition to the Los Angeles City Council. Theo recalled that the council's reaction was to "pat them on the head. 'They're just kids.

45 We'll accept their petition. Maybe we'll do something. Maybe we won't.'"

condescending

disdainful; patronizing

This **condescending** response was discouraging, but the twins did not give up. They attended every council meeting to express their outrage about gun violence.

50 Finally, in 2002, the council took some action. In a partial victory for Niko, Theo, and their fellow activists, resulting legislation outlawed the sale in Los Angeles of ammunition for high-powered weapons.

By this time, the twins were in high school. They

advocate

support an idea

55 continued to **advocate** for stricter regulations on gun and ammunition sales. Meanwhile, Kidz Voice–LA launched other projects. One project raised money to fill 5,000 backpacks with necessities for homeless young people.

idealists

people guided more by ideals than by practicial considerations

As Theo once said, the twins will likely "always be

60 **idealists** and activists." Having developed a taste for politics, he and Niko spent the summer of 2003 in Washington, D.C., working as pages in the House

of Representatives. In 2004, Theo was elected to his community's neighborhood council.

65 TARA CHURCH, ANGELICA ROQUE, AND TREE MUSKETEERS: ONE MILLION TREES AND COUNTING

Realizing what one individual could accomplish by planting one tree gave me a sense of power. I didn't feel that my individual efforts could make a difference until that moment.

70 —Tara Church, an attorney in her twenties, a Harvard Law School graduate, and a founding member of Tree Musketeers

In 1987, Tara Church was only eight years old. Yet she and 12 other Brownies from El Segundo, California, 75 sprouted Tree Musketeers, a nonprofit group that's still flourishing today.

Youth managers such as President Angelica Roque, 18, run Tree Musketeers. Adults help, but kids make all the decisions and do most of the work. They sprout, nurture, 80 and plant seedlings and trees all over the U.S. And they provide support for children around the world who wish to better their communities by planting trees.

Some of the trees and groves that the Tree Musketeers plant are dedicated to loved ones who've passed away or

In 2000, the Tree Musketeers planted their one-millionth tree.

85 societal ideals such as world peace. The group also comes
to the aid of communities devastated by forest fires.

In working for the organization, young volunteers learn
how to raise funds, run an office, maintain a Web site*, and
plan projects. Leaders such as Roque train younger kids to
90 take their places when they move on to college and careers.

The first tree the group planted was given a name:
Marcie the Marvelous Tree. Church and her Brownie
cohorts planted Marcie, a sycamore, as an apology to
Mother Nature. On a camping trip, a drought forced the
95 troop to use paper plates, since there wasn't enough water
for dishwashing. The girls knew where paper plates came
from, and they wanted to make up for the resources they'd
used. Later, Marcie, the tree, inspired them to plant a ring

shield

protect with a
physical barrier

of trees to **shield** their community from airport noise and
100 pollution. Planting trees energized the girls so much that
they kept on doing it.

In 2000, Tree Musketeers met an impressive goal. On
Capitol Hill in Washington, D.C., the group planted its one-
millionth tree. In order to reach this milestone, a million
105 kids donated a million hours of volunteer work.

*treemusketeers.org

TODD RABKIN GOLDEN'S PROSTHESIS DESIGN FOR VIETNAMESE CHILDREN

*. . . some 3.5 million landmines [are] still scattered across
[Vietnam] . . . These remnants of past wars continue to*
110 *kill and maim dozens and possibly even hundreds of*
Vietnamese children every year. . . .
—UNICEF, 2002

In San Francisco, it's common to see people in wheelchairs
begging for money. In Vietnam, you see people begging, but
115 *they don't have wheelchairs and many don't have legs.*
—Todd Rabkin Golden, a high-school senior in 2002

In 2001, teenager Todd Rabkin Golden took a summer
trip to Vietnam, a land of breathtaking natural beauty. But
Todd also saw many Vietnamese kids who had lost their

120 legs to exploded land mines. They had accidentally set off the mines while playing where the land mines had been placed long ago and forgotten. Now, these children without legs used pieces of old tires tied to their hands as makeshift protection as they dragged themselves along the ground.

125 Instead of fretting about and then forgetting this tragedy, Rabkin Golden decided to act. He attended San Francisco's Lick-Wilmerding High School, which emphasizes community service in its curriculum. For his senior project, Todd proposed to make below-the-knee

130 **prostheses** for maimed Vietnamese children. His proposal fit well with Lick's requirement that senior projects must involve technology and design.

prostheses
artificial limbs

Few of the professionals whom Todd consulted offered encouragement,
135 but as his mother, Dr. Elizabeth Rabkin, says, he is a "go-for-it kind of kid." It took Todd four months and fifty dollars worth of materials to design and build a prosthesis.

140 This is not an artificial limb, but a strong aluminum "peg leg" designed for children aged 11 to 18. The prosthesis has eight holes that enable the user to shorten or lengthen it. Since few
145 Vietnamese people are wealthy, Todd assumed that a child's prosthesis would have to be adjustable—and sturdy enough—to last until adulthood.

During the research and design
150 phase of his project, Rabkin Golden asked his little sister to be his foot and leg model. He used her measurements from knee to foot as a starting point to construct a mold.

David Clifford, Todd's metal and woodworking
155 teacher, provided guidance. So did Charles McIntyre, a certified prosthetist at the University of California at San Francisco. In his years at Lick-Wilmerding, Clifford said, no other student of his has come up with an idea that

Rabkin Golden teaches free first-aid classes to his fellow students.

combines intellect with compassion so perfectly. McIntyre
160 commented, "I don't think Todd is going to revolutionize
prosthetics, but he may provide a basic product that is very
much needed."

Originally, Todd planned to build about two dozen
prostheses. Yet the process was so time consuming that he
165 was able to finish only one before his high school graduation.
"I only created one leg," Todd said, "but maybe it will mean
that one person will not have to crawl across the street." He
looks upon his "one leg" as a prototype and continues to
work toward mass-producing prostheses based on his design.
170   Rabkin Golden seems headed for a lifetime of social
activism. An anthropology major at Dartmouth College in
New Hampshire, he serves as Student Body Vice President.
After Todd earned certification as an emergency medical
technician, one of his first thoughts was to share his skills
175 and knowledge with others. On top of studying, playing
sports, and serving in student government, he finds time
to teach free first-aid classes to fellow students.

Think About It

1. Recall that the Milonopoulos brothers devised an "alternate strategy" for solving the problem of gun violence in Los Angeles. Tell what their new strategy was, and explain why the twins felt it was needed.

2. Identify the personal traits the boys had that helped make them successful as youth activists. Give examples of actions that demonstrate these traits.

3. Compare the activism of the Tree Musketeers to that of the Milonopoulos brothers. Identify one similarity and one difference.

4. Define in your own words the problem Todd Rabkin Golden attempted to find a solution for, and summarize the challenges his goal presented.

5. Todd's woodworking teacher said that Todd's prosthesis was "an idea that combined intellect and compassion." Discuss the meaning of this statement. Then evaluate the Milonopoulos brothers' actions, using the same criteria.

6. Suppose you had the opportunity to start a nonprofit organization dedicated to helping people, animals, or the environment. What kind of organization would you start? What would be the main goal?

Stand Alone or Join the Crowd

It's natural to want to feel included—part of the group. How does social pressure affect your feelings and, ultimately, your behavior? Read these stories and consider the choices made by the characters.

5 **THE FAIRLY INTELLIGENT FLY**   A Fable by James Thurber

A large spider in an old house built a beautiful web in which to catch flies. Every time a fly landed on the web and was **entangled** in it the spider **devoured** him, so that when another fly came along he would think the
10 web was a safe and quiet place in which to rest. One day a fairly intelligent fly buzzed around above the web so long without lighting that the spider appeared and said, "Come on down." But the fly was too clever for him and said, "I never light where I don't see other flies and I don't see any
15 other flies in your house." So he flew away until he came to a place where there were a great many other flies. He was about to settle down among them when a bee buzzed up and said, "Hold it, stupid, that's flypaper. All those flies are trapped." "Don't be silly," said the fly, "they're dancing." So
20 he settled down and became stuck to the flypaper with all the other flies.

Moral: Look where you are going before you follow the crowd.

BOOH'S STORY

Korea is a small Asian nation that has suffered
25 centuries of political unrest and economic hardship.

> **entangled**
> caught; intertwined

> **devoured**
> ate up greedily

By its own historians' accounts, the peninsula has been
invaded nine hundred times. Following World War II, the
United States and the Soviet Union divided the country
in two—North Korea and South Korea. The Korean War,
30 *fought between 1950 and 1953, involved North Korea and*
China fighting against South Korea and a U.S.-commanded
multinational *United Nations force. Although the economy*
of South Korea has improved tremendously since that time,
some South Koreans have immigrated to the United States
35 *in search of a better life. In 1987, Sook, a South Korean*
teenager, and her family came to America because her
family felt there were more opportunities here: for her sister
who is hearing-impaired, and for Sook, too. In this first-
person account, Sook tells about her experience of attending
40 *a new high school in Chicago.*

The first day of school I was walking down the hallway,
when I heard someone say "Hi" in Korean. I turned around
and then I realized that there were other Koreans and other
Asians in this school. At first I was so excited, I said "Hi,"
45 but then almost right away it got weird.

They could tell by my last name that I was Korean. But
at this school they think they have to keep company with
just themselves. They don't want to **mingle** with people
from anywhere but Korea. They don't want to join other
50 people. And that's part of the problem. They could be a big
help for people who just moved here. They were supposed
to help me. When a new Korean person comes, the newer
ones help the newest ones. It keeps going on and on.

But I found out it's not always like that. These kids
55 formed a **clique**. They immediately started saying things
like, "Where does she come from?" "I don't think she just
moved here." "I don't like the way she dresses, the way she
talks, the way she acts." "I can't stand her." Some of them
saw me say "Hi" to a black girl. They said, "Why did you say
60 'Hi' to her? She's black!" I said, "My life is living here. I need
to open my mind to all people."

Once in my English class, where I sit, someone had left
me this long letter. It was in Korean and filled with curses.

multinational

involving more than
two countries

mingle

move around in a
group of people; mix

clique

a group of people
who keep others out

I couldn't believe it. It said, "Who do you think you are?
65 Someone special? Don't be snotty." All the time they would
talk about me behind my back. They'd look for me in the
hallway. They'd give me dirty looks. I made friends with
a Chinese girl and four Korean girls told her to stay away
from me. I hated it.

70   I decided I don't need their help. I want to live here
and I want to speak this language. I like English. It sounds
soft and romantic. Anyway, some of them who moved
here five or six years ago still really can't speak English. I
was shocked. I thought, they never use English. They only
75 hear and use it with their teachers. Even when they watch
TV, they watch Korean cable! If I just try to look for all
the people who came from my same country, and I stay
with them the way I did in my country, there will be no
difference between being there and living here.

80   For me, and maybe for all immigrants, what's best I
decided is that once you move here, you have to be like one
of these American people. Try to hang around with people
who speak English. It doesn't have to be just American
people, but with people who speak good English and who
85 act like Americans. That wasn't the reason, though, that I
noticed my new boyfriend.

    He's an American-born Chinese, **second generation**.
He knows how to say "Hello" in Chinese and that's about
it. He's in my math class and I liked him right away. I didn't
90 say anything, because it was embarrassing. In Korea, much
more than here, the man is the boss. It's always more

second generation
born from parents
who are immigrants

important to have a boy child than a girl. The opportunities go to men first. And they are supposed to ask you out first. So we just talked, and then finally around Christmas,
95 he asked me out. I was acting like—excited! It's been six months now.

My mom knows and my dad does, too, but he doesn't take it too seriously. He just makes a lot of faces. We are only allowed to go out once a week on Fridays, and I have
100 to be home at ten or eleven. We go out to a movie, get pizza, or go bowling. But then maybe twice the whole year if there's a party, I can stay out a little later. The important thing is that they know where I am. Then, they don't really mind. I'm the oldest one and the oldest one has to be
105 perfect to show the younger ones.

I try to be a good example. I have a part-time job as a cashier in a little grocery store where I work ten hours each day on Saturdays and Sundays. We got the class transcript and I was ranked fifteenth out of more than four hundred
110 students. I got a pass from the dean and I called my dad. He was so happy, too.

He said, "What do you want?"

"I want a car."

"Bye," and he hung up the phone laughing. But I knew
115 he was proud.

Think About It

1. Describe the fly's attitude toward being part of a group. Does this attitude work well for the fly?

2. Why do you think James Thurber titled his fable "The Fairly Intelligent Fly" instead of "The Very Intelligent Fly"?

3. What other moral could readers infer from "The Fairly Intelligent Fly"?

4. Compare Sook's attitude about immigrating to the United States with the attitude of the other Korean girls at her high school.

5. Choose three words that describe Sook's character, and identify one action or statement that illustrates each.

6. What advice about sticking with your own kind do you think Sook would give to the fairly intelligent fly?

Enjoy the View

Phonemic Awareness and Phonics

Unit 28 introduces vowel phonograms and more letter combinations for connectives.

Vowel Phonograms

Some syllables contain a **vowel phonogram**.

- In some syllables, the vowel phoneme is spelled with two vowel letters.

- The vowel sound represented by the two vowel letters is usually long, but can represent other sounds.

- The vowel phonograms in this unit occur infrequently in English.
    aw for / ô / as in **saw**
    au for / ô / as in **pause**
    ew for / $\overline{oo}$ / as in **chew** and for / $y\overline{oo}$ / as in **few**
    eu for / $\overline{oo}$ / as in **sleuth** and for / $y\overline{oo}$ / as in **eulogy**
    eu for / $\overline{oo}$ / as in **neuron**

Connectives

The sound-spelling patterns are **du** for / $j\overline{oo}$ / and / jə /, and **tu** for / $ch\overline{oo}$ / and / chə /.

This often occurs when the letter **u** is used as a connective between a base word or root and a suffix. Examples: gradual, pendulum, punctuate, fortunate

Word Recognition and Spelling

Prefixes

We can expand words and change meaning by adding **prefixes**. These word parts are added to the beginnings of words. Example: **anti** + freeze = antifreeze

(See Step 3: Vocabulary and Morphology for links to meaning.)

> **Unit 28 Prefixes**
> **anti-, mal-**

Suffixes

We can expand words and change meaning by adding **suffixes**. These word parts are added to the ends of words. Example: nature + **al** = natural

(See Step 3: Vocabulary and Morphology for links to meaning.)

> **Unit 28 Suffixes**
> **-al, -ial, -ual**

Roots

We can build words using **roots**. Roots carry the most important part of a word's meaning. We usually attach a prefix or suffix to make a root into a word. Example: re + **fer** + al = referral

(See Step 3: Vocabulary and Morphology for links to meaning.)

> **Unit 28 Roots**
> **fer; tend/tens/tent; grad/gress**

> ### Unit 28 Essential Words
>
> | | | |
> |---|---|---|
> | aunt | brought | source |
> | bought | caught | view |

Spelling Lists

The Unit 28 spelling lists contain four categories:

1. Words with vowel phonograms: **aw**, **au**, **ew**, and **eu**

2. Words with connectives spelled **du** and **tu**

3. Essential Words (in italics)

4. Words with prefixes, roots, and suffixes

Spelling Lists

Lessons 1–5		Lessons 6–10	
aunt	eulogy	aggression	intended
because	few	antibiotic	malpractice
bought	neutron	applauded	medical
brought	new	contentious	punctual
caught	*source*	doctoral	referee
century	statue	editorial	teleconference
draw	*view*	extensive	upgraded
educate		graduates	

Vocabulary and Morphology

Unit Vocabulary

Sound-spelling correspondences from this unit and previous units make up this unit's vocabulary.

- What do these words mean?
- Do some of them mean more than one thing? Which ones?

UNIT Vocabulary

aw
awful
awning
claw
crawl
dawn
draw
drawer
hawk
jaw
law
lawn
lawyer
outlaw
paw
raw
saw
sawmill
seesaw
slaw
straw
thaw
yawn

au
applaud
auction
authentic
author

automatic
automobile
because
cause
caution
clause
exhaust
faucet
fault
fraud
hydraulic
launch
laundry
pause
restaurant
sauce
saucer
sausage

ew for / o͞o /
blew
chew
crew
drew
flew
grew
jewel
new
newborn

news
newspaper
renew
screw
threw

ew for / yo͞o /
curfew
few
pewter

eu for / o͞o /
deuce
leukemia
maneuver
neutralize
neutron
outmaneuver
sleuth

eu for / yo͞o /
eucalyptus
eulogy

eu for / o͞o /
neuron
neurotic

du for / jo͞o /
arduous
assiduous
deciduous

graduate
module
undergraduate

du for / jə /
educate
fraudulent
incredulous
modulate
pendulum

tu for / cho͞o /
accentuate
fluctuate
impetuous
punctuate
situate
statue
statute
virtual

tu for / chə /
capitulate
century
congratulate
fortune
saturate
spatula
unfortunate

Word Relationships

Synonyms are words that have the same or similar meanings.
Example: teach/educate

Antonyms are words that have opposite meanings.
Example: many/few

Meaning Parts

Prefixes

Prefixes can add to or change the meanings of words. The Unit 28 prefixes have the following meanings.

Unit 28 Prefixes	Meanings	Examples
anti-	opposite; against	antifreeze, antiperspirant, antitrust
mal-	bad, badly; abnormal	malfunction, malnutrition, malodorous

Suffixes

Suffixes can add to or change the meanings of words. When added to a base word or root, they can change the base word or root to an adjective.

Unit 28 Suffixes	Meanings	Examples
-al	relating to; characterized by	educational, formal, natural
-ial	relating to; characterized by	adverbial, collegial, residential
-ual	relating to; characterized by	actual, effectual, eventual

Roots

Roots form the basic meaning part of a word. Roots of English words often come from another language, especially Latin. A root usually needs a prefix or suffix to make it into a word. Example: re + **gress** = regress (re = back; gress = to step; regress = to step back)

Unit 28 Roots	Meanings	Examples
fer	to bear; carry	confer, defer, infer
tend/tens/tent	to stretch; strain	attend, extensive, pretentious
grad/gress	to step; degree	degradation, aggressive, congress

Challenge Morphemes

Roots	Meanings	Examples
spir	to breathe	conspire, inspire, transpire
capit/capt	to head; chief	capital, captain, caption
aud	to hear, listen	audible, audio, audit

STEP 4

Grammar and Usage

Adjectives

Review: Adjectives describe nouns. They answer the questions: **Which one? What kind?** and **How many?** They can be:

■ Single words. Examples: **cautious, raw, hydraulic**

■ Prepositional phrases that function as adjectives. For example, **of the world** is a prepositional phrase that answers the question **Which one?** It is a prepositional phrase in *form*, but it *functions* as an adjective.

Pronouns

Review: **Pronouns** are function words that take the place of nouns. They can be **nominative** (subject), **object**, or **possessive**. Most pronouns have antecedents—nouns to which they refer.

Indefinite pronouns refer to unspecified or unknown people or things. They can be nominative or object pronouns. Indefinite pronouns do not have antecedents.

Relative pronouns begin dependent clauses. A relative pronoun relates back to a noun or pronoun that has already been mentioned in the independent clause. This noun or pronoun is the antecedent. Relative pronouns include: **that, which, who, whom,** and **whose.**

Relative Pronouns

The front of the eyeball has a hole **that** lets in light.
That is a relative pronoun referring back to the noun **hole.**

Helen Keller, **who** lost her sight, was an amazing person.
Who is a relative pronoun referring back to the proper noun **Helen Keller.**

Present Perfect

If the past participle is part of a verb phrase with the helping verb **have** or **has,** the verb phrase is in the **present perfect tense.** The **present perfect** describes an action occurring at an unspecified time in the past or an action starting in the past and continuing in the present.

> **Present Perfect**
>
> Adams **has taken** many photographs.
>> The action in this sentence was completed at an
>> unspecified time in the past.
>
> Luis and Jack **have waited** for over an hour.
>> The action in this sentence started in the past and is
>> still continuing.

Participles

Review: The **present participle** is formed by adding **-ing** to the base verb. Example: chew + **ing** = chewing

The **past participle** of regular verbs is formed by adding **-ed** to the base verb. Example: chew + **ed** = (have) chewed. Some past participles are irregular; their forms must be memorized. Example: bring—(have) brought

Note: The *form* of a participle is the same as the *form* of the progressive: both forms use the **-ing** suffix. The *function* of the participle as an adjective and the *function* of the progressive tense are different.

Phrases

Review: A **phrase** is a group of words that functions as a single word. A phrase cannot stand alone. Example: an award-winning photograph

A **participial phrase** begins with a participle and is followed by a word (or group of words) that modifies it or receives its action. A participial phrase functions as an adjective because it modifies a noun or pronoun. It can come before or after the word it modifies. Example: **Approaching the dock**, the ship clanged its bells.
> The ship, **approaching the dock**, clanged its bells.

Clauses

Review: A **clause** is a group of words that contains a subject and a predicate. An **independent clause** has one subject and one predicate; it represents a complete thought. A **dependent clause** cannot stand alone. It combines with an independent clause to create meaning.

Some dependent clauses function as adjectives. An **adjectival clause**:

- Answers the question **Which one?** or **What kind?**
- Usually begins with a relative pronoun.

> **Adjectival Clause**
>
> Ansel Adams, **who was a famous photographer**, made extraordinary photos of American vistas.
>
> The clause **who was a famous photographer** is an adjectival clause. It begins with the relative pronoun **who**.

Sentence Pattern

Review: A **simple sentence** is an independent clause that contains a subject and a predicate and is a complete thought. Example: The fighters were close friends.

Adjectival clauses can vary sentence structure.

> **Sentences With Adjectival Clauses**
>
> The boys, **who were best friends**, fought each other in the boxing competition.
>
> The clause **who were best friends** describes the **boys**.

A **complex sentence** has one independent clause and one or more dependent clauses. Dependent clauses can be adverbial or adjectival. Adverbial clauses at the beginning of a sentence are followed by a comma. Adjectival clauses are separated from the independent clause by commas if not essential to the meaning of the independent clause.

Confusing Word Pairs

Less and **fewer** are often confused. **Less** means "not as great in amount or quantity." **Less** expresses uncountable amounts and is used with singular nouns. **Fewer** means "a smaller number of things or people." **Fewer** expresses countable amounts and is used with plural nouns.

> There was **less** light in the room than needed for the photograph.
> **Fewer** people came to see the paintings than were expected.

See the Appendix, page xx, for more on count and noncount nouns.

Bring and **take** are also often confused. **Bring** means "to carry something from a distant place to a closer place." **Take** means "to carry something from a nearby place to a place that is farther away."

> The performer will **bring** a puppet from Europe to our local theater.
> Later, someone will **take** the puppet back to Europe.

Listening and Reading Comprehension

Informational Text

■ Some **informational text** is nonfiction written about a specific topic, event, experience, or circumstance. It is often accompanied by visual information in the form of charts, graphs, or illustrations. The visual information provides additional content about the subject matter. "**A View of the Eye**" uses visual information to enhance the text content.

Vocabulary in Context

■ Context clues help us understand new vocabulary. Pronoun referents, meaning signals, and visuals, such as charts and graphs, provide meaning links.

Signal Words

■ Different types of sentences can help us think about new information and ideas in different ways. Identifying signal words within sentences can improve comprehension.

See the Appendix, page A20, for a complete list of signal words based on Bloom's Taxonomy.

Literary Terms and Devices

📖 **Genres** are types or categories of literature. Unit 28 features narrative and fiction.

■ A **narrative** is a story told by a narrator, or storyteller. A narrative has characters, a setting, events, conflict, and a resolution. A narrative told from the "first-person point of view" means that the story is told from the perspective of the storyteller. "**My First View of Ellis Island**" is told from the perspective of the narrator.

■ **Fiction** is the literary genre that includes imaginary stories. Some fiction is based on real people, places, and events. "**Amigo Brothers**" is an example of fiction.

Plot Analysis

■ **Plot** is the sequence of events in a narrative or drama. The author develops the plot to create the story. The plot guides the reader through the story.

- **Characters** and **setting** are introduced early in the story. They create the necessary background information for a reader. The characters, which can be people, animals, or things, interact in a story. The setting is the story's time and place. Characters and setting comprise the introduction—the first element of plot development.

- To understand how a plot develops, we must first identify a story's main **problem** and its **solution**. Without a problem, or conflict, there would be no story—everything would remain the same.

- After we become proficient in identifying a story's main problem and solution, we will learn more about plot development and apply it in our writing.

- Plot development usually consists of five elements:

    Introduction (characters and setting);

    Conflict (rising action);

    Climax (turning point);

    Resolution (falling action);

    Conclusion (the situation at the end of the story, with a look to the future).

STEP

6

Speaking and Writing

Signal Words

■ Different types of sentences require different responses, depending on the focus of **signal words**. Identifying signal words within sentences improves the accuracy of our responses to oral and written questions.

See the Appendix, page A20, for a complete list of signal words based on Bloom's Taxonomy.

Composition Organization

■ Some compositions tell a story. This type of writing is called a **narrative**. A narrative is a story that relates a series of events. Some narratives are true; others are fictitious.

■ A narrative has the same elements as a story:

Conflict: The major problem faced by the main characters. The conflict starts with an initiating event. The conflict is also called rising action because the conflict in a story usually keeps rising until the characters reach a turning point.

Climax: A sequential point in narrative literature. It is the turning point in a story, the point at which tension drops and the falling action begins.

Resolution: This is the part of the story after the turning point. It is also called falling action.

Conclusion: This is how the story ends.

■ Narratives use **transition phrases** to introduce events, create rising action, or signal a climax in the story.

> **Transition Phrases for Narratives**
>
> It all started when . . .
>
> Things were going well until . . .
>
> Gradually, I began to suspect that . . .
>
> Suddenly, I . . .

More About Words

- **Bonus Words** use the same sound-spelling correspondences that we have studied in this unit and previous units.

- **Idioms** are common phrases that cannot be understood by the meanings of their separate words—only by the entire phrase.

- **Why? Word History** tell about the phrase **point of view**.

UNIT Bonus Words

<u>aw</u>	augment	<u>ew</u> **for / $\overline{oo}$ /**	neurology
bawl	auspicious	anew	neurosis
bylaw	autism	cashew	pleurisy
coleslaw	automate	corkscrew	<u>du</u> **for / $j\overline{oo}$ /**
dawdle	autopsy	dew	incredulity
drawback	baulk	mildew	nodule
drawl	caucus	newcomer	
flaw	cauliflower	newscast	<u>du</u> **for / jə /**
hacksaw	caulk	newsprint	adulate
in-law	caustic	screwdriver	coeducation
jigsaw	cautious	shrewd	credulous
lawbreaker	daunt	steward	undulate
lawsuit	default	strew	<u>tu</u> **for / $ch\overline{oo}$ /**
overdraw	flaunt		conceptualize
pawn	gaunt	<u>ew</u> **for / $y\overline{oo}$ /**	constituent
sawdust	gauze	askew	infatuate
sawhorse	haul	ewe	perpetuate
scrawl	haunt	mew	picturesque
scrawny	implausible	skew	presumptuous
shawl	launder	spew	tumultuous
southpaw	overhaul	<u>eu</u> **for / $\overline{oo}$ /**	virtuoso
spawn	plausible	leukocyte	virtuous
sprawl	precaution	neuter	<u>tu</u> **for / chə /**
withdraw	raucous	<u>eu</u> **for / $y\overline{oo}$ /**	botulism
<u>au</u>	taunt	eureka	futuristic
applause	taut	feud	misfortune
auburn	trauma	<u>eu</u> **for / $\overline{oo}$ /**	naturalize
audacious	vault	neuritis	tarantula

Idioms

Idiom	Meaning
break new ground	do or discover something new
draw a blank	be unable to remember something
draw straws	decide by a lottery with straws of unequal lengths
fly the coop	make a getaway; escape
have a grandstand view	be in a position where you can see something very well
hit a raw nerve	upset someone by talking about a particular subject
make your skin crawl	make you feel afraid or disgusted
take a dim view of	disapprove of something
throw caution to the wind	take a huge risk; be very daring; act recklessly and hastily
turn over a new leaf	make a new start; abandon your faults

 Word History

Point of View—The English word **view** comes from the Latin, *vedere*, meaning "to see" or "to consider." A **point of view** originally meant a place from which a landscape could be viewed. Today, it refers to the perspective or attitude from which a person considers an object or a topic. Some professionals, such as scientists, present information from an *objective* point of view: they convey the facts of a subject without disclosing how they feel about it personally.

Artists often work from a *subjective* point of **view**. This means that the way they present a subject is how they think and feel about it personally. Ansel Adams' point of view is revealed in the way he takes photographs. He doesn't photograph exactly what he sees. Instead, he strives to produce an image that he visualizes in his mind.

A VIEW OF THE EYE

Human beings probably rely more on their sense of sight than on their other senses. Most people, however, don't know much about how their eyes work. The eye is an amazing organ.

5   Sometimes we call the eye an "eyeball." Your eye is a ball about one inch in diameter. Most of the ball is covered by a tough white bag. This is called the *sclera*, or the white of the eye. At the front of the ball is a hole that lets in light. This hole is called the *pupil*. It appears as a black dot in the

10 middle of your eye. It isn't really colored black. Looking into the pupil is like looking through the door into a dark room. The pupil is black because there is no light inside the eye to make things visible.

Sometimes the pupil changes size. Sometimes it is

15 as big as a pea. Other times it is as small as the head of a pin. Like a window, your eye has a curtain to control the amount of light that enters it. The colored ring around the pupil acts like a curtain. It is called the *iris*. In dim light, the iris opens to let in more light. In bright light, the iris

20 closes to let in less light.

The pupil is covered with a clear layer of skin called the *cornea*. Behind the cornea is a clear disk called the *lens*. The lens in your eye is shaped like a magnifying glass. It

would fit neatly on the tip of your finger. The job of the lens
25 and the cornea is to gather light and focus it on a special
spot at the back of the eye. This spot is called the *retina*.

The retina is a special layer of cells about the size
of a nickel. If you thought of the eye as a movie camera,
the retina would be the film in the camera. When you
30 take a picture with a camera, you must develop the film.
To develop this film, the light focused onto the retina is
changed into nerve impulses. These impulses are sent to
the brain through the *optic nerve*. The brain develops the
impulses into visual images.

35 In fact, you see things with your brain just as much
as you view them with your eyes. Your eyes collect visual
information. Your brain makes sense out of it. The process
happens so quickly and easily that you don't need to think
about it.

Adapted from "Eye See: Experiments in Seeing" by Linda Allison

HOW THE EYE SEES A FLOWER

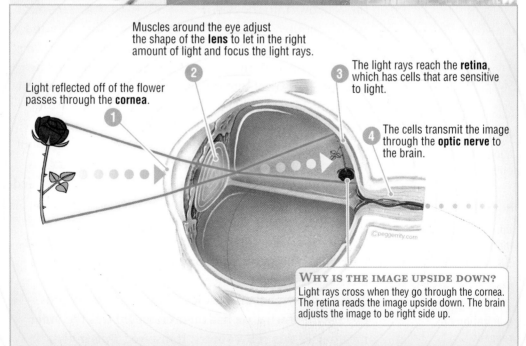

Muscles around the eye adjust
the shape of the **lens** to let in the right
amount of light and focus the light rays.

Light reflected off of the flower
passes through the **cornea**.

The light rays reach the **retina**,
which has cells that are sensitive
to light.

The cells transmit the image
through the **optic nerve** to
the brain.

WHY IS THE IMAGE UPSIDE DOWN?
Light rays cross when they go through the cornea.
The retina reads the image upside down. The brain
adjusts the image to be right side up.

My First View
of Ellis Island

My first impressions of the new world will always remain etched in my memory, particularly that hazy October morning [in 1907] when I first saw Ellis Island. The steamer *Florida* was fourteen days out of Naples. It
5 was filled to capacity with sixteen hundred natives of Italy. It had weathered one of the worst storms in our captain's memory; and glad we were, both children and grown-ups, to leave the open sea. We were glad to come at last through the Narrows into the Bay.

10 My mother, my stepfather, my brother Giuseppe, and my two sisters, Liberta and Helvetia, were happy that we had come through the storm safely. We clustered on the foredeck for fear of separation and looked with wonder on this miraculous land of our dreams.

15 Giuseppe and I held tightly to stepfather's hands. Liberta and Helvetia clung to mother. Passengers all about us were crowding against the rail. Jabbered conversation, sharp cries, laughs, and cheers—a steadily rising **din** filled the air. Mothers and fathers lifted up the babies so that
20 they, too, could see the Statue of Liberty.

I looked at that statue with a sense of **bewilderment**, half doubting its reality. It loomed shadowy through the mist. It brought silence to the decks of the *Florida*. This was a symbol of America. This was an enormous
25 expression of what we had all been taught was the inner meaning of this new country. It inspired **awe** in the

din
a loud, persistent noise

bewilderment
confusion; puzzle-ment

awe
a feeling of great admiration or respect

hopeful immigrants. Many older persons among us were burdened with a thousand memories of what they were leaving behind. They had been openly weeping ever since

30 we began our final approach toward the unknown. Now somehow steadied, I suppose, by the concreteness of the symbol of America's freedom, they dried their tears.

Directly in front of the *Florida*, half visible in the haze, rose an even greater challenge to the imagination.

35 "Mountains!" I cried to Giuseppe. "Look at them!"

"They're strange," he said, "why don't they have snow on them?" He was craning his neck and standing on tiptoe to stare at the New York skyline.

Stepfather looked toward the skyscrapers and smiled.

40 He assured us that they were not mountains but buildings. They were "the highest buildings in the world."

Every side of the harbor offered its marvels. Tugs, barges, sloops, lighters, sluggish freighters, and giant ocean liners moved in different directions. They managed to

45 dart in and out and up and down without **colliding**. They spoke to us through the varied sounds of their whistles. The *Florida* replied with a deep echoing voice. Bells clanged through our ship. This caused a new flurry among our fellow passengers. Many of these people had come from

50 provinces far distant from ours. They were shouting to one another in dialects strange to me. Everything combined to increase our excitement. We rushed from deck to deck, fearful lest we miss the smallest detail of the scene.

Finally the *Florida* veered to the left. It turned

55 northward into the Hudson River. Now the incredible buildings of lower Manhattan came very close to us.

The officers of the ship, mighty and unapproachable beings they seemed to me, went striding up and down the decks shouting orders. They drove the immigrants before

60 them. Scowling and gesturing, they pushed and pulled the passengers. They herded us into separate groups as though we were animals. A few moments later we came to our dock, and the long journey was over.

> **colliding**
> crashing; hitting against something with force

Adapted from "When I First Saw Ellis Island" by Edward Corsi

The New Colossus
by Emma Lazarus

brazen

shocking and annoying

Not like the **brazen** giant of Greek fame

65 With conquering limbs astride from land to land;

Here at our sea-washed, sunset gates shall stand

A mighty woman with a torch, whose flame

Is the imprisoned lightning, and her name

Exiles

deportees; refugees

Mother of **Exiles**. From her beacon-hand

70 Glows world-wide welcome; her mild eyes command

The air-bridged harbor that twin cities frame,

"Keep, ancient lands, your storied pomp!" cries she

With silent lips. *"Give me your tired, your poor,*

Your huddled masses yearning to breathe free,

75 *The wretched refuse of your teeming shore,*

Send these, the homeless, tempest-tossed to me,

*I lift my lamp beside the golden door!"**

*The section of the poem in italics appears on a plaque on the base of the Statue of Liberty.

Between 1892 and 1924, over 22 million people came through Ellis Island and the Port of New York.

Answer It

1. Form a hypothesis about why Edward and his family decided to immigrate to the United States.

2. Make an inference about what Edward thought the Statue of Liberty symbolized.

3. Explain the significance of the target word "view" in this story.

4. Paraphrase the last five lines of the poem "The New Colossus," starting with the phrase "Give me your tired, your poor."

5. Assess the significance of the message communicated in the poem. Keep in mind that the poem is inscribed on the Statue of Liberty.

AMIGO BROTHERS

BY PIRI THOMAS

Viewing Each Other

Human beings are competitive by nature. In families, children experience sibling rivalry. As we grow up and participate in academic, athletic, and social interaction, we are always encouraged to try our best. The result of our
5 *efforts brings out our natural competitive nature.*

Some humans, the best among us, view each other differently. They don't see others merely as competitors; rather, they rise above competition. In this story, a pair of 17-year-old friends from Manhattan's lower east side
10 *teach us to view each other first as human beings and only secondarily as competitors.*

Antonio Cruz and Felix Vargas were both seventeen years old. They were so together in friendship that they felt themselves to be brothers. They had known each other
15 since childhood, growing up on the lower east side of Manhattan in the same tenement building on Fifth Street between Avenue A and Avenue B.

Antonio was fair, lean, and lanky, while Felix was dark, short, and husky. Antonio's hair was always falling over his
20 eyes, while Felix wore his black hair in a natural Afro style.

Each youngster had a dream of someday becoming lightweight champion of the world. Every chance they had the boys worked out, sometimes at the Boys Club on 10th Street and Avenue A and sometimes at the pro's gym on 14th Street. Early morning sunrises would find them running along the East River Drive, wrapped in sweat shirts, short towels around their necks, and handkerchiefs Apache style around their foreheads.

While some youngsters were into street negatives, Antonio and Felix slept, ate, rapped, and dreamt positive. Between them, they had a collection of *Fight* magazines second to none, plus a scrapbook filled with torn tickets to every boxing match they had ever attended, and some clippings of their own. If asked a question about any given fighter, they would immediately zip out from their memory banks divisions, weights, records of fights, knock-outs, technical knock-outs, and draws or losses.

Each had fought many bouts representing their community and had won two gold-plated medals plus a silver and bronze medallion. The difference was in their style. Antonio's lean form and long reach made him the better boxer, while Felix's short and muscular frame made him the better slugger. Whenever they had met in the ring for sparring sessions, it had always been hot and heavy.

Now, after a series of elimination bouts, they had been informed that they were to meet each other in the division finals that were scheduled for the seventh of August, two weeks away—the winner to represent the Boys Club in the Golden Gloves Championship Tournament.

The two boys continued to run together along the East River Drive. But even when joking with each other, they both sensed a wall rising between them.

One morning less than a week before their bout, they met as usual for their daily work-out. They fooled around with a few jabs at the air, slapped skin, and then took off, running lightly along the dirty East River's edge.

Antonio glanced at Felix who kept his eyes purposely straight ahead, pausing from time to time to do some fancy leg work while throwing one-twos followed by upper

60 cuts to an imaginary jaw. Antonio then beat the air with a **barrage** of body blows and short devastating lefts with an overhand jaw-breaking right.

barrage

a heavy outpouring

After a mile or so, Felix puffed and said, "Let's stop a while, bro. I think we both got something to say to
65 each other."

Antonio nodded. It was not natural to be acting as though nothing unusual was happening when two *ace-boon buddies*[1] were going to be blasting each other within a few short days.

70 They rested their elbows on the railing separating them from the river. Antonio wiped his face with his short towel. The sunrise was now creating day.

Felix leaned heavily on the river's railing and stared across to the shores of Brooklyn. Finally, he broke the silence.
75 "Man, I don't know how to come out with it."

Antonio helped. "It's about our fight, right?"

"Yeah, right." Felix's eyes squinted at the rising orange sun.

"I've been thinking about it too, *panin*[2]. In fact, since we
80 found out it was going to be me and you, I've been awake at night, pulling punches on you, trying not to hurt you."

"Same here. It ain't natural not to think about the fight. I mean we both are *cheverote*[3] fighters and we both want to win. But only one of us can win. There ain't no draws in the
85 eliminations."

Felix tapped Antonio gently on the shoulder. "I don't mean to sound like I'm bragging, bro. But I wanna win, fair and square."

Antonio nodded quietly. "Yeah. We both know that in
90 the ring the better man wins. Friend or no friend, brother or no."

Felix finished it for him. "Brother, Tony, let's promise something right here. Okay?"

"If it's fair, *hermano*[4], I'm for it." Antonio admired
95 the courage of a tug boat pulling a barge five times its welterweight size.

---

[1] ace-boon buddies—best friends
[2] panin—pal, buddy
[3] cheverote—cool, fine
[4] hermano—brother

"It's fair, Tony. When we get into the ring, it's gotta be like we never met. We gotta be like two heavy strangers that want the same thing and only one can have it. You understand, don'tcha?"

"*Si*, I know." Tony smiled. "No pulling punches. We go all the way."

"Yeah, that's right. Listen, Tony. Don't you think it's a good idea if we don't see each other until the day of the fight? I'm going to stay with my Aunt Lucy in the Bronx. I can use Gleason's Gym for working out. My manager says he got some sparring partners with more or less your style."

Tony scratched his nose **pensively** . "Yeah, it would be better for our heads." He held out his hand, palm upward. "Deal?"

"Deal." Felix lightly slapped open skin.

"Ready for some more running?" Tony asked lamely.

"Naw, bro. Let's cut it here. You go on. I kinda like to get things together in my head."

"You ain't worried, are you?" Tony asked.

"No way, man." Felix laughed out loud. "I got too much smarts for that. I just think it's cooler if we split right here. After the fight, we can get it together again like nothing ever happened."

pensively
thoughtfully

120   The *amigo*[5] brothers were not ashamed to hug each other tightly.

"Guess you're right. Watch yourself, Felix. I hear there's some pretty heavy dudes up in the Bronx. *Sauvecito*[6], okay?"

"Okay. You watch yourself too, *sabe*[7]?"

125   Tony jogged away. Felix watched his friend disappear from view, throwing rights and lefts. Both fighters had a lot of psyching up to do before the big fight.

The days in training passed much too slowly. Although they kept out of each other's way, they were aware of each
130   other's progress via the ghetto grapevine.

The evening before the big fight, Tony made his way to the roof of his tenement. In the quiet early dark, he peered over the ledge. Six stories below the lights of the city blinked and the sounds of cars mingled with the curses and the
135   laughter of children in the street. He tried not to think of Felix, feeling that he had succeeded in psyching his mind. But only in the ring would he really know. To spare Felix hurt, he would have to knock him out, early and quick.

Up in the South Bronx, Felix decided to take in a movie
140   in an effort to keep Antonio's face away from his fists. The flick was *The Champion* with Kirk Douglas, the third time Felix was seeing it.

The champion was getting the daylights beat out of him. He was saved only by the sound of the bell.

145   Felix became the champ and Tony the challenger.

The movie audience was going out of its head. The champ hunched his shoulders grunting and sniffing red blood back into his broken nose. The challenger, confident that he had the championship in the bag, threw a left. The
150   champ countered with a dynamite right.

Felix's right arm felt the shock. Antonio's face, superimposed on the screen, was hit by the awesome force of the blow. Felix saw himself in the ring, blasting Antonio against the ropes. The champ had to be forcibly
155   **restrained** . The challenger fell slowly to the canvas.

restrained

stopped from moving freely

5 amigo—friend
6 Sauvecito—Take it easy; be cool
7 sabe—you know?

When Felix finally left the theatre, he had figured out how to psyche himself for tomorrow's fight. It was Felix the Champion vs. Antonio the Challenger.

He walked up some dark streets, deserted except for
160 small pockets of wary-looking kids wearing gang colors. Despite the fact that he was Puerto Rican like them, they eyed him as a stranger to their turf. Felix did a fast shuffle, bobbing and weaving, while letting loose a torrent of blows that would demolish whatever got in its way. It seemed to
165 impress the brothers, who went about their own business.

Finding no takers, Felix decided to split to his aunt's. Walking the streets had not relaxed him, neither had the fight flick. All it had done was to stir him up. He let himself quietly into his Aunt Lucy's apartment and went straight
170 to bed, falling into a fitful sleep with sounds of the gong for Round One.

Antonio was passing some heavy time on his rooftop. How would the fight tomorrow affect his relationship with Felix? After all, fighting was like any other profession.
175 Friendship had nothing to do with it. A gnawing doubt crept in. He cut negative thinking real quick by doing some speedy fancy dance steps, bobbing and weaving like mercury. The night air was blurred with perpetual motions of left hooks and right crosses. Felix, his *amigo* brother, was
180 not going to be Felix at all in the ring. Just an opponent with another face. Antonio went to sleep, hearing the opening bell for the first round. Like his friend in the South Bronx, he prayed for victory, via a quick clean knock-out in the first round.

185   Large posters plastered all over the walls of local shops announced the fight between Antonio Cruz and Felix Vargas as the main bout.

The fight had created great interest in the neighborhood. Antonio and Felix were well liked and
190 respected. Each had his own loyal following.

Antonio's fans had unbridled faith in his boxing skills. On the other side, Felix's admirers trusted in his dynamite-packed fists.

Felix had returned to his apartment early in the
195 morning of August 7th and stayed there, hoping to avoid
seeing Antonio. He turned the radio on to *salsa* music
sounds and then tried to read while waiting for word from
his manager.

The fight was scheduled to take place in Tompkins
200 Square Park. It had been decided that the gymnasium
of the Boys Club was not large enough to hold all the
people who were sure to attend. In Tompkins Square Park,
everyone who wanted could view the fight, whether from
ringside or window fire escapes or tenement rooftops.

205 The morning of the fight Tompkins Square was a
beehive of activity with numerous workers setting up
the ring, the seats, and the guest speakers' stand. The
scheduled bouts began shortly after noon and the park had
begun filling up even earlier.

210 The local junior high school across from Tompkins
Square Park served as the dressing room for all the
fighters. Each was given a separate classroom with desk
tops, covered with mats, serving as resting tables. Antonio
thought he caught a glimpse of Felix waving to him from a
215 room at the far end of the corridor. He waved back just in
case it had been him.

The fighters changed from their street clothes into
fighting gear. Antonio wore white trunks, black socks, and
black shoes. Felix wore sky blue trunks, red socks, and
220 white boxing shoes. Each had dressing gowns to match
their fighting trunks with their names neatly stitched on
the back.

The loudspeakers blared into the open windows of the
school. There were speeches by dignitaries, community
225 leaders, and great boxers of yesteryear. Some were well
prepared, some improvised on the spot. They all carried the
same message of great pleasure and honor at being part of
such a historic event. This great day was in the tradition of
champions emerging from the streets of the lower east side.

230 Interwoven with the speeches were the sounds of the
other boxing events. After the sixth bout, Felix was much

relieved when his trainer Charlie said, "Time change. Quick knock-out. This is it. We're on."

Waiting time was over. Felix was escorted from the
235 classroom by a dozen fans in white T-shirts with the word FELIX across their fronts.

Antonio was escorted down a different stairwell and guided through a roped-off path.

As the two climbed into the ring, the crowd exploded
240 with a roar. Antonio and Felix both bowed gracefully and then raised their arms in acknowledgement.

Antonio tried to be cool, but even as the roar was in its first birth, he turned slowly to meet Felix's eyes looking directly into his. Felix nodded his head and Antonio
245 responded. And both as one, just as quickly, turned away to face his own corner.

Bong—bong—bong. The roar turned to stillness.

"Ladies and Gentlemen, *Señores y Señoras.*"

The announcer spoke slowly, pleased at his bilingual
250 efforts.

"Now the moment we have all been waiting for—the main event between two fine young Puerto Rican fighters, products of our lower east side.

"In this corner, weighing 134 pounds, Felix Vargas. And
255 in this corner, weighing 133 pounds, Antonio Cruz. The winner will represent the Boys Club in the tournament of champions, the Golden Gloves. There will be no draw. May the best man win."

The cheering of the crowd shook the window panes of
260 the old buildings surrounding Tompkins Square Park. At the center of the ring, the referee was giving instructions to the youngsters.

"Keep your punches up. No low blows. No punching on the back of the head. Keep your heads up. Understand. Let's
265 have a clean fight. Now shake hands and come out fighting."

Both youngsters touched gloves and nodded. They turned and danced quickly to their corners. Their head towels and dressing gowns were lifted neatly from their shoulders by their trainers' nimble fingers. Antonio crossed
270 himself. Felix did the same.

BONG! BONG! ROUND ONE. Felix and Antonio
turned and faced each other squarely in a fighting pose.
Felix wasted no time. He came in fast, head low, half
hunched toward his right shoulder, and lashed out with a
275 straight left. He missed a right cross as Antonio slipped the
punch and countered with one-two-three lefts that snapped
Felix's head back, sending a mild shock coursing through
him. If Felix had any small doubt about their friendship
affecting their fight, it was being neatly **dispelled**.

280   Antonio danced, a joy to behold. His left hand was like
a piston pumping jabs one right after another with seeming
ease. Felix bobbed and weaved and never stopped boring
in. He knew that at long range he was at a disadvantage.
Antonio had too much reach on him. Only by coming in
285 close could Felix hope to achieve the dreamed-of knockout.

    Antonio knew the dynamite that was stored in his
amigo brother's fist. He ducked a short right and missed
a left hook. Felix trapped him against the ropes just
long enough to pour some punishing rights and lefts to
290 Antonio's hard midsection. Antonio slipped away from
Felix, crashing two lefts to his head, which set Felix's right
ear to ringing.

dispelled
caused to go away

Bong! Both *amigos* froze a punch well on its way, sending up a roar of approval for good sportsmanship.

295   Felix walked briskly back to his corner. His right ear had not stopped ringing. Antonio gracefully danced his way toward his stool none the worse, except for glowing glove burns, showing angry red against the whiteness of his midribs.

300   "Watch that right, Tony." His trainer talked into his ear. "Remember Felix always goes to the body. He'll want you to drop your hands for his overhand left or right. Got it?"

Antonio nodded, spraying water out between his teeth. He felt better as his sore midsection was being

305 firmly rubbed.

Felix's corner was also busy.

"You gotta get in there, fella." Felix's trainer poured water over his curly Afro locks. "Get in there or he's gonna chop you up from way back."

310   *Bong! Bong!* Round two. Felix was off his stool and rushed Antonio like a bull, sending a hard right to his head. Beads of water exploded from Antonio's long hair.

Antonio, hurt, sent back a blurring barrage of lefts and rights that only meant pain to Felix, who returned with

315 a short left to the head followed by a looping right to the body. Antonio countered with his own flurry, forcing Felix to give ground. But not for long.

Felix bobbed and weaved, bobbed and weaved, occasionally punching his two gloves together.

320 Antonio waited for the rush that was sure to come. Felix closed in and feinted with his left shoulder and threw his right instead. Lights suddenly exploded inside Felix's head as Antonio slipped the blow and hit him with a pistonlike left, catching him flush on the point of his chin.

325 Bedlam broke loose as Felix's legs momentarily buckled. He fought off a series of rights and lefts and came back with a strong right that taught Antonio respect.

Antonio danced in carefully. He knew Felix had the habit of playing possum when hurt, to sucker an opponent 330 within reach of the powerful bombs he carried in each fist.

A right to the head slowed Antonio's pretty dancing. He answered with his own left at Felix's right eye that began puffing up within three seconds.

Antonio, a bit too eager, moved in too close and Felix 335 had him entangled into a rip-roaring, punching toe-to-toe slugfest that brought the whole Tompkins Square Park screaming to its feet.

Rights to the body. Lefts to the head. Neither fighter was giving an inch. Suddenly a short right caught Antonio 340 squarely on the chin. His long legs turned to jelly and his arms flailed out desperately. Felix, grunting like a bull, threw wild punches from every direction. Antonio, groggy,

evading

avoiding; dodging

bobbed and weaved, **evading** most of the blows. Suddenly his head cleared. His left flashed out hard and straight,
345 catching Felix on the bridge of his nose.

Felix lashed back with a haymaker right off the ghetto streets. At the same instant, his eye caught another left hook from Antonio. Felix swung out trying to clear the pain. Only the frenzied screaming of those along ringside
350 let him know that he had dropped Antonio. Fighting off the growing haze, Antonio struggled to his feet, got up, ducked, and threw a smashing right that dropped Felix flat on his back. Felix got up as fast as he could in his own corner, groggy but still game. He didn't even hear the count. In a
355 fog, he heard the roaring of the crowd, who seemed to have gone insane. His head cleared to hear the bell sound at the end of the round. He was very glad. His trainer sat him down on the stool.

In his corner, Antonio was doing what all fighters do
360 when they are hurt. They sit and smile at everyone.

The referee signaled the ring doctor to check the fighters out. He did so and then gave his okay. The cold water sponges brought clarity to both *amigo* brothers. They were rubbed until their circulation ran free.
365 *Bong!* Round three—the final round. Up to now it had been tic-tac-toe, pretty much even. But everyone knew there would be no draw and that this round would decide the winner.

This time, to Felix's surprise, it was Antonio who came
370 out fast, charging across the ring. Felix braced himself but couldn't ward off the barrage of punches. Antonio drove Felix hard against the ropes.

The crowd ate it up. Thus far the two had fought with *mucho corazón*[8]. Felix tapped his gloves and commenced
375 his attack anew. Antonio, throwing boxer's caution to the winds, jumped in to meet him.

Both pounded away. Neither gave an inch and neither fell to the canvas. Felix's left eye was tightly closed. Claret red blood poured from Antonio's nose. They fought toe-
380 to-toe.

[8] mucho corazón—a lot of heart

The sounds of their blows were loud in contrast to the silence of a crowd gone completely mute.

Bong! Bong! Bong! The bell sounded over and over again. Felix and Antonio were past hearing. Their blows 385 continued to pound on each other like hailstones.

Finally the referee and the two trainers pried Felix and Antonio apart. Cold water was poured over them to bring them back to their senses.

They looked around and then rushed toward each other. 390 A cry of alarm surged through Tompkins Square Park. Was this a fight to the death instead of a boxing match?

The fear soon gave way to wave upon wave of cheering as the two *amigos* **embraced**.

No matter what the decision, they knew they would 395 always be champions to each other.

BONG! BONG! BONG! "Ladies and Gentlemen, *Señores* and *Señoras*. The winner and representative to the Golden Gloves Tournament of Champions is . . ."

The announcer turned to point to the winner and 400 found himself alone. Arm in arm the champions had already left the ring.

embraced
hugged

Answer It

1. Compare and contrast the characteristics of Antonio and Felix.

2. Justify Antonio and Felix's decision not to see each other before their boxing match.

3. Discuss the significance of the ending of the story.

4. Revise the prediction you made in Step 5 of Lesson 6 about how the story would end.

5. Compose an alternate ending to the story.

Ansel Adams: View Through a Lens

medium

a specific artistic technique

One bright spring Yosemite day in 1927 I made a photograph that was to change my understanding of the **medium**. My soon-to-be wife, Virginia, our friends Cedric Wright, Arnold Williams, and Charlie Michael, and I
5 started out quite early that morning on a hike to the Diving Board. A magnificent slab of granite on the west shoulder of Half Dome, the Diving Board overlooks Mirror Lake thousands of feet below. Several years before I had climbed to the Diving Board with Francis Holman, and since then
10 I had thought of that staggering view of Half Dome and knew it would make a good photograph.

We decided to climb via the LeConte Gully, just north of Grizzly Peak. This route would be relatively free from snow though it is very steep and rough, and much easier
15 to ascend than to descend, as I had discovered with Bill Zorach in 1920. My camera pack alone weighed some forty pounds, as I was carrying my Korona view camera, several lenses, two filters, six holders containing twelve glass plates, and a heavy wooden tripod.

20 At the top of the gully, we removed our packs for the difficult final climb of several hundred feet to the summit of Grizzly Peak. This craggy rock tower gave us

panorama

a large, open view of a wide area

a rather startling **panorama**: four waterfalls, the great mass of Glacier Point, Half Dome rising thousands of feet

25 higher, and the many peaks of the Sierra, dominated by Mount Florence and Mount Clark. Everything above seven thousand feet was covered with snow. I regretted leaving my camera below the summit.

30   We returned to the intermediate base, took up our packs and proceeded up the long, partially snowy rise of Half Dome's shoulder. I stopped often to set up and compose pictures. I had several failures,
35 but did get one rather handsome telephoto image of Mount Galen Clark. By the time I had finished that picture, which took two exposures, added to the six errors I had already made, I had only four plates left for
40 my prime objective of the trip.

Monolith, The Face of Half Dome, *Yosemite National Park, 1947.*

    We reached the Diving Board at about noon, tired and hungry. It was beautiful, but the enormous face of Half Dome was entirely in shade, and I felt I must wait a few hours until the sun revealed the
45 **monolith** . It was one of those rare occasions when waiting was justified.

monolith

a very large block of stone that stands alone

    Following lunch washed down with water from melting snowbanks, I made a picture of Virginia standing on one of the thrusts of the Diving Board. The camera was pointed
50 to the west, and with the first plate I forgot to shield the lens from the direct sun. I made a second plate to be sure. I now had only two plates left for one of the grandest view-experiences of the Sierra, the face of Half Dome itself.

    At about two-thirty I set up the camera at what seemed
55 to be the best spot and composed the image. My 8½-inch Zeiss Tessar lens was very sharp but, as usual with lenses of this design, did not have much covering power; the image formed by the lens was just large enough to cover my glass plate when centered thereon. I had to use the rising-front
60 of the camera, as tilting the camera up more than a small amount would create the unwanted effect of **convergence** of the trees. Over the lens I placed a conventional K2 yellow filter, to slightly darken the sky. I finally had everything

convergence

a process of coming together

ready to go. The shadow effect on Half Dome seemed right,
65 and I made the exposure.

As I replaced the slide, I began to think about how the
print was to appear, and if it would transmit any of the
feeling of the monumental shape before me in terms of its
expressive-emotional quality. I began to see in my mind's
70 eye the finished print I desired: the brooding cliff with a
dark sky and the sharp rendition of distant, snowy Tenaya
Peak. I realized that only a deep red filter would give me
anything approaching the effect I felt emotionally.

I had only *one* plate left. I attached my other filter, a
75 Wratten #29(F), increased the exposure by the sixteen-
times factor required, and released the shutter. I felt I had
accomplished something, but did not realize its significance
until I developed the plate that evening. I had achieved my
first true visualization! I had been able to realize a desired
80 image: not the way the subject appeared in reality but how
it *felt* to me and how it must appear in the finished print.
The sky had actually been a light, slightly hazy blue and
the sunlit areas of Half Dome were moderately dark gray in
value. The red filter dramatically darkened the sky and the
85 shadows on the great cliff. Luckily I had with me the filter
that made my visualized image possible.

The date was April 17, 1927 and the results of this
excursion were three very good plates: *Monolith, The Face
of Half Dome, Mount Galen Clark*, and the one of Virginia
90 on the edge of the Diving Board, *On the Heights*.

Monolith has led a charmed life. It survived my
darkroom fire in 1937 with only charred edges that are
cropped from the final print anyway. I have not dropped
the glass plate nor sat on it. It rests in my vault, still
95 printable, and represents a personally historic moment in
my photographic career.

Visualization is not simply choosing the best filter.
To be fully achieved it does require a good understanding
of both the craft and **aesthetics** of photography. I was
100 asked by *Modern Photography* to write an article about
creative photography for their 1934–5 annual. This was my
definition of visualization.

aesthestics

artistically beautiful
or pleasing appear-
ance

The camera makes an image-record of the object before it.
It records the subject in terms of the optical properties of the
105   lens, and the chemical and physical properties of the negative
and print. The control of that record lies in the selection by the
photographer and in his understanding of the photographic
processes at his command. The photographer visualizes his
conception of the subject as *presented in the final print.*
110   He achieves the expression of his visualization through his
technique—aesthetic, intellectual, and mechanical.

The visualization of a photograph involves the **intuitive**
search for meaning, shape, form, texture, and the projection
of the image-format on the subject. The image forms in
115   the mind—is visualized—and another part of the mind
calculates the physical processes involved in determining the
exposure and development of the image of the negative and
anticipates the qualities of the final print. The creative artist
is constantly roving the worlds without, and creating new
120   worlds within.

intuitive
related to feeling;
not learned knowl-
edge

From *Ansel Adams: An Autobiography* with Mary Street Alinder

Think About It

1. Ansel Adams says that this visit to Yosemite in 1927 was very significant for him. Identify where he states this, and then paraphrase his idea.

2. Recall that Ansel Adams said he had one prime objective on the Yosemite trip. What was the thing that he most wanted to photograph?

3. Compare the view Ansel Adams had of Half Dome with the image he visualized.

4. In lines 103–111, Ansel Adams writes that to successfully express a visualization, an artist requires aesthetic, intellectual, and mechanical abilities. Explain this idea using your own words.

5. In lines 118–120, Ansel Adams writes, "The creative artist is constantly roving the worlds without, and creating new worlds within." Provide an example from a creative art other than photography that illustrates this quote.

6. Judge whether or not you feel that it is helpful first to visualize what you want to achieve before setting out to reach that goal.

*An ant's-eye view through a basement window is
vastly different from an eagle's-eye view from the top of a
tower. Try rolling a sheet of paper like a telescope and look
through it to see how it reduces and changes a view. Artists*
5 *have always made choices about how to "see" a scene,
and looking through a window is one way to* **heighten**
dramatic or emotional effects in paintings.

heighten
intensify; increase

Through the Window
1992, Tilly Willis (English)

Tilly Willis captures a peaceful moment of a mother
with her child pausing to look through a window. Willis
10 lives in England, but a passion for travel has taken her to
the **remote** parts of Africa, the Middle East, and Russia.
This travel has been the source of inspiration for her work.
She is a fellow of the Royal Geographic Society because she
is keenly interested in the people, places, and cultures of
15 the world. She creates dramatic paintings of the lives and
the environments she encounters. She is known for using
the rich, vibrant colors often seen in African art to great
effect in her work.

remote
far-away; distant

Through the Window, *1993*.

The Red Cape, *about 1868–1875.*

The Red Cape
about 1868–1875, Claude Monet (French)

A woman in a red cape has almost passed this window
20 when she pauses to look **wistfully** inside. She is Camille
Doncieux, the favorite model, and wife, of the Impressionist
painter Claude Monet. Monet's placement of Camille and
his contrast of cold weather outside with warmth inside the
studio may have been influenced by Hiroshige, the Japanese
25 printmaker, whose works Monet collected. Painting
through a window was not Monet's favorite way to see. He
most often went outdoors, in almost any weather, to catch
the fleeting qualities of light in the bold brush strokes of
Impressionist technique.

wistfully

pensively; with
wishful desire

Paris Through the Window
1913, Marc Chagall (Russian)

30   This yellow cat with a human head studies Paris at
night through the window. A ghostly image of the Eiffel
Tower **dominates** the city, as it has since 1889 when the
tower was completed. The artist Marc Chagall had come to

dominates

stands out with a
decidedly superior
position

Paris Through the Window, *1913*.

The Human Condition, *1933*.

Paris from his village of Vitebsk in Russia. His Paris studio
35 was in a twelve-sided building where many artists lived.
They sang, recited poetry, played guitars, and created art.
Chagall feverishly painted fantastic scenes of Vitebsk—and
his new home in Paris. Some say that the two-headed face
in blue is the artist himself, wondering if he should stay in
40 this foreign land or return to Russia. He said he was the
color of a potato when he arrived, but after four years in
Paris he became glowingly colorful!

The Human Condition
1933, René Magritte (Belgian)

Through this window the Surrealist painter René
Magritte shows a canvas being painted in front of a
45 window. Or is the window the scene and the canvas
and easel only make-believe? Magritte is using two of
his favorite themes: "windows" and "a painting within
a painting." The name of this painting, *The Human
Condition*, was meant to indicate a dreamlike condition,
50 a painting within a painting. Magritte usually chose
common objects and scenes, then changed them to
something puzzling. All of Magritte's sense of mystery
and imagination went into his paintings.

View to Santorini
1998, Barbara McCann (American)

View to Santorini, *1998*.

Imagine stepping out of this
55   room and into the colorful, sun-
drenched scene beyond. Where will
you go? Whitewashed buildings
invite you to wander up the hills.
The blue Aegean draws you down
60   toward its shore. "I am obsessed
with light and shadow," says artist
Barbara McCann. This painting
depicts a lush and **vibrant** world
in which everything—buildings,
65   flowers, sea, even the window
itself—is washed in shadows and
light. Like the Impressionists of the
19th century, McCann's paintings
capture the feelings a place evokes
70   instead of making an exact record
of how it looks. Her use of a palette knife contributes to
this effect. Broad smears of paint create the suggestion of
clouds. It's hard to view this impression of a Greek island
without feeling as though you are there, looking through
75   the window with the artist.

vibrant
intense; colorful

Reflection (12:00 to 12:55)
1999–2001, Ann Hamilton (American)

Ann Hamilton is an installation artist, which means
that she sets up different materials in space to make her
artwork. To create a series of 12 photographs, she set up
a piece of wavy glass in front of the American pavilion in
80   Venice. The glass **distorted** the view into and out of the
building. Hamilton took a photo through the glass every
five minutes for a total of 12 photos. The shadowy figure
behind the glass in this photo is the artist herself. The light
and blurred waves in the photo suggest the reflection of a
85   figure in water. Unlike traditional photography, Hamilton
wasn't trying to capture one moment in time but several
moments over time.

distorted
twisted; bent out
of shape

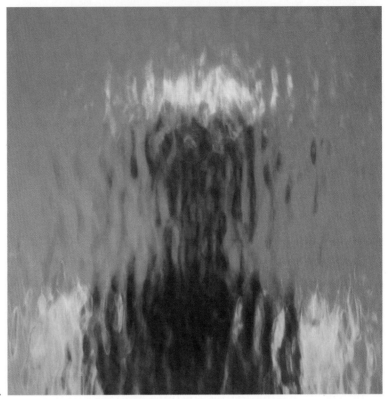

Reflection, *1999–2001.*

What exciting new views will artists of the future reveal when they paint and photograph what they see through 90 windows?

Adapted from "Through the Window in Art" by Marjorie Jackson

Think About It

1. Choose a painting and explain the significance of the window in that painting.

2. Hypothesize why the woman in the red cape in the Monet painting stopped to look in the window.

3. Why do people say that the two-headed face in Chagall's painting, *Paris Through the Window*, represents the artist himself (lines 38–42)?

4. Make an inference about why Magritte painted the window to appear as a painting in his painting *The Human Condition*.

5. Do you think McCann's painting looks exactly like the scene does in real life? Explain.

6. Explain how Hamilton created her work of art.

Unit
29
Give a Call

STEP
1

Phonemic Awareness and Phonics

Unit 29 introduces the phonograms in which the letters **l**, **qu**, **r**, and **w** influence the pronunciation of **a**.

Phonograms

Some syllables contain a **phonogram**. A phonogram is a set of letters that consistently represents a set of sounds.

■ Some consonants—**l**, **qu**, **r**, and **w**—combine with a vowel to produce a new sound.

■ In some syllables, the vowel phoneme is spelled with two letters— a vowel and one of these specific consonants.

■ The phonograms in this unit occur infrequently in English:

> **all** and **al** for / ôl / as in **call** or **salt**
>
> **alk** for / ôk / as in **talk**
>
> **wa** for / wŏ / as in **swap** or / wô / as in **water**
>
> **qua** for / kwŏ / as in **quad** or / kwô / as in **quart**
>
> **war** for / wôr / as in **ward** or / wər / as in **backward**
>
> **wor** for / wûr / as in **word**

STEP 2

Word Recognition and Spelling

Prefixes

We can expand words and change meaning by adding **prefixes**. These word parts are added to the beginnings of words. Example: **semi** + annual = semiannual

(See Step 3: Vocabulary and Morphology for links to meaning.)

> **Unit 29 Prefix**
> **semi-**

Suffixes

We can expand words and change meaning by adding **suffixes**. These word parts are added to the ends of words. Example: occur + **ence** = occurrence

(See Step 3: Vocabulary and Morphology for links to meaning and Step 4: Grammar and Usage for function.)

> **Unit 29 Suffixes**
> **-ure, -ance, -ence**

Roots

We can build words using roots. Roots carry the most important part of the word's meaning. We usually attach a prefix or suffix to make a root into a word. Example: dis + **rupt** = disrupt

> **Unit 29 Roots**
> **struct, rupt**

Essential Words

> **Unit 29 Essential Words**
>
> | | | |
> |---|---|---|
> | oh | whole | whose |
> | straight | whom | wolf |

Spelling Lists

The Unit 29 spelling lists contain three categories:

1. Words with phonograms: **all**, **al**, **alk**, **wa**, **qua**, **war**, and **wor**

2. Essential Words (in italics)

3. Words with prefixes, roots, and suffixes

Spelling Lists

Lessons 1–5		Lessons 6–10	
already	warm	admittance	reward
call	water	composure	semiannual
forward	*whole*	disruption	semicircle
oh	*whom*	influenced	sidewalk
qualify	*whose*	instructor	structure
straight	*wolf*	lecture	workshop
talk	world	literature	worldwide
want		quarterback	

Vocabulary and Morphology

Unit Vocabulary

Sound-spelling correspondences from this unit and previous units make up this unit's vocabulary.

- What do these words mean?
- Do some of them mean more than one thing? Which ones?

UNIT Vocabulary

all for / ôl /
all
ball
call
fall
hall
install
mall
overall
recall
small
smallpox
so-called
stall
swallow
tall
wall
wallet

al for / ôl /
already
also
alter
alternate
alternative
altogether
always
bald
cobalt

false
falter
halt
palsy
salt
saltwater

alk for / ôk /
chalk
jaywalker
sidewalk
stalk
talk
walk
walkie-talkie

wa for / wŏ /
dishwasher
swamp
swan
waffle
wand
wander
want
wash
wasp
watch
watt

wa for / wô /
freshwater
walnut
walrus
water

qua for / kwŏ /
quadrangle
qualify
qualitative
quality
quantify
quantity
squad
squadron
squat

qua for / kwô /
quarrel
quarry
quart
quarterback
quartz

war for / wôr /
award
reward
swarm
war
warden

warm
warm-blooded
warn
warp
warrant
wart

war for / wər /
awkward
backward
forward
inward

wor for / wûr /
framework
network
underworld
word
work
workshop
world
worldwide
worm
worry
worse
worship
worst
worth
worthwhile

Multiple Meanings

Even the smallest words in English can have multiple meanings. For example, the meanings of the word **call** include: (a) the characteristic cry of an animal, (b) a decision made by a referee, (c) communication by telephone, (d) a shout for someone, (e) a strong attraction to an activity or environment. These meanings use **call** as a *noun*. There are also meanings of this word as a *verb* and *phrasal verb*. The specific meaning of the word is important to understand a sentence; the context of the sentence helps to clarify which meaning is intended.

> Which meaning of **call**?
>
> The wolf was drawn by the **call** of the wild.
>
> In this sentence the word **call** means (e) a strong attraction to an environment.

Meaning Parts

Prefixes

Prefixes can add to or change the meanings of words. The Unit 29 prefix has the following meaning.

Unit 29 Prefix	Meaning	Examples
semi-	half	semiannual, semicircle, semitone

Suffixes

Suffixes can add to or change the meanings of words. When added to a base word or root, they can change the base word or root to a noun.

Unit 29 Suffixes	Meanings	Examples
-ure	state of; process; function; office	departure, closure, legislature
-ance	act or condition of	acceptance, insurance, performance
-ence	action; state; quality	influence, existence, difference

Roots

Roots form the basic meaning part of a word. Roots of English words often come from another language, especially Latin. A root usually needs a prefix or suffix to make it into a word.

Example: dis + **rupt** = disrupt (dis = apart; rupt = to break; disrupt = to break apart)

Unit 29 Roots	Meanings	Examples
struct	to build	construct, instruction, obstruct
rupt	to break, burst	disrupt, interrupt, erupt

Challenge Morphemes

Roots	Meanings	Examples
frac	to break	fraction, fracture, refraction
junct	to join	adjunct, injunction, juncture

STEP 4

Grammar and Usage

Adjectives

Review: **Adjectives** describe nouns. They answer the questions:
Which one? What kind? and **How many?** They can be:

■ Single words. Examples: **awkward, bald, warm**

■ Can be prepositional phrases that function as adjectives. For
   example, **with a cobalt stripe** is a prepositional phrase that
   answers the question **What kind?** It is a prepositional phrase in
   form, but it *functions* as an adjective.

Pronouns

Review: **Pronouns** are function words that take the place of nouns.

They can be **nominative** (subject), **object**, or **possessive**. Most
pronouns have antecedents—nouns to which they refer.

Indefinite pronouns refer to unspecified or unknown people or
things. They can be nominative or object pronouns. Indefinite
pronouns do not have antecedents.

Relative pronouns begin dependent clauses. A relative pronoun is
related to a noun or pronoun that has already been mentioned in the
independent clause. This noun or pronoun is called an antecedent.
Relative pronouns include: **that, which, who, whom,** and **whose**.

> **Relative Pronouns**
>
> The cell phone advertisement was one **that** we had seen many
> times.
>
> > **That** is a relative pronoun referring back to the noun **one**.

Participles

Review: The **present participle** is formed by adding **-ing** to the base
verb. Example: call + **ing** = calling

The **past participle** of a regular verb is formed by adding **-ed** to the
base verb. Example: call + **ed** = (have) called

Note: The *form* of a participle is the same as the *form* of the progressive:
both *forms* use the **-ing** suffix. The *function* of the participle as an
adjective and the *function* of the progressive tense are different.

Past Perfect

Review: If the past participle is part of a verb phrase with the helping verbs **have** or **has**, the verb phrase is in the **present perfect tense**. The **present perfect** describes an action occurring at an unspecified time in the past or an action starting in the past and continuing in the present. Example: **I have waited** for a call for over an hour.

The **past perfect tense** uses the past participle of a verb with **had** (the past tense of the verb **have**). The **past perfect** describes an action completed in the past before another past action took place. A sentence with a past perfect verb often has two verbs expressing actions in the past, one in an independent clause and one in a dependent clause. In the sentence, the action described by the past perfect verb was completed before the action described by the other verb.

> **Past Perfect**
>
> Carlos **had called** his friend before he **left** for school.
>
> In this sentence, **had called** is in the past perfect tense. The action **called** occurred before he **left**.

Phrases

Review: **A phrase** is a group of words that functions as a single word. A phrase cannot stand alone. Example: a call from the wild

A **participial phrase** begins with a participle and is followed by a word (or group of words) that modifies it or receives its action. A participial phrase functions as an adjective because it modifies a noun or pronoun. It can come before or after the noun or pronoun that it modifies.
Examples:
   Ringing unexpectedly, the cell phone broke the silence.
   The cell phone, **ringing unexpectedly**, broke the silence.

Clauses

Review: A **clause** is a group of words that contains a subject and a predicate. An **independent clause** has one subject and one predicate; it represents a complete thought. A **dependent clause** cannot stand alone. It combines with an independent clause to create meaning.

Some dependent clauses function as adjectives. An **adjectival clause**:

■ Answers the questions **Which one?** or **What kind?**

■ Usually begins with a relative pronoun.

■ Occurs near the noun it modifies.

> **Adjectival Clause**
>
> Cell phones, **which are unwelcome at the movies,** began to ring.

Sentence Pattern

Review: A **simple sentence** is an independent clause that contains a subject and a predicate and is a complete thought. Example: The poet wrote a poem about a calling.

Adjectival clauses can vary sentence structure. They occur near the noun they modify.
Example: The poem had a message **that the students understood**.

A **complex sentence** has one independent clause and one or more dependent clauses. The dependent clauses can be adverbial or adjectival. If an adverbial clause comes at the beginning of a sentence, it is separated from the independent clause by a comma. An adjectival clause is separated from the independent clause by commas if it is not essential to the meaning of the independent clause.

Confusing Word Pairs

Already and **all ready** are frequently confused when writing. **Already** is an adverb and means "by this time or previously." In a verb phrase, **already** is often placed between the helping or linking verb and the past participle. **All ready** is a phrase that acts as an adjective. **All ready** means "prepared or available for action."

The advertisements for next season's television shows have **already** started.

The team was **all ready** to leave when the call came.

The relative pronouns **who** and **which** are frequently used incorrectly. **Who** refers to people, while **which** refers to things.

The advertisers, **who** target young people, are very persuasive.

Advertisements, **which** are everywhere, come in many forms.

Listening and Reading Comprehension

Informational Text

■ Some **informational text** is nonfiction material about a specific topic, event, experience, or circumstance. It is often accompanied by visual information in the form of charts, graphs, or illustrations. The visual information provides additional content about the subject matter. "**It's Your Call**" uses visual information in the form of an advertisement to illustrate the content of the text.

Vocabulary in Context

■ **Context clues** help us understand new vocabulary. Pronoun referents, meaning signals, and visuals, such as charts and graphs, provide meaning links.

Signal Words

■ Different types of sentences can help us think about new information and ideas in different ways. Identifying signal words within sentences can improve comprehension.

See the Appendix, page A20, for a complete list of signal words based on Bloom's Taxonomy.

Literary Terms and Devices

 Genres are types or categories of literature. Unit 29 features persuasive essays and poetry.

■ A **persuasive essay** is a form of writing designed to influence the reader. In a persuasive essay, the writer takes a position and then provides reasons and supporting facts or examples to make each reason convincing. "**Cell Phones for Teens: A Good Call for Safety**" is an example of a persuasive essay.

■ **Poetry** is a literary genre that contains some or all of these six elements: thought, imagery, mood, melody, meter, and form. These elements are illustrated in "**A Call to Poetry.**"

Thought is the element that contains the poem's message. One component of thought is the **theme**, which is often stated as a universal truth—unlimited by time or space.

Imagery refers to the poem's creation of mental pictures, or images, for the reader. Metaphor, simile, and personification are examples of techniques that poets use to create imagery.

Mood: Poems evoke emotions and set an atmosphere or a tone for the reader. This element is called mood.

Melody is the element created by a poet's use of sound. Alliteration, rhyme, assonance, consonance, and onomatopoeia are examples of devices used to create melody in poetry.

Meter: Patterns of stressed and unstressed syllables in a poem create meter or poetic rhythm.

Form is the element that defines the poem's actual structure. Examples of poetic forms include quatrain, sonnet, blank verse, limerick, ballad, and free (open) verse.

Figurative Language

Figurative language is language that is not literally true. It includes literary devices such as simile, metaphor, personification, and symbol.

Simile: A figure of speech that makes a comparison. A simile always uses the words **like** or **as**. Examples: He took off like a rocket. She is as sharp as a tack. "Postscript" in "**A Call to Poetry**" uses simile.

Metaphor: A figure of speech that compares people, places, things, or feelings without using the words **like** or **as**. Examples: I have butterflies in my stomach. "All the world's a stage" (William Shakespeare). All three poems in "**A Call to Poetry**" use examples of metaphor.

Personification: Figurative language that assigns human characteristics to an animal, idea, or thing. Examples: Fear is your worst enemy. Time is a thief who steals each day one by one. "The Calling" in "**A Call to Poetry**" uses examples of personification.

Symbol: An image, figure, or object that represents a different thing or idea. There are many cultural symbols. Examples: the American flag symbolizes independence and democracy; the American bald eagle symbolizes freedom and strength; a dove or an olive branch symbolizes peace. In "**The New Colossus**," the Statue of Liberty is a symbol of freedom and opportunity. "Story from Bear Country" in "**A Call to Poetry**" uses examples of symbol.

Symbols and metaphors are very similar. Here is one way to tell the difference: In metaphor, both things compared are usually named ("The day was a heavy weight on my shoulders"). In contrast, the idea that a symbol represents is often not named directly; it is simply understood through the context. For example, in a poem about a sad day, the color gray may symbolize sadness.

Speaking and Writing

Signal Words

■ Different types of sentences require different responses, depending on the focus of **signal words**. Identifying signal words within sentences improves the accuracy of our responses to oral and written questions.

See the Appendix, page A20, for a complete list of signal words based on Bloom's Taxonomy.

Composition Organization

■ Some compositions attempt to persuade or convince. This type of writing is called a **persuasive essay.**

■ A persuasive essay has specific components:

Statement of position: The writer takes a stand or states a position on a topic.

Reasons and supporting facts or examples: The writer provides reasons to explain his or her position, as well as facts or examples to make each reason convincing.

Anticipated objections: The writer addresses objections that he or she anticipates, or expects certain people to raise in response.

Call for action: The writer makes a request for people to act based on the reasons provided.

More About Words

- **Bonus Words** use the same sound-spelling correspondences that we have studied in this unit and previous units.

- **Idioms** are common phrases that cannot be understood by the meanings of their separate words—only by the entire phrase.

- **Why? Word History** tells the origins of the phrase **call-and-response**.

UNIT Bonus Words

all for / ôl /
appall
ballpark
ballroom
befall
crestfallen
enthrall
fallback
gall
hallway
handball
landfall
mothball
pall
pitfall
pratfall
seawall
shortfall
stonewall
wallaby
walleye
wallflower
wallow
windfall

al for / ôl /
altercate
balsam
exalt

falsify
halter
malt
paltry
saltbox
saltine
saltshaker
scald

alk for / ôk /
balk
crosswalk
floorwalker
jaywalk
skywalk
sleepwalk
walkout
walkover
walkup
walkway

wa for / wŏ /
awash
backwash
brainwash
hogwash
swab
swashbuckler
swat
swatch

wan
wanderlust
washcloth
watchdog
watchmaker
watchman
wattle
whitewash
wishy-washy

wa for / wô /
backwater
kilowatt
megawatt
waltz

qua for / kwŏ /
quad
quadraphonic
quadriceps
quadrilateral
quadruple
quaff
quandary
quantum
quatrain
squab
squabble
squalid
squall

squalor
squander
squash
squawk

qua for / kwô /
quarantine
quark
quarterly

war for / wôr /
forewarn
swarthy
thwart
warble
warbler
wardrobe

war for / wər /
afterward
onward
outward

wor for / wûr /
workbook
workmanship
workroom
worrywart

Idioms

Idiom	Meaning
be a fly on the wall	be somewhere secretly to see and hear what happens
be all thumbs	be awkward, especially with your hands
be on call	be available when summoned for service
call into question	raise doubts about
call it a day	stop whatever you have been doing for the rest of the day
come straight from the horse's mouth	come from the person who has direct personal knowledge of the matter
fall through the cracks	pass unnoticed, neglected, or unchecked
open a can of worms	set unpleasant events in motion
see the writing on the wall	see the dark side of the course of future events
throw the baby out with the bath water	throw out something valuable along with something useless

 **Word History**

Call-and-Response—Call-and-response is a way of communicating. It begins with a call: a line of a poem, a statement made by a person, or a phrase of a song's melody. What follows the call is a response. This doesn't mean simply an answer. It may be an affirmation of the call, the repetition of the call, or some other repeated response, by another person or group of people.

Africans brought the tradition of call-and-response communication to the New World. Over the centuries, they have transformed call-and-response in various formats. Many modifications of call-and-response can be heard in public gatherings; in children's rhymes; in religious observance; and in forms of African-American music—gospel, blues, rhythm and blues, and jazz.

Call-and-response constitutes the pattern of democratic participation in West African cultures. In public gatherings, in religious rituals, and in musical expression, call-and-response is the format for interaction. It evokes active participation by the audience. Today, call-and-response is reflected in literature, music, and much of modern culture.

How much do you know about advertising? Chances are that you already know a lot. An average American sees or hears 560 advertisements each day!

Ads come in many forms. One form is the print ad.
5 Much space in magazines and newspapers is used for ads. Print ads use pictures and words to persuade readers to buy products and services. Other ads are broadcast on the radio. Between songs, companies try to sell products and services. TV is another medium filled with ads. Shows are frequently
10 interrupted for commercials. Some companies even pay to have their products appear in the shows themselves. This strategy is called product placement. It is a way for companies to slip their products into consumers' minds.

Advertising is often aimed at young people. Young
15 people spend billions of dollars every year. They also influence how their parents spend money. It is important to look critically at ads that are aimed at you. While ads do inform you about products, they also try to persuade you to buy them. Advertisers try to make you think that buying
20 their product will make you happy and improve your life. Of course, not many products will deliver on these promises.

How can you look at ads critically? When you see or hear a commercial, think about its message. Think about

who created it. Think about what they want you to do or
25 buy. Also, think about the strategy the ad is using to grab
your attention. Is it using humor to make you feel good
about what it is selling? Is it using a celebrity to connect
with you? Is it making claims that seem too good to be
true? Recognizing these strategies makes it easier for you to
30 evaluate products in ads.

When you look at or hear an ad, ask yourself:
What is really being offered?
How good is it, really?
Do I need it?
35 Is it worth the price?
Are there any catches?

Your answers will help you figure out if a company is
selling its product with facts or just persuasion. Then you
can make a good call about whether or not to buy it.
40 Here are two ads for cell phones. Look critically at
each one.

When you read an advertisement, ask yourself: Are there any catches?

Andre: Hey, how much did you pay for your cell phone?

Manolo: I got a pretty good price.

Andre: As good as nothing?

Manolo: As good as what?

Andre: I just got my IM Wireless phone for free.

Manolo: One of those bare-bones phones?

Andre: Wrong! It has a built-in camera!

Manolo: For free? But you can't text-message.

Andre: Wrong again!

Manolo: Then it must have those ordinary rings, right?

Andre: Nope. I can download the coolest new tones.

Andre: Excuse me, I'm getting a call. (to phone)
Hey, hold on for a second.

Manolo: Man, you have all the luck.

Andre: It's not luck; it's IM Wireless.

Manolo: How do I get my free phone?

Andre: Just call 1-555-IMPHONE for your free phone! (to phone)
Sorry about that; what's going on?

Announcer: Free cell phone offer requires purchase of regularly priced phone. Mail-in rebate required. Taxes and fees are extra. A two-year service agreement is required. Additional charges may apply.

CELL PHONES FOR TEENS:

A GOOD CALL FOR SAFETY?

This persuasive essay takes the position that there are good reasons for teens to have cell phones. As you read the article, weigh the pros and cons of the argument.

Imagine this: It's a frigid, rainy winter night. Your
5 teenager is riding in a car. The car gets a flat tire on an infrequently patrolled highway. The nearest call box is two miles away. Now imagine this: Your teenager has a cell phone. The **scenario** looks a lot less frightening, doesn't it? This is just one of many potentially dangerous situations
10 in which a cell phone is indispensable. Every young person should have a cell phone when he or she is out alone.

In fact, because of the realities of family life today, cell phones should be **standard** pocket gear for all young people. The majority of parents now work outside the
15 home. This means that more and more kids must spend at least part of the day alone. According to the United States Census Bureau, one out of five children between the ages of 5 and 14 has no adult supervision for at least part of the day. These kids need to be able to get in touch
20 with their parents at a moment's notice. Even kids whose parents do not work outside the home have reason to carry cell phones. Murphy's law says, "Anything that can go wrong probably will go wrong." This statement isn't always true. Still, unexpected problems do arise: a missed bus, a
25 problem with a pet, sudden stomach flu at a baseball game.

scenario

a description of events

standard

commonly accepted as normal; usual

assistance

aid; help in doing something

rate

a cost of something; amount

valid

convincing; sound

titans

powerful companies and those who run them

Difficulties requiring adult **assistance** are part of life. Without a cell phone, a child in one of these situations may be miserably stuck.

Many parents will take issue with the proposition that
30 kids need cell phones. They see cell phones as expensive time-wasters. Some will argue that cell phones and the **rate** plans that come with them are too expensive. Others will assert that the phones are loaded with gadgets such as digital cameras and ring options. These options have no
35 benefit in the area of personal safety.

The objections are **valid** . They should not stand in the way of cell phones becoming safety equipment for kids, however. Cell phone companies need to listen to these concerns and take them as a call to action. The giants
40 of the wireless networks should get busy designing and marketing an affordable bare-bones cell phone and calling plan. Instead of just targeting young people with eye-popping features and flashy advertising campaigns, they should work to make safety-first cell phones available and
45 affordable for all families. Yes, cellular **titans** , even if you don't have a teenager who is out and about at night, you'll sleep better knowing that you've done something to make a positive difference for families everywhere.

Answer It

1. Identify the author's main reason for why kids should have cell phones.

2. Outline the main points the author makes to support her view that kids should have cell phones.

3. Critique the author's point that cell phones will make young people safer.

4. Explain the generalization that the author is making about phone companies when she writes, "Instead of just targeting young people with eye-popping features and flashy advertising campaigns, they should work to make safety-first cell phones available and affordable for all families."

5. In the third paragraph of the essay, the author gives several reasons why parents might not want their children to have cell phones. Make an inference about why the author takes parents' concerns into account in her essay.

A CALL TO POETRY

A call can come in the form of a ringing telephone. A call can be an inner voice that suddenly inspires you. Or, a call can be an unseen force that draws you forward into a new world. The poems that follow explore what it means
5 *to be called in different ways. As you read each poem, ask yourself these questions: What kind of call is the poet describing? How is the poet affected by receiving it?*

POSTSCRIPT

by Naomi Shihab Nye

1.

I wish I had said nothing.
10 Had not returned the call.
Had left the call **dangling**, a shirt from one pin.

And settled into the deep pink streaks of sundown
without a single word flying from my mouth.
The thousand small birds of January

15 in their smooth soaring cloud
finding the trees.

2.

Or if I had to say something,
only a tiny tiny thing. A well-shaped phrase.
Smoothed off at the edges like a child's wooden
20 cow.
That nobody would get a splinter from.

> **dangling**
> hanging uncertainly; remaining unresolved

THE CALLING   by Luis J. Rodriguez

languished

became downcast;
pined

25

The calling came to me
while I **languished**
in my room, while I
whittled away my youth
in jail cells
and damp *barrio* fields.

captivity

confinement

30

It brought me to life,
out of **captivity**,
in a street-scarred
and tattooed place
I called body.

clamor

a loud, noisy outcry

35

Until then I waited silently,
a deafening **clamor** in my head,
but voiceless to all around;
hidden in America's eyes,
a brown boy without a name.

40

45

I would sing into a solitary
        tape recorder,
music never to be heard.
I would write my thoughts
in scrambled English;
I would take photos in my mind—
        plan out new parks,

bushy green, concrete free,
new places to play
and think.

Waiting.
50 Then it came.
The calling.
It brought me out of my room.
It forced me to escape
night captors
55 in street prisons.

It called me to war,
to be writer,
to be scientist
and march with the soldiers
60   of change.

It called me from the shadows,
out of the wreckage
of my barrio—from among those
who did not exist.

65 I waited all of 16 years
for this time.

Somehow, unexpected,
I was called.

STORY FROM BEAR COUNTRY   by Leslie Marmon Silko

70   You will know
        when you walk
        in bear country
        By the silence
        flowing swiftly between the juniper trees
75   by the sundown colors of sandrock
        all around you.

        You may smell damp earth
        scratched away
        from yucca roots
80   You may hear snorts and growls
        slow and massive sounds
        from caves
        in the cliffs high above you.

        It is difficult to explain
85   how they call you
        All but a few who went to them
        left behind families
                grandparents
                and sons
90   a good life.

        The problem is
        you will never want to return
        their beauty will overcome your memory
        like winter sun
95   melting ice shadows from snow
        and you will remain with them
        locked forever inside yourself
                your eyes will see you
                dark shaggy and thick.

100   We can send bear priests
        loping after you
        their medicine bags
        bouncing against their chests

Naked legs painted black
105   bear claw necklaces
rattling against
their capes of blue spruce.

They will follow your trail
into the narrow canyon
110   through the blue-gray mountain sage
to the clearing
where you stopped to look back
and saw only bear tracks
behind you.

115   When they call
faint memories
will **writhe** around your heart
and startle you with their distance.
But the others will listen
120   because bear priests sing
beautiful songs
They must
if they are ever to call you back.

They will try to bring you
125   step by step
back to the place you stopped
and found only bear prints in the sand
where your feet had been.

Whose voice is this?
130   You may wonder
hearing this story when
after all
you are alone
hiking in these canyons and hills
135   while your wife and sons are waiting
back at the car for you.

faint
unclear; weak

writhe
to twist and turn

But you have been listening to me
for some time now
from the very beginning in fact
140   and you are alone in this canyon of stillness
not even cedar birds flutter.

See, the sun is going down now
the sandrock is washed in its colors
Don't be afraid
145   we love you
              we've been calling you
              all this time
Go ahead
turn around
150   see the shape
of your footprints
in the sand.

"Postscript," from *19 Varieties of Gazelle* by Naomi Shihab Nye
"The Calling," from *Cool Salsa* edited by Lori M. Carlson
"Story from Bear Country," from *Storyteller* by Leslie Marmon Silko

Answer It

1. Interpret the image described in lines 17–20 of "Postscript."

2. Review the metaphor that Luis J. Rodriguez presents in lines 56–60 of "The Calling." Discuss how writers and scientists might be considered "soldiers of change."

3. Draw on images in the poem "The Calling" to contrast how the speaker felt about his life before the calling with how he feels about his life after he got the calling.

4. In "Story from Bear Country," do you think bears might symbolize some deep instinctual connection with nature? Justify your response.

5. Identify a main theme in "Story from Bear Country." State it as a universal truth.

THE CALL OF THE WILD
CHAPTER 6: FOR THE LOVE OF A MAN
BY JACK LONDON

Call of the Wild Summary

Buck, a large, strong dog, has been living a comfortable
life in the home of Judge Miller in Santa Clara, California
when he is kidnapped and sold on the black market. The
5 *Gold Rush is on in Alaska and the Yukon, and he is sent*
there to work as a sled dog. Buck has strength and pride,
and he bridles under mistreatment by various owners, who
try to beat him into submission. Buck learns to survive and
work as the lead dog of a sled team. John Thornton rescues
10 *Buck from the cruel treatment of one of his masters, and*
Buck gives him his loyalty in return. Buck's devotion to John
is tempered by his visions of retreating to the forest, joining
a wolf pack, and breaking his ties forever with humankind.
Will Buck heed the call of the wild?

15   For a long time after his rescue, Buck did not like
Thornton to get out of his sight. From the moment he left
the tent to when he entered it again, Buck would follow at
his heels. His transient masters since he had come into the
Northland had bred in him a fear that no master could be
20 permanent. He was afraid that Thornton would pass out
of his life as Perrault and François and the Scotch half-

breed had passed out. Even in the night, in his dreams, he
was haunted by this fear. At such times he would shake
off sleep and creep through the chill to the flap of the
25 tent, where he would stand and listen to the sound of his
master's breathing.

But in spite of this great love he bore John Thornton,
which seemed to bespeak the soft civilizing influence,
the strain of the primitive, which the Northland had
30 aroused in him, remained alive and active. Faithfulness
and devotion, things born of fire and roof, were his; yet
he retained his wildness and wiliness. He was a thing of
the wild, come in from the wild to sit by John Thornton's
fire, rather than a dog of the soft Southland stamped with
35 the marks of generations of civilization. Because of his
very great love, he could not steal from this man, but from
any other man, in any other camp, he did not hesitate an
instant; while the **cunning** with which he stole enabled
him to escape detection.

cunning

careful deception;
shrewdness

40 His face and body were scored by the teeth of many
dogs, and he fought as fiercely as ever and more shrewdly.
Skeet and Nig were too good-natured for quarrelling,
—besides, they belonged to John Thornton; but the
strange dog, no matter what the breed or valor, swiftly
45 acknowledged Buck's supremacy or found himself
struggling for life with a terrible antagonist. And Buck
was merciless. He had learned well the law of club and
fang, and he never forewent an advantage or drew back
from a foe he had started on the way to Death. He had
50 lessoned from Spitz, and from the chief fighting dogs of
the police and mail, and knew there was no middle course.
He must master or be mastered; while to show mercy was
a weakness. Mercy did not exist in the **primordial** life. It
was misunderstood for fear, and such misunderstandings
55 made for death. Kill or be killed, eat or be eaten, was the
law; and this mandate, down out of the depths of Time,
he obeyed.

primordial

basic; connected
with an early stage
of development

He was older than the days he had seen and the breaths
he had drawn. He linked the past with the present, and the
60 eternity behind him throbbed through him in a mighty

rhythm to which he swayed as the tides and seasons swayed. He sat by John Thornton's fire, a broad-breasted dog, white-fanged and long-furred; but behind him were the shades of all manner of dogs, half-wolves and wild

65 wolves, urgent and prompting, tasting the savor of the meat he ate, thirsting for the water he drank, scenting the wind with him, listening with him and telling him the sounds made by the wild life in the forest, dictating his moods, directing his actions, lying down to sleep with him

70 when he lay down, and dreaming with him and becoming themselves the stuff of his dreams.

So peremptorily did these shades **beckon** him, that each day mankind and the claims of mankind slipped farther from him. Deep in the forest a call was sounding,

75 and as often as he heard this call, mysteriously thrilling and luring, he felt compelled to turn his back upon the fire and the beaten earth around it, and to plunge into the forest, and on and on, he knew not where or why; nor did he wonder where or why, the call sounding **imperiously**, deep

beckon
motion or signal to

imperiously
arrogantly; in an overbearing manner

80 in the forest. But as often as he gained the soft unbroken
earth and the green shade, the love for John Thornton drew
him back to the fire again.

Thornton alone held him. The rest of mankind was as
nothing. Chance travellers might praise or pet him; but he
85 was cold under it all, and from a too demonstrative man he
would get up and walk away. When Thornton's partners,
Hans and Pete, arrived on the long-expected raft, Buck
refused to notice them till he learned they were close to
Thornton; after that he tolerated them in a passive sort
90 of way, accepting favors from them as though he favored
them by accepting. They were of the same large type as
Thornton, living close to the earth, thinking simply and
seeing clearly; and ere they swung the raft into the big eddy
by the saw-mill at Dawson, they understood Buck and his
95 ways, and did not insist upon an intimacy such as obtained
with Skeer and Nig.

For Thornton, however, his love seemed to grow and
grow. He, alone among men, could put a pack upon Buck's
back in the summer travelling. Nothing was too great for
100 Buck to do, when Thornton commanded. One day (they
had grub-staked themselves from the proceeds of the raft
and left Dawson for the head-waters of the Tanana) the
men and dogs were sitting on the crest of a cliff which fell
away, straight down, to naked bed-rock three hundred feet
105 below. John Thornton was sitting near the edge, Buck at
his shoulder. A thoughtless **whim** seized Thornton, and
he drew the attention of Hans and Pete to the experiment
he had in mind. "Jump, Buck!" he commanded, sweeping
his arm out and over the chasm. The next instant he was
110 grappling with Buck on the extreme edge, while Hans and
Pete were dragging them back into safety.

"It's uncanny," Pete said, after it was over and they had
caught their speech.

Thornton shook his head. "No, it is splendid, and it is
115 terrible, too. Do you know, it sometimes makes me afraid."

"I'm not hankering to be the man that lays hands on
you while he's around," Pete announced conclusively,
nodding his head toward Buck.

whim

a sudden idea or desire

"Py Jingo!" was Hans's contribution. "Not mineself
120 either."

It was at Circle City, ere the year was out, that Pete's
apprehensions were realized. "Black" Burton, a man evil-
tempered and malicious, had been picking a quarrel with
a tenderfoot at the bar, when Thornton stepped good-
125 naturedly between. Buck, as was his custom, was lying in
a corner, head on paws, watching his master's every action.
Burton struck out, without warning, straight from the
shoulder. Thornton was sent spinning, and saved himself
from falling only by clutching the rail of the bar.

130 Those who were looking on heard what was neither
bark nor yelp, but a something which is best described
as a roar, and they saw Buck's body rise up in the air as
he left the floor for Burton's throat. The man saved his
life by instinctively throwing out his arm, but was hurled
135 backward to the floor with Buck on top of him. Buck
loosed his teeth from the flesh of the arm and drove in
again for the throat. This time the man succeeded only
in partly blocking, and his throat was torn open. Then
the crowd was upon Buck, and he was driven off; but
140 while a surgeon checked the bleeding, he prowled up
and down, growling furiously, attempting to rush in, and
being forced back by an array of hostile clubs. A "miner's
meeting," called on the spot, decided that the dog had
sufficient **provocation** , and Buck was discharged. But his
145 reputation was made, and from that day his name spread
through every camp in Alaska.

provocation
a reason to protest
or fight

Later on, in the fall of the year, he saved John Thornton's
life in quite another fashion. The three partners were lining
a long and narrow poling-boat down a bad stretch of rapids
150 on the Forty-Mile Creek. Hans and Pete moved along the
bank, snubbing with a thin Manila rope from tree to tree,
while Thornton remained in the boat, helping its descent by
means of a pole, and shouting directions to the shore. Buck,
on the bank, worried and anxious, kept abreast of the boat,
155 his eyes never off his master.

At a particularly bad spot, where a ledge of barely
submerged rocks jutted out into the river, Hans cast off

the rope, and, while Thornton poled the boat out into the
stream, ran down the bank with the end in his hand to
160 snub the boat when it had cleared the ledge. This it did,
and was flying down-stream in a current as swift as a mill-
race, when Hans checked it with the rope and checked
too suddenly. The boat flirted over and snubbed in to the
bank bottom up, while Thornton, flung sheer out of it, was
165 carried down-stream toward the worst part of the rapids, a
stretch of wild water in which no swimmer could live.

    Buck had sprung in on the instant; and at the end
of three hundred yards, amid a mad swirl of water, he
overhauled Thornton. When he felt him grasp his tail,
170 Buck headed for the bank, swimming with all his splendid
strength. But the progress shoreward was slow; the progress
down-stream was amazingly rapid. From below came the
fatal roaring where the wild current went wilder and was
rent in shreds and spray by the rocks which thrust through
175 like the teeth of an enormous comb. The suck of the water
as it took the beginning of the last steep pitch was frightful,
and Thornton knew that the shore was impossible. He
scraped furiously over a rock, bruised across a second, and
struck a third with crushing force. He clutched its slippery

180 top with both hands, releasing Buck, and above the roar of
the churning water shouted: "Go, Buck! Go!"

Buck could not hold his own, and swept on down-
stream, struggling desperately, but unable to win back.
When he heard Thornton's command repeated, he partly

185 reared out of the water, throwing his head high, as though
for a last look, then turned obediently toward the bank. He
swam powerfully and was dragged ashore by Pete and Hans
at the very point where swimming ceased to be possible
and destruction began.

190 They knew that the time a man could cling to a
slippery rock in the face of that driving current was a
matter of minutes, and they ran as fast as they could up the
bank to a point far above where Thornton was hanging on.
They attached the line with which they had been snubbing

195 the boat to Buck's neck and shoulders, being careful that
it should neither strangle him nor impede his swimming,
and launched him into the stream. He struck out boldly,
but not straight enough into the stream. He discovered the
mistake too late, when Thornton was abreast of him and

200 a bare half-dozen strokes away while he was being carried
helplessly past.

Hans promptly snubbed with the rope, as though Buck
were a boat. The rope thus tightening on him in the sweep
of the current, he was jerked under the surface, and under

205 the surface he remained till his body struck against the
bank and he was hauled out. He was half drowned, and
Hans and Pete threw themselves upon him, pounding the
breath into him and the water out of him. He staggered
to his feet and fell down. The faint sound of Thornton's

210 voice came to them, and though they could not make out
the words of it, they knew that he was in his extremity.
His master's voice acted on Buck like an electric shock. He
sprang to his feet and ran up the bank ahead of the men to
the point of his previous departure.

215 Again the rope was attached and he was launched, and
again he struck out, but this time straight into the stream.
He had miscalculated once, but he would not be guilty of
it a second time. Hans paid out the rope, permitting no

slack, while Pete kept it clear of coils. Buck held on till he
220 was on a line straight above Thornton; then he turned, and
with the speed of an express train headed down upon him.
Thornton saw him coming, and, as Buck struck him like a
battering ram, with the whole force of the current behind
him, he reached up and closed with both arms around the
225 shaggy neck. Hans snubbed the rope around the tree, and
Buck and Thornton were jerked under the water. Strangling,
suffocating, sometimes one uppermost and sometimes the
other, dragging over the jagged bottom, smashing against
rocks and snags, they veered in to the bank.
230   Thornton came to, belly downward and being violently
propelled back and forth across a drift log by Hans and
Pete. His first glance was for Buck, over whose limp and
apparently lifeless body Nig was setting up a howl, while
Skeet was licking the wet face and closed eyes. Thornton
235 was himself bruised and battered, and he went carefully
over Buck's body, when he had been brought around,
finding three broken ribs.
     "That settles it," he announced. "We camp right here."
And camp they did, till Buck's ribs knitted and he was able
240 to travel.

Answer It

1. Hypothesize a reason why Buck is so loyal to John Thornton.

2. Review lines 27–39. Paraphrase the author's contrast between the "soft
   civilizing influence" and "the strain of the primitive."

3. Explain why Buck's loyalty made Thornton nervous.

4. The story gives multiple examples of how Buck is loyal to Thornton. Describe
   one way that Thornton shows his loyalty to Buck.

5. Compare and contrast the first and last attempts Buck made to save Thornton.
   Tell why the final attempt was successful and the first one was not.

6. Thornton commands Buck to return to shore after Buck's first attempt to save
   him. Explain why Buck followed the order instead of continuing to try to save
   his master.

THE CALL OF THE WILD

CHAPTER 7: THE SOUNDING OF THE CALL

BY JACK LONDON

Spring came on once more, and at the end of all their wandering they found, not the Lost Cabin, but a shallow placer in a broad valley where the gold showed like yellow butter across the bottom of the washing-pan. They sought
5 no farther. Each day they worked earned them thousands of dollars in clean dust and nuggets, and they worked every day. The gold was sacked in moose-hide bags, fifty pounds to the bag, and piled like so much firewood outside the spruce-bough lodge. Like giants they toiled, days flashing on
10 the heels of days like dreams as they heaped the treasure up.

There was nothing for the dogs to do, save the hauling in of meat now and again that Thornton killed, and Buck spent long hours musing by the fire. The vision of the short-legged hairy man came to him more frequently, now
15 that there was little work to be done; and often, blinking by the fire, Buck wandered with him in that other world which he remembered.

The **salient** thing of this other world seemed fear. When he watched the hairy man sleeping by the fire, head
20 between his knees and hands clasped above, Buck saw that he slept restlessly, with many starts and awakenings, at which times he would peer fearfully into the darkness and fling more wood upon the fire. Did they walk by the beach

> **salient**
> most obvious or noticeable

of a sea, where the hairy man gathered shell-fish and ate
25 them as he gathered, it was with eyes that roved everywhere
for hidden danger and with legs prepared to run like the
wind at its first appearance. Through the forest they crept
noiselessly, Buck at the hairy man's heels; and they were
alert and vigilant, the pair of them, ears twitching and
30 moving and nostrils quivering, for the man heard and
smelled as keenly as Buck. The hairy man could spring up
into the trees and travel ahead as fast as on the ground,
swinging by the arms from limb to limb, sometimes a
dozen feet apart, letting go and catching, never falling,
35 never missing his grip. In fact, he seemed as much at home
among the trees as on the ground; and Buck had memories
of nights of **vigil** spent beneath trees wherein the hairy
man roosted, holding on tightly as he slept.

And closely **akin** to the visions of the hairy man was
40 the call still sounding in the depths of the forest. It filled
him with a great unrest and strange desires. It caused him
to feel a vague, sweet gladness, and he was aware of wild
yearnings and stirrings for he knew not what. Sometimes
he pursued the call into the forest, looking for it as though
45 it were a **tangible** thing, barking softly or defiantly, as
the mood might dictate. He would thrust his nose into the
cool wood moss, or into the black soil where long grasses
grew, and snort with joy at the fat earth smells; or he would
crouch for hours, as if in concealment, behind fungus-
50 covered trunks of fallen trees, wide-eyed and wide-eared
to all that moved and sounded about him. It might be,
lying thus, that he hoped to surprise this call he could not
understand. But he did not know why he did these various
things. He was impelled to do them, and did not reason
55 about them at all.

Irresistible impulses seized him. He would be lying in
camp, dozing lazily in the heat of the day, when suddenly his
head would lift and his ears cock up, intent and listening,
and he would spring to his feet and dash away, and on and
60 on, for hours, through the forest aisles and across the open
spaces where the wildflowers bunched. He loved to run
down dry watercourses, and to creep and spy upon the bird

vigil
a period of waiting

akin
like; similar to

tangible
touchable, real

life in the woods. For a day at a time he would lie in the underbrush where he could watch the partridges drumming
65 and strutting up and down. But especially he loved to run in the dim twilight of the summer midnights, listening to the subdued and sleepy murmurs of the forest, reading signs and sounds as man may read a book, and seeking for the mysterious something that called—called, waking or
70 sleeping, at all times, for him to come.

One night he sprang from sleep with a start, eager-eyed, nostrils quivering and scenting, his mane bristling in recurrent waves. From the forest came the call (or one note of it, for the call was many noted), distinct and definite as
75 never before, —a long-drawn howl, like, yet unlike, any noise made by husky dog. And he knew it, in the old familiar way, as a sound heard before. He sprang through the sleeping camp and in swift silence dashed through the woods. As he drew closer to the cry he went more slowly, with caution in
80 every movement, till he came to an open place among the trees, and looking out saw, erect on haunches, with nose pointed to the sky, a long, lean, timber wolf.

He had made no noise, yet it ceased from its howling and tried to sense his presence. Buck stalked into the
85 open, half crouching, body gathered compactly together, tail straight and stiff, feet falling with unwonted care. Every movement advertised commingled threatening and overture of friendliness. It was the menacing **truce** that marks the meeting of wild beasts that prey. But the wolf
90 fled at the sight of him. He followed, with wild leapings, in a frenzy to overtake. He ran him into a blind channel, in the bed of the creek, where a timber jam barred the way. The wolf whirled about, pivoting on his hind legs after the fashion of Joe and of all cornered husky dogs, snarling and
95 bristling, clipping his teeth together in a continuous and rapid succession of snaps.

Buck did not attack, but circled him about and hedged him in with friendly advances. The wolf was suspicious and afraid; for Buck made three of him in weight, while
100 his head barely reached Buck's shoulder. Watching his chance, he darted away, and the chase was resumed. Time

truce

a temporary stopping of hostilities; respite

and again he was cornered, and the thing repeated, though
he was in poor condition, or Buck could not so easily have
overtaken him. He would run till Buck's head was even
105 with his flank, when he would whirl around at bay, only to
dash away again at the first opportunity.

But in the end Buck's pertinacity was rewarded; for the
wolf, finding that no harm was intended, finally sniffed
noses with him. Then they became friendly, and played
110 about in the nervous, half-coy way with which fierce beasts
belie their fierceness. After some time of this the wolf
started off at an easy lope in a manner that plainly showed
he was going somewhere. He made it clear to Buck that he
was to come, and they ran side by side through the sombre
115 twilight, straight up the creek bed, into the gorge from which
it issued, and across the bleak divide where it took its rise.

On the opposite slope of the watershed they came down
into a level country where were great stretches of forest and
many streams, and through these great stretches they ran
120 steadily, hour after hour, the sun rising higher and the day
growing warmer. Buck was wildly glad. He knew he was
at last answering the call, running by the side of his wood

belie

misrepresent;
picture falsely

brother toward the place from where the call surely came. Old memories were coming upon him fast, and he was
125 stirring to them as of old he stirred to the realities of which they were the shadows. He had done this thing before, somewhere in that other and dimly remembered world, and he was doing it again, now, running free in the open, the unpacked earth underfoot, the wide sky overhead.

130 They stopped by a running stream to drink, and, stopping, Buck remembered John Thornton. He sat down. The wolf started on toward the place from where the call surely came then returned to him, sniffing noses and making actions as though to encourage him. But Buck
135 turned about and started slowly on the back track. For the better part of an hour the wild brother ran by his side, whining softly. Then he sat down, pointed his nose upward, and howled. It was a mournful howl, and as Buck held steadily on his way he heard it grow faint and fainter until
140 it was lost in the distance.

John Thornton was eating dinner when Buck dashed into camp and sprang upon him in a frenzy of affection, overturning him, scrambling upon him, licking his face, biting his hand—"playing the general tom-fool," as John
145 Thornton characterized it, the while he shook Buck back and forth and cursed him lovingly.

For two days and nights Buck never left camp, never let Thornton out of his sight. He followed him about at his work, watched him while he ate, saw him into his blankets
150 at night and out of them in the morning. But after two days the call in the forest began to sound more imperiously than ever. Buck's restlessness came back on him, and he was haunted by recollections of the wild brother, and of the smiling land beyond the divide and the run side by
155 side through the wide forest stretches. Once again he took to wandering in the woods, but the wild brother came no more; and though he listened through long vigils, the mournful howl was never raised. . . .

Answer It

1. Identify one reason that the call was so strong for Buck at this time.

2. Draw a conclusion about whether Buck's visions of the hairy man are based on things that Buck actually experienced in his own life.

3. Predict what will happen to Buck if the men and dogs continue to stay where they are, and give a reason for your prediction.

4. Unlike humans, wild animals do not use words to communicate. List three ways that Buck and the timber wolf communicated with each other.

5. Identify the thing in the story that triggered Buck's running away, and then identify what made him decide to turn back.

6. In Lesson 9 you made a prediction about what Buck would do if the men remained camped. Now that you have read the rest of the selection, do you think that Buck will remain with Thornton or return to the wild again? Why or why not?

Celebrate the Individual

STEP

1

Phonemic Awareness and Phonics

Unit 30 introduces variant spellings for the sounds / k /, / f /, and / s /.

Multiple Spellings for / k /, / f /, and / s /

Review:

- The letters **c**, **k**, and -**ck** represent the sound / k /. Examples: cat, kid, track

- The letter **f** represents the sound / f /. Example: fat

- The letter **s** represents the sound / s /. Example: sat

The / k / sound is also represented by the sound-spelling patterns **ch** and **que**. Examples: chord, oblique

The / f / sound is also represented by the letter combinations **ph** and **gh**. Examples: phone, enough

The / s / sound is also represented by the letter combination **sc**. Examples: science, scissors

STEP 2

Word Recognition and Spelling

Prefixes, Suffixes, and Roots

We can expand words and change meaning by adding **prefixes** and **suffixes**.

- Prefixes are added to the beginning of words.

- Suffixes are added to the end of words.

- **Roots** are the basic meaning part of words. We usually attach a prefix or suffix to make the root a word.

Refer to page A16 for a list of prefixes, roots, and suffixes and their meanings.

Prefix Review

ad-	antiheroic	**post-**
adapter	antihistamine	postdoctoral
adhesive		posthumous
administrative	**mal-**	postimpressionism
admonish	maladaptive	postoperative
	maladjustment	
ad- (assimilates)	malediction	**semi-**
accidental	malfeasance	semitonic
affronted		
aggravatingly	**ob-**	**sub-**
annexation	objectivity	subgroup
approvable	oblige	subhuman
arrived	observance	submissive
assailable	obsessively	subsequent
attainability		
	ob- (assimilates)	**sub- (assimilates)**
anti-	occupied	successive
antibody	offering	suggestively
antidepressant	opponents	suppose
	opposed	sustenance

Suffix Review

-age
bandage
linkage
verbiage
village

-al
correctional
eternal
marginal
thermal

-ance
compliance
continuance
exuberance
resonance

-ence
benevolence
diffidence

divergence
malevolence

-ial
binomial
colloquial
polynomial
terrestrial

-ible
edible
incredible
indelible
sensible

-ic
dogmatic
endemic
geometric
patriotic

-ity
commodity
equanimity
fidelity
levity

-ive
descriptive
extensive
repulsive
speculative

-sion /shŭn/
aggression
expansion
mansion
repercussion

-sion /zhŭn/
corrosion
excursion

immersion
propulsion

-tion
fraction
moderation
presumption
procrastination

-ual
habitual
lingual
monolingual
subtextual

-ure
architecture
pressure
restructure

Root Review

cept/capt/ceit
interceptor
susceptibly
capably
capacities
conceitedly
deceitfulness

cred
accreditation
discredited
incredibly

fer
circumference
fertilizer
preferential

grad/gress
biodegradable
grader
ungraded

aggressor
digression
regression

mis/mit
compromise
dismissal
permissive
committee
intermittent
transmitter

plic/pli/plex
complicity
replicate
compliance
multiplication
perplexed
perplexity

pos/pon/pound
depository
exposition

proposal
exponential
exponentially
compounded
impound

rupt
bankruptcy
corruption
erupted

sist/sta/stit
insistence
persistent
constantly
standardization
institute
instituting

struct
indestructible
obstruction
structural

ten/tin/tain
contentedness
discontentedly
untenable
continuation
discontinuing
pertinence
abstain
attainment
entertainment

tend/tens/tent
attendance
contender
extensively
intensification
attention
inattentively

Essential Words

Unit 30 Essential Words

| behalf | broad | sew |
| bouquet | mountain | shepherd |

Spelling Lists

The Unit 30 spelling lists contain three categories:

1. Words with phonograms: **ch**, **que**, **ph**, **gh**, and **sc**

2. Essential Words (in italics)

3. Words with prefixes, roots, and suffixes

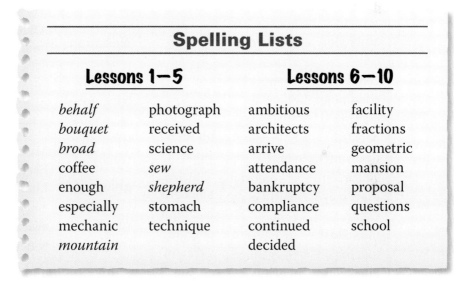

Spelling Lists

Lessons 1–5

behalf	photograph
bouquet	received
broad	science
coffee	*sew*
enough	*shepherd*
especially	stomach
mechanic	technique
mountain	

Lessons 6–10

ambitious	facility
architects	fractions
arrive	geometric
attendance	mansion
bankruptcy	proposal
compliance	questions
continued	school
decided	

3 Vocabulary and Morphology

Unit Vocabulary

Sound-spelling correspondences from this unit and previous units make up this unit's vocabulary.

- What do these words mean?
- Do some of them mean more than one thing? Which ones?

UNIT Vocabulary

Review Words	**ch for / k /**	technician	philosophy	scientists
actually	ache	technology	phone	scissors
ambitious	anchor		photo	
cells	architect	**que for / k /**	photograph	**African Loan Words**
cents	chaos	clique	phrase	bark
conditions	chemical	critique	physical	gum
continued	chemist	opaque	telegraph	sack
decided	chemistry	technique	telephone	zebra
drawing	chloride	**ph for / f /**	triumph	
education	chorus	alpha	trophy	**Middle Eastern Loan Words**
especially	chromosome	alphabet		
exciting	chronic	bibliography	**gh for / f /**	abbot
individual	echo	biography	enough	algebra
lodging	hierarchy	dolphin	rough	coffee
questions	mechanic	elephant	tough	cork
received	mechanism	emphasis	**sc for / s /**	cotton
resource	melancholy	emphasize	adolescence	giraffe
revenue	orchestra	geography	crescent	jar
substances	schedule	graph	descend	mask
suggested	scheme	microphone	discipline	mirror
tools	scholar	nephew	muscle	monkey
workers	school	phantom	scene	soda
	stomach	phase	scent	zero
	technical	phenomenon	science	

English Loan Words From African and Middle Eastern Languages

English has often borrowed words from other languages based on the meanings of those loan words. This happens when a word from another language labels an object whose origin is in a country where that language is spoken—the language that originated the word. Words in this unit include words borrowed from African or Middle Eastern languages.

Meaning Parts

Prefixes

Prefixes can add to or change the meanings of words.
A prefix + a base word or root = a new word with a new meaning.
Examples: **ob** + ject = object; **anti** + body = antibody

Suffixes

Suffixes can change the meaning or function of words.
Examples: verb to noun: press + **ure** = pressure
noun to adjective: margin + **al** = marginal
verb to adjective: speculate + **ive** = speculative

Roots

A **root** is the basic meaning part of a word. It usually attaches to a prefix or suffix to create a word. Roots of English words often come from other languages, especially Latin.

Example: sub + **cept** + ible = susceptible (sub = below, **cept** = to take, ible = capable of) susceptible = capable of being influenced

Refer to page A16 for a list of prefixes, roots, and suffixes and their meanings.

Grammar and Usage

Pronouns

Review: **Pronouns** are function words that take the place of nouns. They can be **nominative** (subject), **object**, or **possessive**. Most pronouns have antecedents—nouns to which they refer.

Indefinite pronouns refer to unspecified or unknown people or things. They can be nominative or object pronouns. Indefinite pronouns do not have antecedents.

Relative pronouns begin dependent clauses. They include: **that**, **which**, **who**, **whom**, and **whose**. A relative pronoun is related to a noun or pronoun already mentioned in the independent clause. This noun or pronoun is called an antecedent. Example: Camels, **which** provide transportation in the desert, are prized possessions.

Future Perfect

Review: The **present perfect** uses the helping verb **have** or **has** and the past participle of a verb. It describes an action occurring at an unspecified time in the past, or an action that starts in the past and continues in the present. Example: I have waited for a call for an hour.

Review: The **past perfect tense** uses the past participle of a verb with **had** (the past tense of the verb **have**). The **past perfect** describes an action completed in the past before another past action took place. A sentence with a past perfect verb often has two verbs expressing actions in the past: one in an independent clause and one in a dependent clause. In the sentence, the action described by the past perfect verb was completed before the action described by the other verb. Example: He had called before he left for the train.

The **future perfect tense** is a verb phrase that uses the future of the verb **have** (**will have**) and the past participle of a verb. It expresses an action that will be completed in the future before another future action.

> **Future Perfect**
>
> By the time the pig is fully grown, it **will have become** extremely heavy.
>
> > In this sentence, the action of becoming heavy will occur before the future action of becoming full grown.

Conjunctions

Review: Conjunctions are function words that join words, phrases, or clauses in a sentence or across two sentences. **Coordinating conjunctions** (**and**, **or**, and **but**) join words or groups of words that are equal or grammatically similar.

Subordinating conjunctions establish the relationship between two clauses that are not equal. The idea in one clause is dependent on the idea in the other. Subordinating conjunctions include: **although**, **as**, **because**, **if**, **since**, **than**, **unless**, **until**, **when**, **where**, and **while**. An adverbial clause usually begins with a subordinating conjunction. Example: The brothers fought over the camels **because** they did not understand their father's instructions.

Clauses

Review: A **clause** is a group of words that contains a subject and a predicate. An **independent clause** has one subject and one predicate; it represents a complete thought. A **dependent clause** cannot stand alone. It combines with an independent clause to create meaning.

Some dependent clauses function as adverbs. An **adverbial clause**:

- Answers the questions: **How? When? Where? Why?** or **Under what conditions?**
- Expands the predicate part of the sentence.
- Usually begins with a subordinating conjunction.
- Can occur at the beginning or end of a sentence.

> **Adverbial Clause**
> The brothers argued **until they had solved their problem**.

Other dependent clauses function as adjectives. An **adjectival clause**:

- Answers the question **Which one?** or **What kind?**
- Usually begins with a relative pronoun.
- Occurs near the noun it modifies.

> **Adjectival Clause**
> The brothers, **who were arguing**, finally resolved their disagreement.

Sentence Pattern

Review: A **simple sentence** is an independent clause that contains a subject and a predicate and is a complete thought. Example: Kibuka received the pig as a gift.

A **compound sentence** consists of two independent clauses joined by the conjunction **and**, **but**, or **or**. Sentences that are similar use the conjunction **and**. Sentences with contrasting ideas use the conjunction **but**. Sentences that offer a choice use the conjunction **or**. Example: Kibuka treated the pig well, and the neighbors were amused.

A **complex sentence** consists of one independent clause and one or more dependent clauses. The dependent clauses can be adverbial or adjectival. If an adverbial clause is at the beginning of a sentence, it is separated from the independent clause by a comma. An adjectival clause is separated from the independent clause by commas if it is not essential to the meaning of the independent clause.

> **Complex Sentence With an Adjectival Clause**
>
> Kibuka, who was lonely in retirement, was delighted to see his grandson.

Punctuation

Review: Commas, colons, and semicolons are special punctuation marks.

- **Commas** are used in a series, in dates, addresses, and in compound and complex sentences.
- **Colons** are used after the greeting in a business letter, before a list following an independent clause, and to separate the hour from the minutes when writing time.
- **Semicolons** can be used to join two related independent clauses.

Confusing Word Pairs

Your and **you're** are frequently confused in writing. **Your** is a possessive adjective. It indicates ownership. **You're** is a contraction of **you are**. It is part of the present tense of the verb **be**.

Is this **your** book?

You're late for class.

There, **their**, and **they're** are also frequently confused in writing. **There** is an adverb meaning "in that place." **Their** is a possessive adjective and indicates ownership. **They're** is a contraction of **they are**.

Place the book **there**.

The brothers would not sell **their** camels.

They're very thirsty.

STEP

Listening and Reading Comprehension

Informational Text

- Some **informational text** is nonfiction material about a specific topic, event, experience, or circumstance. It is often accompanied by visual information in the form of charts, graphs, or illustrations. The visual information provides additional content about the subject matter. The use of visual information helps solve the mathematical word problem in "**The Eighteenth Camel.**"

Vocabulary in Context

- **Context clues** help us understand new vocabulary. Pronoun referents, meaning signals, and visuals, such as charts and graphs, provide meaning links.

Signal Words

- Different types of sentences can help us think about new information and ideas in different ways. Identifying signal words within sentences can improve comprehension.

  See the Appendix, page A20, for a complete list of signal words based on Bloom's Taxonomy.

Literary Terms and Devices

- **Genres** are types or categories of literature. Unit 30 features fiction.

- **Fiction** is the literary genre that includes imaginary stories. Some fiction is based on real people, places, and events. "**The Pig**" is an example of fiction.

Plot Analysis

- **Plot** is the sequence of events in a narrative or drama. The author develops the plot to create the story. The plot guides the reader through the story.

- **Characters** and **setting** are introduced early in the story. They create the necessary background information for a reader. The characters, which can be people, animals, or things, interact in a story. The setting is the story's time and place. Characters and setting comprise the introduction—the first element of plot development.

At a Glance 225

■ To understand how a plot develops, we must first identify a story's main **problem** and its **solution**. Without a problem, or conflict, there would be no story—everything would remain the same.

■ After we become proficient in identifying a story's main problem and solution, we will learn more about plot development and apply it in our writing.

■ Plot development usually consists of five elements:

Introduction (characters and setting);

Conflict (rising action);

Climax (turning point);

Resolution (falling action);

Conclusion (the situation at the end of the story, with a look to the future).

Speaking and Writing

Signal Words

■ Different types of sentences require different responses, depending on the focus of the signal words. Identifying signal words within sentences improves the accuracy of our responses to oral and written questions.

See the Appendix, page A20, for a complete list of signal words based on Bloom's Taxonomy.

Composition Organization

■ Some compositions are written in response to literature. This type of writing summarizes the text and then analyzes or evaluates it.

■ A story summary incorporates the main elements of plot analysis. It includes:

An introduction to the story, including the title, author, and setting;

A description of the event that initiates the action in the plot or story;

A description of the major events that lead to the climax;

A description of the climax and how the problem is resolved.

A response to literature expresses the reader's reaction to the story. When writing a response to fictional literature, the writer often expresses opinions about the characters, the plot, the ideas, or other aspects of the story that were summarized.

More About Words

- **Bonus Words** use the same sound-spelling correspondences that we have studied in this unit and previous units.

- **Idioms** are common phrases that cannot be understood by the meanings of their separate words—only by the entire phrase.

- **Why? Word History** tells the origins of the word **algebra**.

UNIT Bonus Words

Review Words
adage
agile
aloof
elicit
equable
facetious
fraudulent
illicit
imbalance
incite
maudlin
solace
uproot

ch for / k /
archaic
chasm
cholera
cholesterol
chord
chrome
chromium
chrysalis
conch
schematic
scholastic

que for / k /
baroque

brusque
grotesque
masquerade
mystique

ph for / f /
amphibian
amphitheater
asphalt
autobiography
autograph
cacophony
calligraphy
catastrophe
cellophane
decipher
digraph
diphthong
epitaph
graphite
headphones
hyphen
lymph
metaphor
morpheme
nymph
orphan
pamphlet
periphery
pharmacy

phobia
phoneme
phonetics
phonics
phonograph
phony
phosphate
prophet
saxophone
siphon
sophomore
sphinx
stenographer
symphony
topography
typhoon
typhus

gh for / f /
roughage
roughhouse
slough
toughen

sc for / s /
ascertain
ascetic
discern
incandescent
miscellaneous

scenery
scythe

**African
Loan Words**
aye-aye
barge
gorilla
scoff

**Middle Eastern
Loan Words**
abbey
admiral
almanac
arsenal
average
caramel
cipher
hazard
mattress
mummy
muslin
racket
satin
sequin
sherbet
sheriff
sofa
syrup

Idioms	
Idiom	**Meaning**
be a tough act to follow	be so good it is not likely that anyone or anything else that comes after will be as good
be a tough nut to crack	be a difficult problem to solve
have a memory like an elephant	be able to remember things easily and for a long period of time
have butterflies in your stomach	have a feeling of unease or nausea caused by fearful anticipation
move mountains	achieve something that is very difficult
not have the stomach for something	not feel brave or determined enough to do something unpleasant
set the scene	describe a situation where something is going to happen soon
steal the scene	be the most popular or the best part of an event or situation
strike a chord	remember something because it is similar to what you are talking about
take the rough with the smooth	accept the unpleasant parts of a situation as well as the pleasant parts

Why? Word History

Algebra—Algebra is a branch of mathematics in which symbols, usually letters of the alphabet, represent numbers and are used to represent quantities and to express relationships. Solving an algebra problem involves finding the number or numbers that make both sides of a particular equation equal. So, it's fitting that the word **algebra** comes from the term *al-jabr*, which in Arabic means "balancing" or "reuniting."

Al-Khwarizmi is considered the Father of Algebra because he wrote the first comprehensive book on the subject. This book, composed around AD 830, was called *Hisab al-jabr w'al-muqabala*, which translates to *"The Compendious Book on Calculation by Completion and Balancing."* It was this book that introduced algebra to the world.

The Eighteenth Camel

For thousands of years, camels have served as vehicles.
They have furnished transportation for many peoples
of the Arabian deserts. The beasts have served in other
ways, too. Camels have been valued for their milk, meat,
5 and skins. The beasts have had great importance in the
desert economy. A Bedouin can measure his wealth by the
number of camels he owns.

A tale is told of a certain wealthy Bedouin who, upon
his death, left seventeen camels. These were to be divided
10 among three sons. The first son was to get half of the
camels. The second would get a third. The third son would
get one-ninth of the lot.

By such a division, the first son would get eight and a
half camels. The second son would get five and two-thirds
15 camels. The third son would inherit only one and eight-
ninths of a camel. The situation seemed impossible to
solve. None of the sons would sell his share to the others.
Certainly none of them wanted to kill any of the camels.
The beasts were much more valuable alive than dead.
20 Tempers flared. Angry words were spoken.

Now, in the area lived a wealthy Arabian woman.
Distressed by the fighting, she offered the brothers one of her
own camels. She hoped it would help to settle the dispute.

They now had eighteen camels to share. The first son
25 received his half. This consisted of nine camels. The second
son received six camels—his one-third share. And the last
son received two camels, one-ninth of the eighteen.

To their surprise, they found that there was one camel left. For, when added together, nine plus six plus two equals
30 only seventeen. So they returned the woman's camel with their thanks.

Without her camel, the inheritance would not have been peacefully resolved. It seemed that she had done nothing—for she had neither lost nor gained an animal.
35 But the woman was a wise individual. An individual is what is often needed to bring about an action. An individual can be a catalyst. The catalytic effect had great value. Its worth was greater than any other gift she might have given to the brothers.

Adapted from "The Eighteenth Camel: A Retelling of an Old Bedouin Folk Tale" by Thelma Schmidhauser

THE PIG:

An Individual Dilemma

by Barbara Kimenye

Old Kibuka had long believed that retirement was no sort of life for a man like himself, who would, so he modestly believed, pass for not a day over forty-five. He had held a responsible post at the Ggombolola Headquarters,
5 until the Government had sent somebody from the Public Service Commission to nose around the offices and root out all employees over retirement age. Then the next thing Kibuka knew, despite his youthfully dyed hair, he had a **pension**, a Certificate of Service, but no longer a job.

10 He still worried about the state his filing system must be in today, for having once called in at the Headquarters, merely to see if the youngster who had replaced him needed any advice or help, he had been appalled at the lack of order. Papers were scattered everywhere, confidential
15 folders were open for all the world to read, and his successor was flirting madly with some pin-brained girl at the other end of the newly installed telephone.

The visit had not been anything near a success, for not even his former colleagues showed anything but superficial
20 interest in what Kibuka had to say.

So there he was, destined to waste the remainder of his life in the little cottage beside the Kalasanda stream, with plenty indeed to look back on, but not very much to look

pension

a regular payment made by a business or government to a retired person

forward to, and his greatest friend, Yosefu Mukasa, was
25 away in Buddu County on business.

The self-pitying thought "I might as well be dead" kept
recurring in his mind as he pumped his pressure stove to
boil a kettle of tea. Then the noise of a car, grinding its way
along the narrow, uneven track, heading in his direction,
30 sent him eagerly to the door. It was his eldest grandson who
climbed out of the battered Landrover. A tall, loose-limbed
young man in a khaki shirt and blue jeans. Old Kibuka
practically choked with happiness as his frail fingers were
squeezed in a sinewy grip, and the bones of his shoulders
35 almost snapped under an affectionate hug.

"What a wonderful surprise! Come in, my boy. I was
just making a cup of tea."

"Grandfather, this is a very short visit. I'm afraid I
can't stay more than a few minutes." The boy's voice was
40 musically deep, very much like his grandfather's once had
been, before the tremor of age had changed it. "I just came
to see how you are getting on, and I brought you a present."

"That's very kind of you, son!" The unexpected visit
and now a present: in a matter of seconds Kibuka had
45 completely reversed his opinion that life was no longer
worth living. He was **aglow** with excitement.

aglow
delighted; radiating
excitement

"Yes. It's one of the piglets from the Farm School. The sow doesn't seem able to feed this new litter, so I thought you might like one for eating; it should make an excellent meal."

50 The boy strode back to the Landrover and returned with a black, squealing bundle under his arm.

Kibuka was more delighted than ever. He had never seen so small a pig before, and he spent a good ten minutes marveling at its tiny twinkling eyes, its minute hoofs, and 55 its wisp of a tail. When his grandson drove away, he waved happily from the doorstep, the piglet clutched tenderly to his chest.

He had told his grandson that he would take the creature up to the Mukasas and ask Miriamu to prepare 60 it as a special "welcome home" supper for Yosefu, but he soon sensed a certain reluctance within himself to do this, because the piglet followed him about the house or squatted trustingly at his feet each time he sat down. Moreover, it obviously understood every word Kibuka said 65 to it, for, whenever he spoke, it listened gravely with its dainty forefeet placed lightly upon his knee.

By nightfall Kibuka was enchanted with his new companion, and would have as much considered eating it as he would consider eating the beloved grandson 70 who had given it to him. He fed the piglet little scraps of food from his own plate, besides providing it with a rich porridge mixture. Nevertheless, within a few days it was clear that the pig's appetite was increasing out of all proportion to its size, and Kibuka had to resort to 75 collecting matoke peelings[1] in an old bucket from his friends and nearest neighbors.

The news that Kibuka was keeping a pig, the first ever actually reared in Kalasanda, caused something of a sensation. In no time at all there was little need for him to 80 cart the bucket from house to house, because the women and children, on their way to draw water from the stream, made a practice of bringing the peelings and food scraps with them as part of the excuse for calling on him, and

[1] matoke peelings—banana or plantain peels

being allowed to fondle the animal and discuss its progress
85 as if it were a dear relative with a delicate hold on life.

No pig had ever had it so good. Fortunately, it proved to be a fastidiously clean creature, and for this reason Kibuka allowed it to spend its nights at the foot of his bed, although he was careful not to let his neighbors know of
90 this. The pig, naturally enough, positively flourished in this cozy atmosphere of good will and personal attention. From a squealing bundle small enough to be held in one hand, it quickly developed into a handsome, hefty porker with eyes which held the faintest glint of **malice** even when it was at
95 its most affectionate with Kibuka.

malice
in a manner to cause intentional harm

However, as the weeks went by, its rapid growth was accompanied by a variety of problems. For instance, it required more and more food, and, having been reared on the leavings of every kitchen in Kalasanda, was inclined to
100 turn up its enormous snout at the idea of having to root in the shamba[2] whenever it felt like something to eat. Every time it started to kick its empty dish about noisily, pausing now and then to glare balefully at old Kibuka and utter snorts of **derision**, the old man was driven to taking up
105 his bucket and trudging forth to see if any scraps in the village had been overlooked.

derision
belittlement; ridicule

[2] shamba—a garden or field where food is grown

Kibuka's pig turned up its snout to rooting in the shamba for something to eat.

remorse

a strong feeling of sadness or guilt

Also, while Kibuka had at first secretly enjoyed the warmth of a cuddly little piglet lying across his feet each night, he found himself at a distinct disadvantage when 110 that same piglet acquired a bulk of some fifty or so pounds, and still insisted upon ponderously hoisting itself onto his bed as of right. Worse still, along with the weight, the piglet also produced a snore which regularly kept poor Kibuka awake until dawn. It was a grave decision he was finally 115 called upon to make, yet one on which he simply dare not waver: in future, the pig would have to stay outside, tethered to a tree.

Who suffered most, Kibuka or his pig, would be hard to tell, for the animal's lamentations, continuing throughout 120 the night, were equal in strength to the black **remorse** and wealth of recrimination churning in Kibuka's bosom. That pig never knew how often it was near to being brought indoors and pacified with a bowl of warm milk.

During the day it still was free to roam about until, 125 that is, it adopted the irritating habit of falling into the stream. There it would be, placidly ambling after Kibuka as he pottered in his small shamba, or gently napping in the shade of a coffee tree, and then, for no apparent reason, off it would go to the water's edge, and either fall or plunge in 130 before anybody could say "bacon."

The Kalasanda stream had no real depth; many Kalasandans often bathed there or waded in; but sometimes, after a drop or two of rain, the current had more strength, and was quite capable of sweeping a child off its feet. The 135 pig seemed always to choose such times for its immersion, and there wasn't anything anybody could really do as it spluttered and floundered with its hoofs flaying madly, and terror written plainly across its broad, black face.

At first, Kibuka would rush back and forth along the 140 bank, calling frantically in the hope that it would struggle towards him, but what usually happened in the end was that a particularly strong eddy would sweep it round the bend into a thicket of weeds and rushes, and then the children playing there would have a good half-hour's fun 145 driving it home.

This happened so often that Kibuka was forced to keep the pig tethered day and night. He visualized the time when no children would be playing in the reeds, and the pig would perhaps become entangled, dragged under and drowned.

150　　　By way of compensation he decided upon a regular evening walk for the animal, so by and by Kalasanda became accustomed to the sight of Kibuka, slight yet patriarchal in his kanzu and black waistcoat[3], sedately traversing the countryside with a huge black pig at the

155　end of a rope, and only strangers saw anything out of the ordinary in it. Without doubt, these walks were a source of great pleasure and exercise to the pig, who found them a wonderful change from the all too familiar view of Kibuka's shamba. Unfortunately, the same could not be

160　said of their effect on old Kibuka. To be frank, Kibuka's corns were killing him, and the excruciating pain of every step sometimes brought tears to his eyes. Still, he tried to bear his discomfort with **stoic** fortitude, for, as he said to Daudi Kulubya, who showed concern over his limp, it was

165　always the same before the heavy rains; in fact, his corns were as good as a barometer when it came to forecasting the weather. But he was always glad to return home, where he could sit for an hour with his poor feet in a bowl of hot water and try to keep his mind off the small fortune he

170　was spending on corn plasters brought to Kalasanda by the peddlers in the market.How long this state of affairs would have continued is anybody's guess. There were occasions when Kibuka actually entertained the notion of parting with his pet at the first good offer from a reputable farmer

175　or butcher. And yet, one trusting glance or look of affection from that waddling hunk of pork was enough for him to feel ashamed of what he regarded as his own **treachery**.

　　　The end came at last in the most unlikely manner. One minute there was Kibuka contemplating the sunset, and,

180　incidentally, giving his feet a rest by one of the obscure paths leading to the Sacred Tree, while the pig scratched happily at the root of a clump of shrubs, its head hidden by **foliage**, while its carcass, broadside on, barricaded

stoic
indifferent; showing little or no reaction

treachery
betrayal; disloyalty

foliage
the leaves of plants and trees

[3] kanzu and black waistcoat—a traditional long cotton garment and black vest worn by Bugandan males

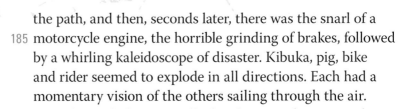

the path, and then, seconds later, there was the snarl of a
185 motorcycle engine, the horrible grinding of brakes, followed
by a whirling kaleidoscope of disaster. Kibuka, pig, bike
and rider seemed to explode in all directions. Each had a
momentary vision of the others sailing through the air.

When Kibuka eventually dared to open his eyes and
190 cautiously move each limb, he was relieved to find he was
still in one piece, although one shoulder felt painfully bruised
and there was blood on both his hands. The rider, whom he
now recognized as a certain Nathaniel Kiggundu, did not
appear to have fared very badly either. He was staggering
195 out of a tangled mass of weeds, wiping mud off his face, and
fingering a long tear in the knee of his trousers.

Somewhere from behind the hedge came the raucous
cries of a pig in distress, and it was in this direction that
both men headed, once they had regained their bearings.
200 They were only just in time to see the injured animal
give up the ghost and join its ancestors in that heavenly
piggery which surely must exist somewhere above. There
was scarcely a mark on it, but its head lay at a strange and
awkward angle, so it can be safely assumed that it died of a
205 broken neck.

Old Kibuka was terribly upset, and the accident had
left him in a generally shaky condition. He sat down
beside the dead animal and wondered what would happen
next. Nathaniel Kiggundu, however, seeing Kibuka was

210 comparatively unhurt, showed more concern over his
motorcycle, which lay grotesquely twisted in a ditch. The
inevitable crowd collected almost as soon as the pig
expired, so there was much coming and going, first to
stare at the fatal casualty, then to stare at the motorbike.

215 Nantondo kept up a running commentary, her version of
how the accident happened, although nobody believed she
had seen it, and by the time Musisi the Ggombolola Chief
arrived on the scene, she had fully adopted the role of
Mistress of Ceremonies.

220   After taking a statement from Kiggundu, Musisi
approached Kibuka and insisted upon taking him home in
the Landrover. "You don't look at all well, Sir. Come. You
can make your statement in the morning, when you have
had a rest."

225   "But I can't leave my pig here." Kibuka refused to budge
from the spot.

    "Well, I can put it in the back of the Landrover, if you
like. Only it would be better to have the butcher cut it
up, because I don't think pork will keep for long in this
230 weather."

    The idea of eating the pig had never entered Kibuka's
mind. While sitting beside the body, he had been seriously
considering just whereabouts in the shamba he could bury
it. Now he opened his mouth to tell Musisi in no uncertain
235 terms that eating one's good friends was a practice reserved
for barbarians; and then, he suddenly had a clear picture
of himself struggling to dig a grave. He was sure no
Kalasandans would want to help him do it. Then came
the realization of the effect a **perpetual** reminder of his
240 porking friend in his shamba would have on him. He did
not think he could stand it. Far better, indeed, to let the
past bury itself and, besides, why deprive his fellow villagers
of a tasty treat? They were, after all, the people who had
nourished the creature on their leftovers.

245   "Very well. Get somebody to carve it up and share it out
among the people who eat pork, and do be sure to send a
whole back leg up to the Mukasas," he said at last, suddenly
feeling too **weary** to care.

inevitable
certain; predictable

perpetual
continuing forever;
constant

weary
tired; fatigued

"Musa the butcher won't do it," Nantondo piped. "He's a
250 Muslim."

"Well, I'll take it along to the Ggombolola Headquarters
and ask one of the askaris[4] to carve it up. Anybody who
wants pork must go there at about seven o'clock tonight,"
declared Musisi, and ordered two of the onlookers to help
250 him lift the carcass into the back of his vehicle.

Back at his cottage, Kibuka rubbed his injured shoulder
with a concoction he used to cure most of his ailments, be
they loose bowels or a sore throat, and then sat brooding
over a cup of tea. He went to bed very early and awoke the
255 next day to find the sun well risen. He decided he had had
the best night's sleep he had enjoyed for many a month.
Musisi arrived as Kibuka was leaving home to see if the leg
of pork had been safely delivered to Yosefu and Miriamu.

"No, I'm taking the meat there now, Sir," Musisi said.
260 "Would you care to come with me?"

Kibuka gladly accepted the lift, although he declined
the lump of pork Musisi had brought for him, personally.
"You have it, son. I'm not a great lover of pork."

Miriamu went into raptures over the leg of pork, and
265 Yosefu showed the keenest interest in the details of the
accident. They pressed both Kibuka and Musisi to stay to
lunch, but Musisi had to leave to attend a committee meeting
in Mmengo, so only Kibuka remained. He and Yosefu, who
lately had not seen as much of each other as usual, had plenty
270 to discuss, and lunch was an exhilarating meal.

"I must say, you really are a wonderful cook!" Kibuka
told Miriamu, helping himself to more food. Miriamu
preened herself, shyly. "Well, that pork was as tender as a
chicken, and very tasty, too!"

dismay

shock; disappointment

275   There was a moment of **dismay** when Kibuka realized
he was eating and thoroughly enjoying the succulence
of his late friend, but it quickly passed, and he continued
piling his plate with meat, smiling to himself at the
knowledge that there would be no need to take a walk in
280 the late afternoon; he could have a good nap instead.

4 askaris—police officers

Reprinted from *Kalasanda Revisited* by Barbara Kimenye

Answer It

1. List some key details that describe the main character, Kibuka.

2. Contrast how Kibuka felt about keeping the young piglet with how he felt about having a full-grown pig.

3. As the story progresses, Kibuka begins to experience conflict as a result of keeping the pig. After reading lines 167–171, stop and predict what may happen next in the story to resolve the problem for Kibuka. Base your prediction on what has already happened in the story, as well as what you might logically expect as a reader.

4. Explain why you think Kibuka allowed Musisi to haul the pig off to Ggombolola Headquarters so that a butcher could carve the pig up.

5. Think about how Kibuka felt about his retirement at the beginning of the story. Infer how the experience of having the pig might have changed how Kibuka viewed retirement.

A REMARKABLE INDIVIDUAL

Erik learned later his summit date of June 27 was Helen Keller's birthday.

"I am only one, but still I am one.
I can not do everything, but still I can do something.
I will not refuse to do the something I can do."

—Helen Keller

5   *What would it feel like to stand atop the highest*
mountains of the world? While many aspire to reach such
heights, few actually go there. Climbers must endure bitter
cold, driving wind, treacherous terrain, and, in many cases,
limited oxygen in their quest to reach each summit. And
10 *after all the effort, the glory at the top is short. Often, there*
is only enough time to snap a few photos before beginning
the perilous trip down the mountain. Less than one hundred
mountaineers have climbed all of the Seven Summits,
which consists of the highest mountains on each of the seven
15 *continents. One of these individuals is Erik Weihenmayer.*
Weihenmayer shares the qualities of this elite group. He is
determined, tenacious, athletic, and remarkably courageous.
But one quality is his own. Weihenmayer is blind. He was
born with retinoschesis, a disorder that caused progressive
20 *degeneration of his retinas. His story is one of triumph*
against seemingly insurmountable circumstances.

Part I

By the fourth day at high camp, we were running out
of food and fuel. We only had three boxes of macaroni and

cheese and a pile of old frozen candy bars we had found
25 stashed in the igloo. The rest of our food was all the way
down at fourteen thousand feet. Lying in the tent next
to Sam, I could feel our opportunity, which was once so
boundless, slipping away like a puny dwindling stack of old
candy bars. "All this work, all our training," I said, "we're so
30 close, and we still may not summit." I couldn't get over this
conflict between my desire to summit and the cold reality
of the mountains. Over the last year, we had put in so much
effort, a part of me felt like it was our right to summit. All
the running, the stair climbing, the practice climbs, the
35 heavy-load carrying, had been a test which we had passed,
but on Denali[1], you could receive a perfect score and still
be turned back. Those who **imposed** their human rules
over the natural laws of the mountain were extremely
lucky if they lived to regret it. During our eighteen days on
40 McKinley, three climbers had died while trying to reach
the top. Just the day before, two climbers had left for the
summit with storm clouds above and went missing for
twenty-four hours. Few ever survived a night out on the
upper mountain, and the **consensus** at high camp was
45 that they were surely dead. Earlier this morning, however,
Chris spotted them, staggering down the snow slope above
the seventeen-thousand-foot basin; they would take a few
flailing steps, fall down, slide a ways, struggle up, and take
a few more steps. "Those two boys are the luckiest fools
50 alive," Chris said matter-of-factly. Miraculously, the two,
lost in a whiteout only a few hours from camp, stumbled
upon a snow cave, built by previous climbers, and had
hunkered inside through the night. Chris and Jeff helped
the two into their tent. While Jeff boiled water, Chris
55 pulled off their boots, socks, and gloves, assessing quickly
that they would both lose some toes and fingers.

 That night we were silent as we heard Base Camp
Annie, our only contact with the outside world, give the
weather report for the next day. It called for a brief break
60 in the storm before it resumed at full force. Chris turned

*Erik Weihenmayer
is one of a few
climbers to conquer
the Seven Summits.*

imposed
placed upon; forced

consensus
an agreement
reached among
members of a group

---

[1] Denali—the Athabascan name for Mount McKinley; the word means "high one."

20,320'

"This environment was both awe-inspiring and inhospitable, clearly unsuitable for the delicate flickering warmth of a human life."

to us and said firmly, "You don't decide when to climb a mountain. The mountain decides."

By the fifth day, however, Denali seemed to be showing its friendlier side. Miraculously the sky was clearer. 65 Lenticular clouds[2] hovered over the summit of Mount Foraker, but because we knew this might be our last shot, we decided to climb to as high as the saddle between the north and south summits, where we could reevaluate the weather. We left at six a.m., roped up into two teams and 70 waded through a field of thigh-deep snow. It was a struggle placing my feet in the deep boot holes that Chris had made. Many times I would miss them and begin veering to the left or right of the trail. This was a horribly inefficient use of energy and I knew that continuously breaking my own trail 75 above seventeen thousand feet would exhaust me quickly.

With my tight fleece hat and the thick elastic strap of my goggles over my ears, combined with the constant wind rolling down from the saddle, I was cut off from the outside world. The frigid stinging air even obliterated my sense 80 of smell. My many layers of fleece and GORE-TEX, three-layer mittens, and huge plastic boots protected me from the forty-below-zero temperature, and felt like a cocoon around me. This environment was both awe-inspiring and **inhospitable**, clearly unsuitable for the delicate flickering 85 warmth of a human life. Although Chris traveled only thirty feet in front of me and Sam thirty feet behind me, I felt as **solitary** as an astronaut exploring the landscape of the moon.

inhospitable

unfriendly; not welcoming

solitary

alone; lonely

2 lenticular clouds—lens-shaped clouds that form when stable moist air flows over a mountain

Next we reached the Autobahn, a steep **traverse**, which
90 led one thousand feet to the saddle. Climbers, constantly
surrounded by death, develop a sick sense of humor. The
Autobahn was named for the large number of German
parties who had pitched off the side of it to their deaths.
Another nearby section of the mountain was named The
95 Orient Express, for similar reasons. "We have to complete
the Autobahn in at least two hours," Chris said, "or it
means we're moving too slow." I tried to force my body to
move more quickly so we wouldn't have to turn around.
Internal monologues would continuously play in my head.
100 "Quit being a baby. You're not so tired. We'll rest in forty
minutes, tops." Eventually, after what seemed like hundreds
of pep talks, I stepped off the traverse onto a flatter section
and Chris told me that this was the saddle. We made it in
one hour and fifty minutes.

105   The weather seemed to be holding, so we made the
decision to keep going, traversing up an endlessly steep
slope, with the snow consolidated into glacier ice, hard
and windblown. With no boot holes to find and only the
repetitive consistency of my eight **crampon** points digging
110 and catching in the smooth hard ice, propelling my body
upward, I began to feel the rhythm of clean, pure, internal
movement. For the first time all morning, I dared to believe
we had a chance.

Finally we came out onto the Football Field, a large
115 gradual slope where nineteen days ago, our first on the
mountain, one of two Taiwanese climbers had died and been
buried somewhere nearby. "Not a place you want to get stuck

traverse
a crossing

crampon
an iron spike
attached to a boot

on," Chris warned. I forced myself to hurry past, fearing, with every step, that I was trespassing on top of his grave.

120   Next was Pig Hill, a six-hundred-foot headwall that was the last grunt before the summit ridge. As we began to climb, Sam, Chris, and I were no longer three individual climbers, but were roped together, moving up the slope like a slithering snake. Each of the parts worked, neither pulling
125 nor tugging, to move the unit forward. Then something very strange happened, something that has never happened to me since, while so near a summit; I began to feel stronger. Halfway up, Chris turned to me and paused for a few seconds. "I don't usually say this, Big E, because I don't
130 want to jinx anything, but I think we're gonna make it."

Think About It

1. The story's introduction gives reasons why mountain climbing is so difficult. Hypothesize how mountain climbing might be more dangerous for a blind climber.

2. Explain what Erik Weihenmayer means when he says ". . . on Denali, you could receive a perfect score and still be turned back." (lines 36–37)

3. After reading about the climbers who died or went missing, state your opinion on whether you believe Erik and his team should continue to reach the summit.

4. Tell why Erik feels solitary and isolated on the climb to the saddle.

5. On the climb up the Autobahn, Erik seems doubtful that they will be able to reach the summit. Locate two things that made him change his mind.

6. Contrast how Erik feels about his team on the climb up Pig Hill to how he felt towards them on the climb to the saddle.

A REMARKABLE INDIVIDUAL

Part II

When we crested Pig Hill, the summit seemed very
close, but I didn't realize the hardest part was yet to come.
Connecting Pig Hill to the summit was the summit ridge,
just a quarter mile long, but only two feet wide, with a
5 thousand-foot drop on one side and a nine-thousand-foot
drop on the other. The good news in this bleak scenario
was that, if I fell, it really wouldn't matter which side it was
off of. Before the ridge Chris huddled us around him and
spoke, his voice unusually calm. "Boys, listen carefully. If
10 you fall here, we all fall. You'll drag us all off the side of
the mountain. So, if I haven't explained myself plainly," he
leaned in toward us as his voice gained momentum, "what
I'm telling you boys is . . . DON'T FALL!" I was nervous,
taking each step slowly and carefully. In my life off the
15 mountain, I could stumble and fall and get up again, but
I knew, on the ridge, the mountain wouldn't tolerate a
mistake. Then I leaned on my pole and it must have been
too close to the edge. The snow gave way under the weight,
and I felt myself sway forward over the side. I quickly
20 recovered and stepped back. "Test it first before you weight
it," Chris yelled, his gruff voice masking his nervousness.

I found my confidence again and slowly placed each
step, testing each by gradually weighting my front foot
while keeping tension on my back leg. After every step,

bearings

position

25 I'd keep my **bearings** by tapping my ice ax against the left edge of the ridge, sliding the tip several inches inward across the slope until it bit firm solid snow, and finally plunging it in. My other hand used my pole to scan for boot holes and monitor the right edge. All my preparation,
30 all my skills seemed to gather together into this moment. The process of scanning, stepping, and breathing was all-consuming, so that the extent of my life was reduced to moving slowly and rhythmically up the narrow ridge, as if there had never been anything more than the tug of the
35 rope, my raw amplified breathing, and the careful crisp bite of my equipment in the firm snow. How beautiful it was in

severity

seriousness;
intensity

its **severity**, my whole being totally consolidated into one purpose. Step. Breathe, breathe, breathe. Step.

I was concentrating so fully, Chris's voice, right in front
40 of me, yelling over the wind, seemed to emerge as if I were waking from a dream. "Congratulations, you're standing on the top of North America." It seems strange that the last step felt no different from the thousands and thousands of previous steps I had taken in the last nineteen days. It was
45 just another step, and then I was there.

Immediately I sat down in the snow, suffering from a gurgling high-altitude cough. Then Sam was next to me. "We're not quite there yet, Big E," he said.

"You're joking," I begged. But before I could protest,
50 everybody's arms were around me and I was being guided up a little embankment. I could hear their breathing and their GORE-TEX crackling in the wind. We all stood as a team on the three-foot-by-three-foot mound of snow, which

marked the true summit of McKinley. Sadly, though, I
55 could feel Ryan's absence, and I reached into my shirt and
felt his HighSights cross warm against my skin[1]. Then we
unfurled the American Foundation for the Blind flag and
posed for a few glory shots[2].

As the last photo clicked, I heard the tiny mechanical
60 buzz of the Cessna plane circling above. An hour before
summitting, we had radioed down to Base Camp Annie,
who radioed out to a small airstrip in Talkeetna where
my family waited. Now as I stood on the top, my dad, my
two brothers, and Ellen[3] were circling above me, sharing
65 in this exhilarating moment. It was strange, knowing that
they were only a few hundred yards away, yet I couldn't
touch them or hear their voices. Later I learned that Mark[4]
had spotted us first, tiny red dots moving slowly against
infinite white. He lifted his oxygen mask for a moment and
70 tapped Ellie. "There they are!" he said, his words trembling
with excitement and vibrating with the plane's engine.
"There they are, Ellie!" Ellie was so nervous for us, she only
managed a nod, the tears spilling down her face as she
peered through the window.
75 My team all wore identical red GORE-TEX shells. And
with our hats and goggles covering our faces, we were
indistinguishable. As the plane swooped by, we all waved
our ski poles and cheered. Then I asked Sam if he thought

"Before the ridge, Chris huddled us around him and spoke, his voice unusually calm. 'Boys, listen carefully. If you fall here, we all fall.'"

indistinguishable
alike; impossible to tell apart

[1] A member of the climbing team, Ryan, had to descend early in the expedition due to unexpected symptoms of a heart condition. He gave Erik a cross, his good luck charm to carry to the summit.

[2] When Erik returned home, he learned that his summit date of June 27 was, in fact, Helen Keller's birthday.

[3] Ellen is Erik's wife.

[4] Mark is Erik's brother.

my family would know which one was me. "I think they
80 will," he laughed. "You're the only one waving your ski pole
in the wrong direction."

Chris's voice was still on edge when he cut into our
celebration. "The weather's changing, boys, and we need
to move. The summit's only the halfway point." My thirty
85 seconds of carefree exhilaration were over. The others
were still hugging and shouting, ice axes drawn toward
the sky. I stood aside from the celebration, a flash of panic
shooting through me like a lightning bolt. You've gotten
up here. Great. Now what do you do? I thought. How do
90 you get down? How will you get down the ridge? Tripping
on a crampon strap or losing my balance on the way up
would probably mean falling into the slope, but falling on
the way down would mean a nine-thousand-foot head-over-
heels tumble, my entire rope team dragging along behind
95 me. As I thought of that gruesome image, tears formed in
my eyes and immediately froze to my eyelashes. Then Jeff
noticed how quiet I was and asked me what was wrong.
"I'm worried about getting down the ridge," I said. "I'm
worried I'll do something stupid." Then everyone gathered
100 around me, putting their hands on my shoulders. "We'll
get down," Chris said, and something in his voice made me
believe him instantly. The concentration game began again
and I carefully lowered each foot into the frozen boot holes
in front of me, knowing that all of our lives depended on an

terrain
land; landscape

105 action so seemingly simple. The **terrain** began to flatten
out, bringing me out of my trance. "How much farther until
the end of the ridge?" I asked Chris. "Boy, you passed the
ridge twenty minutes ago," he answered.

Six hours later we stumbled across the seventeen-
110 thousand-foot basin at the foot of the Autobahn. I tripped
in one of the deep boot holes and fell face-first in the
snow. Knowing we were so close to camp, I just lay there
moaning and laughing. Jeff and Sam followed my lead,
collapsing in the snow as well. We were all moaning and

pathetic
pitiful; not worthy
of respect

115 calling out in **pathetic** voices, "Chris, help us up. We can't
go any farther. Chris, you're my hero." Chris, knowing we
were out of danger, and feeling somehow relieved from

the responsibility of leading, untied himself from the rope and raced energetically toward camp as if he had forgotten 120 the fifteen hours of constant movement. "You boys are the sorriest excuse for climbers that I've ever seen," he yelled as he motored away. Twenty minutes later we staggered into camp. I lay on my belly in the snow, my body beyond exhaustion, not even feeling the temperature that had 125 dropped forty degrees in the last hour.

Later, sitting in the igloo around a pot of freeze-dried spaghetti, Chris loaded our bowls. "Gotta eat," he said. "We've got a death march in the morning." As I piled the last spoonful into my mouth, my wasted body rejected it 130 and I gave the whole meal back to the mountain gods. It lay in a pile in front of the entranceway, quickly freezing into a rock-hard mound in the snow. "Chris, I'm sorry," I said. "First you drag me to the top and then I throw up in your igloo." Chris was silent, sitting a few feet across from me. 135 Then he spoke as if he hadn't heard me. "You're all right, Big E." Then Chris reached across the igloo and slapped his gloved hand against my shoulder. "Anyone," he said, "who stands on the top of North America, I'll crawl through his puke any day."

140 Chris dropped into the doorway and was gone. Then I was alone, the events of the day flooding into my tired brain. The igloo walls enveloped me in a muffled silence, and a feeling of such **intensity** swept over me that I could

"I had never known, never truly known, that this awesome place could exist inside me."

intensity

exceptionally great force or power

feel my body shaking. I had only stood on the summit for a
145 few minutes, but the experience had forged itself into me,
more powerful than any memory, fusing so tight that it
was impossible to distinguish me from it. I could still feel
the blasting wind, the storms, and the staggeringly long
days. I could feel it all, from the bumpy plane ride in, to the
150 immense openness of the summit, and it was all within me,
changing my life forever, no longer a dream but flesh and
bone and blood. I had never known, never truly known,
that this awesome place could exist inside me.

Adapted from *Touch the Top of the World: A Blind Man's Journey
to Climb Farther Than the Eye Can See* by Erik Weihenmayer,
www.touchthetop.com

Think About It

1. Erik has trouble climbing the summit ridge. Judge whether Erik would have had difficulty climbing the ridge had he not been blind.

2. Summarize the reasons for Erik's mixed feelings of joy and sadness upon reaching the summit.

3. Erik reached the summit of Mt. McKinley on Helen Keller's birthday. How are Erik and Helen alike?

4. Describe Erik's reaction to Chris's announcement that the team must head back down the mountain.

5. Contrast Chris's attitude toward Erik and the team at the beginning of the passage and his attitude at the end of the passage.

6. Reread the quotation by Erik Weihenmayer at the end of the selection. (lines 154–164) Paraphrase what Weihenmayer believes a summit symbolizes and assess the value of this image.

"But a summit is so much more than the view. I may
155 be biased, but when people say they summit mountains for
the view, I don't believe them. No one suffers the way one
does on a mountain simply for a beautiful view. A summit
isn't just a place on a mountain. A summit exists in our
hearts and minds. It is a tiny scrap of a dream made real,
160 indisputable proof that our lives have meaning. A summit
is a symbol that with the force of our will and the power of
our legs, our backs, and our two hands, we can transform
our lives into whatever we choose them to be, whatever our
hands are strong enough to create."   by Erik Weihenmayer

*Erik went on to climb the Seven Summits, the highest mountains
on each continent in the world.*

Hike High
by Jorge Arguello and Janan Young

165 We hike Round Mountain.
Brown flowers. Scat. Meandering air.

The place where escaped helium balloons
from carnivals and car dealerships land.

The Manzanita grows so thick
170 boundaries disappear.

We can't pass in some places.
So we take the deer and coyote

trails, the path of life, of love.
The pines are Dr. Seussian

175 and move musically, waving
to the caravanserai of clouds.

Appendix

English Consonant Chart

(Note the voiceless/voiced consonant phoneme pairs)

Mouth Position

Type of Consonant Sound	Bilabial (lips)	Labiodental (lips/teeth)	Dental (tongue between teeth)	Alveolar (tongue behind teeth)	Palatal (roof of mouth)	Velar (back of mouth)	Glottal (throat)
Stops	/p/ /b/			/t/ /d/		/k/ /g/	
Fricatives		/f/ /v/	/th/ /t͟h/	/s/ /z/	/sh/ /zh/		/h/[1]
Affricatives					/ch/ /j/		
Nasals	/m/			/n/		/ng/	
Lateral				/l/			
Semivowels	/ʰw/ /w/[2]			/r/	/y/		

1   Classed as a fricative on the basis of acoustic effect. It is like a vowel without voice.

2   /ʰw/ and /w/ are velar as well as bilabial, as the back of the tongue is raised as it is for /u/.

Adapted with permission from Bolinger, D. 1975. *Aspects of Language* (2nd ed.). Harcourt Brace Jovanovich, p. 41.

English Vowel Chart

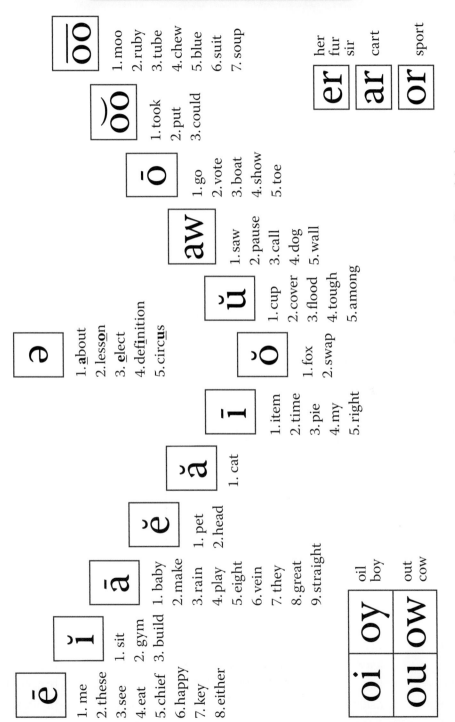

ē
1. me
2. these
3. see
4. eat
5. chief
6. happy
7. key
8. either

ĭ
1. sit
2. gym
3. build

ā
1. baby
2. make
3. rain
4. play
5. eight
6. vein
7. they
8. great
9. straight

ĕ
1. pet
2. head

ə
1. about
2. lesson
3. elect
4. definition
5. circus

ă
1. cat

ī
1. item
2. time
3. pie
4. my
5. right

ŭ
1. cup
2. cover
3. flood
4. tough
5. among

ŏ
1. fox
2. swap

aw
1. saw
2. pause
3. call
4. dog
5. wall

ō
1. go
2. vote
3. boat
4. show
5. toe

o͝o
1. took
2. put
3. could

o͞o
1. moo
2. ruby
3. tube
4. chew
5. blue
6. suit
7. soup

oi oil
oy boy
ou out
ow cow

er her, fur, sir
ar cart
or sport

Note: The order of spelling examples reflects the relative frequency of incidence for that spelling of the phoneme.

Vowel Chart based on Moats, L.C. (2003). *LETRS: Language Essentials for Teachers of Reading and Spelling,* Module 2 (p. 98). Adapted with permission of the author. All rights reserved. Published by Sopris West Educational Services.

Word List: Unit Vocabulary, Essential Words, and Bonus Words

abbey	always	asphalt	balance	bluebird
abbot	ambitious	assiduous	bald	blueblood
absence	amiable	associate	balk	blueprint
accentuate	amino	atrium	ball	boo
access	amnesia	auburn	balloon	book
accident	amphibian	auction	ballpark	bookends
ache	amphitheater	audacious	ballroom	bookkeeper
acid	ampoule	audio	balsam	booklet
acoustic	analogy	augment	bamboo	bookmark
actually	anchor	aunt	bamboozle	bookstore
adage	anesthesia	auspicious	bankbook	boom
adjacent	anew	authentic	barbarian	boomerang
admiral	angel	author	barge	boost
adolescence	anticipate	autism	bark	boot
adulate	antique	autobiography	baroque	booth
advice	anxious	autograph	bassoon	bootstrap
afternoon	apologize	automate	bathroom	botulism
afterward	appall	automatic	baulk	bought
age	applaud	automobile	bawl	boulder
agile	applause	autopsy	because	bounce
algebra	appreciate	avenue	befall	bouquet
all	aquarium	average	beguile	boutique
allegro	archaic	award	behalf	brace
almanac	architect	awash	beneficial	brainwash
aloof	arduous	awful	beret	bravo
alpha	argue	awkward	bibliography	bridegroom
alphabet	armada	awning	bicycle	bridge
already	arrange	aye-aye	billion	broad
also	arsenal	baboon	biography	broccoli
alter	artesian	backward	blew	brood
altercate	artificial	backwash	bloom	brook
alternate	ascertain	backwater	blooper	broom
alternative	ascetic	badge	blue	broomstick
altogether	askew	baggage	bluebell	brought

bruise	century	civil	cookbook	dawn
brusque	ceremony	civilize	cookery	debris
budge	chalet	clause	cookie	deceive
budget	chalk	claw	cool	decide
bylaw	challenge	clique	coolant	decided
cabaret	chance	clue	coop	deciduous
cabbage	change	cobalt	cork	decimal
caboose	chaos	coeducation	corkscrew	decipher
cacophony	charge	coffee	cottage	default
cage	chasm	coincide	cotton	deferential
call	checkbook	coleslaw	cougar	delicious
calligraphy	chemical	college	coupon	dementia
capacity	chemist	commence	courier	descend
capitulate	chemistry	commerce	crawl	desperado
capricious	chew	commercial	credulous	detergent
caramel	childhood	complexion	crescent	detour
carpool	childproof	conceive	crestfallen	deuce
carriage	chili	concentrate	crew	device
cartoon	chloride	concept	critique	dew
cashew	cholera	conceptualize	crook	diagnostician
catastrophe	cholesterol	conch	crooked	dice
caucus	choose	conditions	croon	difference
caught	chord	confetti	croquet	differential
cauliflower	chorus	confidence	crosswalk	differentiate
caulk	chrome	confidential	croup	digraph
cause	chromium	congratulate	crucial	dimension
caustic	chromosome	conscience	cruise	diphthong
caution	chronic	conscious	curfew	discern
cautious	chrysalis	consequential	currency	discipline
cease	cipher	constituent	cycle	disguise
celebrate	circle	continue	damage	dishwasher
cellophane	circumstance	continued	dance	displace
cells	circumstantial	contour	danger	distance
cent	circus	convey	darkroom	dodge
center	cite	convince	daunt	dolphin
cents	city	cook	dawdle	doom

drama	especially	few	gaunt	guidance
draw	essence	fictitious	gauze	guide
drawback	essential	fidget	gender	guidebook
drawer	eucalyptus	finance	general	guideline
drawing	eulogy	fireproof	generate	guile
drawl	eureka	fishhook	generous	guise
drew	ewe	flaunt	gentle	gum
drool	exalt	flaw	geography	gym
droop	exceed	flew	geranium	gymnasium
due	excellent	flexion	giant	hacksaw
dyspepsia	except	floorwalker	giraffe	hall
echo	excess	fluctuate	glacier	hallway
edge	exciting	fluxion	glance	halt
educate	exercise	food	gloom	halter
education	exhaust	fool	glue	handball
efficient	explicit	foolery	good	haul
either	exterior	foolhardy	goodbye	haunt
electrician	eyetooth	foolproof	goody-goody	hawk
electricity	face	foot	goose	hazard
elephant	facetious	football	gooseberry	headphones
elicit	facial	foothill	gooseneck	hedge
emerge	facilitate	force	gorilla	hence
emphasis	fall	forewarn	goulash	hey
emphasize	fallback	fortune	gourmet	hierarchy
enchilada	false	forward	grace	hogwash
encyclopedia	falsehood	four	graduate	hood
energy	falsify	framework	graffiti	hoodwink
enforce	falter	fraud	grapefruit	hoof
engine	fancy	fraudulent	graph	hook
enhance	fantasia	freshwater	graphite	hoot
enough	father	fruit	grew	huge
ensue	faucet	fudge	grey	hydraulic
enthrall	fault	futuristic	groove	hyphen
epitaph	fence	gadget	grotesque	ice
equable	ferocious	gall	group	ideology
especial	feud	gasoline	grouper	igloo

ignorance
illicit
image
imagine
imbalance
impatient
impetuous
implausible
implicit
incandescent
incentive
incidence
incite
incredulity
incredulous
individual
inefficient
inertia
infatuate
infectious
initial
initiate
in-law
install
instance
insufficient
intelligence
international
inward
jar
jaw
jaywalk
jaywalker
jewel
jigsaw
judge

judicial
juice
kangaroo
kilowatt
lagoon
landfall
large
launch
launder
laundry
law
lawbreaker
lawn
lawsuit
lawyer
ledge
legislate
lei
lettuce
leukemia
leukocyte
license
liter
llama
lodge
lodging
logic
look
lookout
loop
loophole
loose
lose
lotion
louver
luggage

lymph
macaroni
machine
magazine
magic
magnesia
malaria
mall
malt
manage
maneuver
margin
marine
marriage
mask
masquerade
mathematician
mattress
maudlin
mechanic
mechanism
media
median
medicine
medium
megawatt
melancholy
menial
mercy
message
metaphor
mew
mezzanine
microphone
mildew
million

mirror
miscellaneous
misfortune
misguide
modulate
module
mongoose
monkey
moo
moon
moose
morpheme
mothball
mould
mountain
mousse
move
movement
movie
mummy
muscle
mushroom
musician
muslin
mystique
nation
naturalize
negotiate
neither
nephew
network
neuritis
neurology
neuron
neurosis
neurotic

neuter
neutralize
neutron
new
newborn
newcomer
news
newscast
newspaper
newsprint
nice
niece
nodule
noodle
noon
notebook
notice
notion
nougat
noxious
nudge
nutritious
nymph
obey
obnoxious
office
official
oh
omniscient
onward
opaque
opinion
orange
orchestra
origin
orphan

ostentatious
outlaw
outmaneuver
outward
overall
overanxious
overdraw
overdue
overhaul
oxygen
page
palace
pall
palsy
paltry
pamphlet
paratroop
parcel
parley
partial
participate
passage
patient
patio
patriotic
pause
paw
pawn
peace
pencil
pendulum
perceive
percent
periphery
pernicious
perpetuate

pewter
phantom
pharmacy
phase
phenomenon
philosophy
phobia
phone
phoneme
phonetics
phonics
phonograph
phony
phosphate
photo
photograph
phrase
physical
piano
picturesque
piece
pigeon
piñata
pitfall
pizza
place
plausible
plaza
pledge
pleurisy
police
policy
politician
pontoon
poodle
pool

posterior
potential
poultry
practice
practitioner
pratfall
precaution
precede
precious
precise
preferential
prejudice
presidential
presumptuous
pretentious
prey
price
prince
principal
principle
proceed
process
produce
proficient
pronounce
proof
proofread
prophet
protein
prove
provincial
punctuate
pursue
quad
quadrangle
quadraphonic

quadriceps
quadrilateral
quadruple
quaff
qualify
qualitative
quality
quandary
quantify
quantity
quantum
quarantine
quark
quarrel
quarry
quart
quarterback
quarterly
quartz
quatrain
questions
quotient
raccoon
race
racial
racket
radio
radius
range
rational
raucous
ravine
raw
recall
receive
received

recoup
recruit
regime
region
register
rein
reindeer
reinforce
rejoice
religion
reluctance
renew
repetitious
replace
reproduce
rescue
residential
residue
resource
restaurant
revenge
revenue
reward
rice
ridge
rigid
romance
roof
room
roommate
roost
root
rough
roughage
roughhouse
route

routine	scrawny	slough	squab	substantial
sack	screw	sludge	squabble	substantiate
sacrifice	screwdriver	small	squad	successor
salsa	scythe	smallpox	squadron	suede
salt	seawall	smooth	squalid	sufficient
saltbox	seesaw	smoulder	squall	suggest
saltine	seize	smudge	squalor	suggested
saltshaker	sentence	so-called	squander	suit
saltwater	sequence	social	squash	suitcase
satin	sequential	soda	squat	superficial
saturate	sequin	sofa	squawk	superior
sauce	serial	solace	stadium	superstitious
saucer	sew	soon	stage	surface
sausage	shampoo	sophomore	stalk	surgeon
sauté	shawl	soufflé	stall	surveillance
saw	shepherd	soul	statue	survey
sawdust	sherbet	soup	statute	suspicion
sawhorse	sheriff	source	stenographer	suspicious
sawmill	shoes	southpaw	steward	swab
saxophone	shook	space	stomach	swallow
scald	shoot	spacious	stonewall	swamp
scene	shortfall	spaghetti	stood	swan
scenery	shoulder	spatial	stool	swarm
scent	shrewd	spatula	stoop	swarthy
schedule	sidewalk	spawn	straight	swashbuckler
schematic	silence	special	strange	swat
scheme	since	specific	strategy	swatch
scholar	siphon	specify	straw	symphony
scholastic	situate	spew	strew	syrup
school	skein	sphinx	studio	tablespoon
science	skew	sponge	subconscious	taboo
scientists	skywalk	spoof	subdue	taco
scissors	slaw	spook	subgroup	talk
scoff	sleepwalk	spool	submarine	tall
scoop	sleuth	spoon	substance	tarantula
scrawl	slice	sprawl	substances	tattoo

taunt	tragic	village	warp	workshop
taut	transfixion	virtual	warrant	world
taxi	trauma	virtuoso	wart	worldwide
teaspoon	trio	virtuous	wash	worm
technical	triumph	voice	washcloth	worry
technician	troop	voyage	wasp	worrywart
technique	trophy	waffle	watch	worse
technology	troupe	walk	watchdog	worship
teenager	trudge	walkie-talkie	watchmaker	worst
telegraph	true	walkout	watchman	worth
telephone	tumultuous	walkover	water	worthwhile
textbook	tycoon	walkup	watt	wound
thaw	typhoon	walkway	wattle	yawn
they	typhus	wall	wedge	you
threw	unconscious	wallaby	whey	youth
thwart	undergraduate	wallet	whitewash	zebra
too	underworld	walleye	whole	zero
took	undue	wallflower	whom	zoo
tool	undulate	wallow	whose	zookeeper
tools	unfortunate	walnut	windfall	
toot	union	walrus	wishy-washy	
tooth	unique	waltz	withdraw	
toothbrush	unveil	wan	wolf	
toothpaste	uproot	wand	wood	
toothpick	urge	wander	woodcutter	
topography	valet	wanderlust	woodland	
torrential	value	want	woodpecker	
toucan	vault	war	woof	
tough	vegetable	warble	wool	
toughen	veil	warbler	word	
tour	vein	warden	work	
tournament	velour	wardrobe	workbook	
tourney	via	warm	workers	
tourniquet	vicious	warm-blooded	workmanship	
trace	view	warn	workroom	

LANGUAGE! Pronunciation Key

Consonants

p	**p**u**p**, ra**pp**ed, **p**ie	zh	vi**si**on, trea**s**ure, a**z**ure
b	**b**o**b**, e**bb**, **b**rother	h	**h**at, **h**ere, **h**ope
t	**t**ire, jump**ed**, hur**t**	ch	**ch**ur**ch**, ma**tch**, bea**ch**
d	**d**ee**d**, ma**d**, file**d**	j	**j**u**dg**e, en**j**oy, **j**ell
k	**c**at, **k**ick, **c**ut	m	**m**op
g	**g**et, **g**ill, ma**g**azine	n	**n**ot
f	**f**lu**ff**, rou**gh**, **ph**oto	ng	si**ng**
v	**v**al**v**e, e**v**ery, ele**v**en	l	**l**and
th	**th**in, **th**ree, ma**th**		
<u>th</u>	**th**is, **th**ere, mo**th**er	w	**w**ith, **w**agon, **w**est
s	**s**od, **c**ity, li**s**t	r	**r**amp
z	**z**ebra, ha**s**, bee**s**	y	**y**ard, **y**es, **y**ellow
sh	**sh**ip, **s**ugar, ma**ch**ine		

Vowels

ē	b**ee**t	(bēt)	ō	b**oa**t	(bōt)
ĭ	b**i**t	(bĭt)	o͝o	p**u**t	(po͝ot)
ā	b**ai**t	(bāt)	o͞o	b**oo**t	(bo͞ot)
ĕ	b**e**t	(bĕt)	oi	b**oi**l	(boil)
ă	b**a**t	(băt)	ou	p**ou**t	(pout)
ī	b**i**te	(bīt)	î	p**ee**r	(pîr)
ŏ	p**o**t	(pŏt)	â	b**ea**r	(bâr)
ô	b**ou**ght	(bôt)	ä	p**a**r	(pär)
ŭ	b**u**t	(bŭt)	ô	b**o**re	(bôr)
ə	r**a**bb**i**t	(ră' bət)	û	p**ea**rl	(pûrl)

The definitions that accompany the readings relate to the context of the readings. They are provided to help students understand the specific reading selection. For complete definitions of these words, consult a dictionary. Pronunciations are taken from the *American Heritage® Dictionary of the English Language*, Fourth Edition.

abolitionists (ăb'ə-lĭsh'ə-nĭs)—reformers who wanted to end slavery

ache (āk)—a dull, lasting pain

adversaries (ăd'vər-sĕr'ēz)—opponents; foes

advocate (ăd'və-kāt')—support an idea

aesthetics (ĕs-thĕt'ĭks)—artistically beautiful or pleasing appearance

aglow (ə-glō')—delighted; radiating excitement

agony (ăg'ə-nē)—great pain

akin (ə-kĭn')—like; similar to

arc (ärk)—a curved line

ashamed (ə-shāmd')—embarrassed

assistance (ə-sĭs'təns)—aid; help in doing something

assured (ə-shoŏrd')—guaranteed; certain

attic (ăt'ĭk)—a space under the roof of a house

auspiciously (ô-spĭsh'əs-lē)—favorably

awe (ô)—a feeling of great admiration or respect

barrage (bə-räzh')—a heavy outpouring

bearings (bâr'ĭngz)—position

beckon (bĕk'ən)—motion or signal to

belie (bĭ-lī')—misrepresent; picture falsely

benefactor (bĕn'ə-făk'tər)—a donor; person who gives something to another

bewilderment (bĭ-wĭl'dər-mənt)—confusion; puzzlement

bore (bôr)—endured with tolerance and patience

brazen (brā'zən)—shocking and annoying

captivity (kăp-tĭv'ĭ-tē)—confinement

central (sĕn'trəl)—in the center; in the middle of

clamor (klăm'ər)—a loud, noisy outcry

clique (klēk)—group of people who keep others out

colliding (kə-līd'ĭng)—crashing; hitting against something with force

concentric (kən-sĕn'trĭk)—having a common center

condescending (kŏn'dĭ-sĕnd'ĭng)—disdainful; patronizing

consensus (kən-sĕn'səs)—an agreement reached among members of a group

consolation (kŏn'sə-lā'shən)—comfort; reassurance

convergence (kən-vûr'jəns)—a process of coming together

convey (kən-vā')—to express; carry

crampon (krăm'pŏn')—an iron spike attached to a boot

cunning (kŭn'ĭng)—careful deception; shrewdness

dangling (dăng'glĭng)—hanging uncertainly; remaining unresolved

deprived (dǐ-prīvd')—denied; kept from having

derision (dǐ-rǐzh'ən)—belittling; ridicule

devoured (dǐ-vourd')—ate up greedily

diminishes (dǐ-mǐn'ǐsh-ǐz)—decreases; lessens

din (dǐn)—a loud, persistent noise

discoloured (dǐs-kǔl'ərd)—changed or spoiled in color; stained

dismay (dǐs-mā')—shock; disappointment

disparity (dǐ-spǎr'ǐ-tē)—difference; inequality

dispelled (dǐ-spěld')—caused to go away

distorted (dǐ-stôrt'ǐd)—twisted; bent out of shape

distributed (dǐ-strǐb'yoot-ǐd)—spread out

dominates (dǒm'ə-nāts')—stands out with a decidedly superior position

emancipated (ǐ-mǎn'sə-pāt'ǐd)—freed; liberated

embraced (ěm-brāst')—hugged

emphasis (ěm'fə-sǐs)—stress; special importance

energy-efficient (ěn'ər-jē ǐ-fǐsh'ənt)—designed to conserve energy

enfranchised (ěn-frǎn'chīzd')—provided with rights, especially the right to vote

enhance (ěn-hǎns')—to improve; add to

entangled (ěn-tǎng'gəld)—caught; intertwined

evading (ǐ-vād'ǐng)—avoiding; dodging

exiles (ěg'zīlz')—deportees; refugees

faint (fānt)—unclear; weak

fidgeting (fǐj'ǐt-ǐng)—moving in a nervous fashion

flout (flout)—to mock; make fun of

foliage (fō'lē-ǐj)—the leaves of plants and trees

frequently (frē'kwənt-lē)—often

gain (gān)—to acquire; increase

gaping (gā'pǐng)—opening wide

genteel (jěn-tēl')—politeness traditionally associated with wealth and education

heighten (hīt'n)—intensify; increase

humility (hyoo-mǐl'ǐ-tē)—meekness; modesty

idealists (ī-dē'ə-lǐs)—people guided more by ideals than by practical considerations

imperiously (ǐm-pîr'ē-əs-lē)—arrogantly; in an overbearing manner

imposed (ǐm-pōzd')—placed upon; forced

incorporates (ǐn-kôr'pə-rāts')—includes, contains

indistinguishable (ǐn'dǐ-stǐng'gwǐ-shə-bəl)—alike; impossible to tell apart

inevitable (ǐn-ěv'ǐ-tə-bəl)—certain; predictable

inhospitable (ǐn-hǒs'pǐ-tə-bəl)—unfriendly; not welcoming

innovative (ǐn'ə-vā'tǐv)—original; ahead of the times

intensity (ǐn-těn'sǐ-tē)—exceptionally great force or power

intuitive (ǐn-too-'ǐ-tǐv)—related to feeling, not learned knowledge

justice (jǔs'tǐs)—a judge

keen (kēn)—splendid; fine

languid (lăng'gwĭd)—listless; lacking energy

languished (lăng'gwĭsht)—became downcast; pined

lax (lăks)—careless; lenient

lopsided (lŏp'sī'dĭd)—sagging; leaning to one side

malice (măl'ĭs)—in a manner to cause intentional harm

massive (măs'ĭv)—huge; great

medium (mē'dē-əm)—a specific artistic technique

mingle (mĭng'gəl)—move around in a group of people; mix

monolith (mŏn'ə-lĭth')—a very large block of stone that stands alone

morality (mə-răl'ĭ-tē)—standards; ideas about right and wrong

mortification (môr'tə-fĭ-kā'shən)—shame; embarrassment

multinational (mŭl'tē-năsh'ə-nəl)—involving more than two countries

panorama (păn'ə-răm'ə)—a large, open view of a wide area

pathetic (pə-thĕt'ĭk)—pitiful; not worthy of respect

pension (pĕn'shən)—a regular payment made by a business or government to a retired person

pensively (pĕn'sĭv-lē)—thoughtfully

perpetual (pər-pĕch'ōō-əl)—continuing forever; constant

porch (pôrch)—a covered structure outside the entrance to a house

primordial (prī-môr'dē-əl)—basic; connected with an early stage of development

profound (prə-found')—intellectually deep; insightful

prominence (prŏm'ə-nəns)—renown; fame

proponents (prə-pō'nənts)—supporters

prostheses (prŏs-thē'sēz)—artificial limbs

provocation (prŏv'ə-kā'shən)—a reason to protest or fight

rate (rāt)—a cost of something; amount

reconciled (rĕk'ən-sīld')—prepared to accept; adjusted to something difficult

regular (rĕg'yə-lər)—having fixed intervals; consistent

remorse (rĭ-môrs')—a strong feeling of sadness or guilt

remote (rĭ-mōt')—far-away; distant

restrained (rĭ-strānd')—stopped from moving freely

retort (rĭ-tôrt')—a quick reply or answer

salient (sā'lē-ənt)—most obvious or noticeable

scenario (sĭ-nâr'ē-ō')—a description of events

second generation (sĕk'ənd jĕn'ə-rā'shən)—person whose parents are immigrants

segments (sĕg'mənts)—sections; separate pieces

self-reliant (sĕlf' rĭ-lī'ənt)—independent; able to take care of oneself

severity (sə-vĕr'ĭ-tē)—seriousness; intensity

shabby (shăb'ē)—worn; threadbare

shield (shēld)—protect with a physical barrier

solitary (sŏl'ĭ-tĕr'ē)—alone; lonely

sordid (sôr'dĭd)—wretched; shameful

sparingly (spâr'ĭng-lē)—in a limited manner

standard (stăn'dərd)—commonly accepted as normal; usual

stoic (stō'ĭk)—indifferent; showing little or no reaction

suffrage (sŭf'rĭj)—the right or privilege of voting

tactics (tăk'tĭks)—plans; strategies

tangible (tăn'jə-bəl)—touchable, real

temporary (tĕm'pə-rĕr'ē)—for a limited time; short-term

terrain (tə-rān')—land; landscape

titans (tīt'nz)—powerful companies and those who run them

tones (tōnz)—sounds

traverse (trə-vûrs')—crossing

treachery (trĕch'ə-rē)—betrayal; disloyalty

triumphant (trī-ŭm'fənt)—victorious; conquering

truce (trōōs)—a temporary stopping of hostilities; respite

valid (văl'ĭd)—convincing; sound

variations (vâr'ē-ā'shənz)—types; kinds

vibrant (vī'brənt)—intense; colorful

vigil (vĭj'əl)—a period of waiting

weary (wîr'ē)—tired; fatigued

whim (hwĭm)—a sudden idea or desire

wistfully (wĭst'fəl-lē)—pensively; with wishful desire

writhe (rīth)—twist and turn

Prefixes, Roots, and Suffixes

Prefixes, Roots, and Suffixes (Units 13–30)

Prefix	Meanings	Examples
ad-	toward; to; near; in	addict, adjust, adverse
anti-	opposite; against	antifreeze, anitperspirant, antitrust
con-	with, together	conflict, contribute
de-	from	decode, deduct
dis-	not, absence of, apart	disgust, disinterest, discuss
ex-	out, from	excavate, expand
fore-	before, in front of	forehand, foretell
in-	not; into, toward	inactive, ingrained, income
inter-	between, among	interact, interstate
mal-	bad, badly; abnormal	malfunction, malnutrition, malodorous
mid-	middle	midsummer, midterm
mis-	wrongly, badly, not	misfile, misprint, misunderstand
non-	not, without	nonstop, nonsense
ob-	down; against; facing; to	oblige, observe, obsolete
over-	beyond, above, too much	overdue, overpass, overslept
per-	through, thoroughly, throughout	perfect, perform, permit
post-	after; behind; following	postdate, postpone, postscript
pre-	before	preregister, preset
pro-	forward, in front of	progress, protect
re-	back, again	return, revisit
semi-	half	semiannual, semicircle, semitone
sub-	under, beneath; below	subcontract, submerge, subway
super-	above, over; superior	supersonic, superhero
trans-	across, through	transfer, transport
un-	not, do the opposite of	unlike, unplug
under-	below, less	underpass, undersized

Root	Meanings	Examples
aud	to hear, listen	audible, audio, audit
cap	to take, hold; catch	capable, captivate, captor
capit/capt	to head; chief	capital, captain, caption
cede	to move; withdraw	concede, precede, recede
ceed	to move; withdraw	exceed, proceed, proceeding
ceit	to take, hold; catch	conceit, deceit, deceitful
cept	to take, hold; catch	except, intercept, percept
cess	to move; withdraw	excess, process, recess
cred	to believe	credible, creditor, incredible
dic/dict	to say, tell	indicate, predict
duc/duct	to lead	educate, conduct
fac	to make, do	facsimile, faculty
fact	to make, do	factory, benefactor
fec	to make, do	affect, defector
fer	to bear; carry	confer, defer, infer
fic	to make, do	difficult, significant
flect	to bend; curve	deflect, inflect, reflect
flex	to bend; curve	flexibility, flexor, reflex
form	to shape	reform, transform
frac	to break	fraction, fracture, refraction
gen	birth; kind; origin	gender, gene, generous
grad/gress	to step; degree	degradation, aggressive, congress
ject	to throw	reject, projectile
junct	to join	adjunct, injunction, juncture
lumen	to light	illuminate, luminous
mis	to send; let go	admission, dismiss, promise
mit	to send; let go	admit, commit, permit
pel/puls	to drive, push	compel, repulse
pend/pens	to hang, pay, weigh	pendulum, compensate, pensive

Root	Meanings	Examples
plex	to fold; twist; weave	complex, duplex, perplex
pli	to fold; twist; weave	pliable, pliant, pliers
plic	to fold; twist; weave	complicate, explicit, implicate
pon	to put; place	component, exponent, proponent
port	to carry	deport, export
pos	to put; place	deposit, disposal, positive
pound	to put; place	compound, expound, impound
rect/reg	right, straight	correct, direct, regal
rupt	to break, burst	disrupt, interrrupt, erupt
scrib/script	to write	inscribe, transcript
sist	to stand; put in place	assist, consist, insist
spect	to look at, see, watch	inspect, prospector, spectator
spir	to breathe	conspire, inspire, transpire
sta	to stand; put in place	constant, obstacle, station
stit	to stand; put in place	constitution, destitute, substitute
struct	to build	construct, instruction, obstruct
tain	to hold	contain, detain, retain
ten	to hold	content, retentive, tenure
tend/tens/tent	to stretch; strain	attend, extensive, pretentious
tin	to hold	continue, discontinue, pertinent
tract	to pull	extract, retract
vers	to turn	converse, reverse, universe
vert	to turn	divert, invert, revert
vid	to see	evident, provide, video
vis	to see	invisible, visitor, visor

Suffix	Meanings	Examples
-able	capable of, can do	dependable, lovable
-age	collection; mass; relationship	baggage, foliage, parentage

Suffix	Meanings	Examples
-al	relating to; characterized by	educational, formal, natural
-ance	act or condition of	acceptance, insurance, performance
-ate	cause to be, having the quality of	illustrate, considerate
-dom	state or condition of being	freedom, stardom
-en	to become, made of, caused to be or have	deepen, stiffen, widen
-ence	action; state; quality	influence, existence, difference
-er	someone who, something that	entertainer, trainer
-ful	full of, characterized by	colorful, painful
-ial	relating to; characterized by	adverbial, collegial, residential
-ible	capable of; can do; able to be	expressible, reducible, responsible
-ic	of; pertaining to; characterized by	economic, historic, symbolic
-ist	someone who	artist, medalist
-ity	state or quality of	finality, legality, rigidity
-ive	causing; making; characterized by	active, impressive, objective
-ize	cause to be, become, resemble	legalize, memorize, humanize
-less	without, lacking	spotless, helpless
-ly	how something is done	quickly, softly
-ment	state, act, or process of	agreement, ailment
-ness	state, quality, condition, degree of	lateness, sweetness, thickness
-or	someone who, something that	director, donor
-ous	full of, having, characterized by	humorous, rigorous, nervous
-sion	act of; state of; result of	collision, depression, permission
-some	characterized by	lonesome, tiresome
-tion	act of; state of; result of	action, condensation, education
-ual	relating to; characterized by	actual, effectual, eventual
-ure	state of; process; function; office	departure, closure, legislature
-y	characterized by, consisting of, the quality or condition of	funny, stormy, tricky

Signal Words Based on Bloom's Taxonomy

Category	Meaning	Location
Remember Units 7–8	Retrieve relevant knowledge from long-term memory	
list	state a series of names, ideas, or events	Unit 7
locate	find specific information	
name	label specific information	
recognize	know something from prior experience or learning	
state	say or write specific information	
describe	state detailed information about an idea or concept	Unit 8
recall	retrieve information from memory to provide an answer	
repeat	say specific infomation again	
retrieve	locate information from memory to provide an answer	
Understand Units 9–12	Construct meaning from instructional messages, including oral, written, and graphic communication	
conclude	arrive at logical end based on specific information	Unit 9
define in your own words	tell the meaning of something in one's own words	
illustrate	present an example or explanation in pictures or words	
predict	foretell new information from what is already known	
tell	say or write specific information	
identify	locate specific information in the text	Unit 10
paraphrase	restate information in somewhat different words to simplify and clarify	
summarize	restate important ideas and details from multiple paragraphs or sources	

Category	Meaning	Location
categorize	place information into groups	Unit 11
classify	organize into groups with similar characteristics	
discuss	talk about or examine a subject with others	
match	put together things that are alike or similar	
sort	place or separate into groups	
compare	state the similarities between two or more ideas	Unit 12
contrast	state the differences between two or more ideas	
explain	express understanding of an idea or concept	
Review **Remember** and **Understand** levels		Unit 12
Apply Units 13–15	Carry out or use a procedure in a given situation	
generalize	draw conclusions based on presented information	Unit 13
infer	draw a logical conclusion using information or evidence	
use	apply a procedure to a task	
show	demonstrate an understanding of information	Unit 14
Review **Apply** level		Unit 15
Analyze Units 16–18	Break material into its constituent parts and determine how the parts relate to one another and to an overall structure or purpose	
distinguish	find differences that set one thing apart from another	Unit 16
select	choose from among alternatives	
arrange	organize information	Unit 17
organize	arrange in a systematic pattern	
outline	arrange information into a systematic pattern of main ideas and supporting details	
Review all levels		Unit 18

Category	Meaning	Location
Evaluate Units 19–21	Require judgments based on criteria and standards	
assess	determine value or significance	Unit 19
justify	prove or give reasons that something is right or valid	
critique	examine positive and negative features to form a judgment	Unit 20
judge	form an opinion or estimation after careful consideration	
Review **Evaluate** level		Unit 21
Create Units 22–24	Assemble elements to form a whole or product; reorganize elements into a new pattern or structure	
compose	make or create by putting parts or elements together	Unit 22
design	devise a procedure to do a task	
plan	devise a solution to solve a problem	
hypothesize	formulate a possible explanation; speculate	Unit 23
revise	modify or change a plan or product	
Review all levels		Unit 24

Elements of Poetry

Poetry is a unique literary genre. A poem uses words purposefully and sparingly. Poems incorporate combinations of six different elements.

Element	Definition	Components/Examples
Thought	Thought encompasses all of the ideas contained in a poem. Often, poems contain a theme, a statement of universal truth that is not bound by time or space.	Poets convey meaning, or thought, in various ways. **Figurative meaning** is symbolic; it is not actual. **Literal meaning** is actual meaning. **Subject** is the topic of the poem. In poetry, the topic may be literal or figurative. **Theme** is a poem's principal message. A theme is usually a universal truth about the way things really are. A thematic statement is not bound by time or space; it has been true for all people, across all time. Example: *People can accomplish more together than they can alone.*
Imagery	Poets use descriptive words and figurative language to paint images in the minds of the reader or listener. Figures of speech are often used to create poetic visions. Figurative language is language that is not literal. It includes literary devices such as hyperbole, irony, metaphor, metonymy, paradox, personification, simile, and symbolism.	Some examples of devices poets use to create imagery: **Hyperbole** is exaggeration used for emphasis. Poets use it to heighten effect. Example: *I wandered, lonely as a cloud.* **Irony** is a figure of speech in which what is said is the opposite of what is really meant. Irony is often used to scorn or to attack ideas. **Metaphor** is a figure of speech that compares people, places, things, or feelings without using the words *like* or *as*. Example: *He is a prince.* **Metonymy** is a figure of speech that uses a word to represent a closely related word. Example: *The White House announced a new crackdown.* **Paradox** is a statement containing seemingly contradictory elements, which on closer inspection may be true. Example: *Nature's first green is gold.* **Personification** is figurative language that assigns human characteristics to an animal, an idea, or a thing. Examples: *Elephants waltzed across the plains, The past spoke to her, The ship protested as it struggled against the rising seas.* **Simile** is a figure of speech that uses *like* or *as* to compare two unlike things that resemble each other in some way. Examples: *He runs like the wind, Her dreams are as big as the ocean.* **Symbolism** is a poetic device in which one thing represents a different thing or idea. In *Moby Dick*, the white whale is the symbol of evil.

Element	Definition	Examples/Components
Mood	The emotion that a poem stirs is its mood. Poets use words, imagery, rhythm, and sound to help establish the mood of a poem.	A poem's mood may be peaceful, somber, joyous, sorrowful, hopeful, pensive, gloomy, longing, hopeful, wistful, or contemplative. A poet sets a tone in the attitude toward the subject. A poet's tone may be playful, ironic, angry, formal, informal, optimistic, or pessimistic.
Melody	The sounds of the words in a poem create its melody. Poets often repeat the same phonemes for special melodic effects.	Some examples of devices poets use to create melody: **Alliteration** is the repetition of initial consonant sounds. Example: *Calm and confident, the carolers came out singing clearly.* **Assonance** is the repetition of vowel sounds without actual rhyme. Example: *Meek but regal, she became queen.* **Consonance** is the repetition of consonant sounds in words. Example: *Some memories of Amy smile at me through time.* **Onomatopoeia** is created when the sound of a word suggests its meaning. Examples: *crash, hush, jiggle, slam, buzz, screech, whirr, sizzle, crunch, wring, wrench, gouge, grind, mangle, bang, bam, crackle, pow, zap, fizz, roar, growl, blip, click.* **Rhyme** is the repetition of all the sounds, beginning with and following a word's first vowel sound. Examples: *ran/ can; version/excursion; string/bring; got/lot; tense/cents.*

Element	Definition	Examples/Components
Meter	Poems often establish a beat or rhythm. In a poem with regular meter, every other syllable or every third syllable is usually accented.	Poets often use meter to create a rhythmic tempo, or cadence. **Rhythm** is created with a pattern of accented and unaccented syllables in a line of poetry. The accent usually falls on every second or every third syllable. The **metric foot** is the basic unit of poetic meter, the rhythmic pattern of stressed and unstressed syllables. A foot consists of a group of two or three syllables. Each syllable is either stressed (/) or unstressed (0). The most common types of metric feet include these: Iamb: 0/ (I think´ that I´ shall ne´ver see´) trochee /0 (By´ the shores´ of Gitch´ee Gu´mee) anapest 00/ (Not a crea´ture was stir´ring, not e´ven a mouse´) dactyl /00 (Cling´ for eter´ nity, each´ to the o´ ther) **Meter**, or versification, is the regular pattern of unstressed and stressed syllables in a line of poetry. The most common meter in English poetry is iambic pentameter. Meter can be classified by the number of metric feet in each line: 1 foot: monometer 6 feet: hexameter 2 feet: dimeter 7 feet: heptameter 3 feet: trimeter 8 feet: octameter 4 feet: tetrameter 9 feet: nonameter 5 feet: pentameter Examples: In ancient Greece, Homer and Virgil wrote in dactylic hexameter. In Elizabethan England, Shakespeare wrote in iambic pentameter. Edgar Allen Poe wrote his famous *The Raven* in trochaic octameter.
Form	Form is the poem's actual structure or appearance on a page.	Poets use many different verse forms. For example, a poem whose shape reinforces its meaning is a concrete poem. Other examples of **verse form** include: ballad, blank verse, cinquain, couplet, haiku, limerick, ode, free verse, sestina, sonnet, and villanelle.

Grammar and Usage References

Noun Form and Function (Units 1, 2, 3, 4, 7, 8, 9, and 11)

Form	Function
Adding the suffix -**s** to most singular nouns	makes a **plural noun**.
• map + s = maps • cab + s = cabs • mast + s = masts	• I had the **maps** at camp. • The **cabs** are fast. • The bats sat on the **masts**.
Adding the suffix -**es** to nouns ending in **s**, **z**, **x**, **ch**, **sh**, or **tch**	makes a **plural noun**.
• dress + es = dresses • fizz + es = fizzes • box + es = boxes • rich + es = riches • dish + es = dishes • match + es = matches	• Rose bought three new **dresses**. • They drank cherry **fizzes**. • The **boxes** were full of books. • The safe contains many **riches**. • The **dishes** fell to the floor. • The wet **matches** did not light.
Adding the suffix -**'s** to nouns	makes a **possessive singular noun**.
• Stan + 's = Stan's • van + 's = van's • man + 's = man's	• **Stan's** stamps are at camp. • The **van's** mat is flat. • The **man's** plan is to get clams.
Adding the suffix -**'s** to nouns	makes a **possessive plural noun**.
• boy + s' = boys' • girl + s' = girls' • dog+ s' = dogs'	• The **boys'** cards were missing. • The **girls'** snacks are on the table. • The **dogs'** bowls are empty.
Adding the **'** to a plural noun ending in -**es**	makes a **possessive plural noun**.
• foxes + ' = foxes' • fishes + ' = fishes'	• The **foxes'** den is snug. • The **fishes'** fins make waves.

Count Nouns—Nouns that can be specifically counted		
Rules	**Form**	**Examples**
• Can be preceded by the indefinite articles in the **singular** form	a an	a **bicycle**, a **cat**, a **table** an **insect**
• Can be made **plural**	-s -es	**bicycles, cats, tables, insects** **dresses, riches, suffixes**
• Can be preceded by the definite article in the **singular** form • Can be preceded by the definite article in the **plural** form when referring to specific objects, groups, or ideas	the	the **pencil**, the **pencils** the **insect**, the **insects** the **truck**, the **trucks**
• Can be preceded by the zero article (Ø) in the **plural** form	zero article (Ø)	(Ø) **Bicycles** are fun to ride. I see (Ø) **stars** in the sky. (Ø) **Insects** are not fun.
• Can be preceded by determiners in the **singular** form	this	This **bicycle** is red. This **lunch** is good. This **table** is round.
	that	That **insect** is big. Do not light that **match**! That **truck** is running.
• Can be preceded by determiners in the **plural**	these those	These **trucks** are red. Those **workers** are strong.
• Can be preceded by quantity adjectives **a lot of**, **any**, **many**, **some**, **a few**, and **fewer**	a lot of any many some a few fewer	He has a lot of **friends**. I don't have any red **pencils**. She has many **cats**. I saw some **stars** in the sky. I need a few **paper clips**. I'd like fewer **slices** of meat.
• Cannot be preceded by the quantity adjectives **much** or a **little**		NOT: She has much apples. There are a little stars in the sky.

Noun Form and Function (*continued*)

Noncount Nouns		
Cannot be specifically counted, but can be measured		
Rules	**Form**	**Examples**
• Can only be used in the singular form	singular	That was **fun**. The plant needs **water**. The pen is out of **ink**.
• Never take indefinite articles **a** and **an**		The room is filled with **smoke**. You need **cash** for the movie. I want **mustard** on my sandwich.
• Sometimes take the definite article **the**, if it refers to a specific object, group, or idea	**the**	Please pass me the **pasta**. The **soup** is on the table. Wash the **dirt** from your hands.
• Can be preceded by determiners **this** and **that**	**this** **that**	This **corn** tastes great! That **water** looks dirty.
• Can be preceded by quantity adjectives **a lot of**, **any**, **much**, **some**, **a little**, and **less**	**a lot of**	There is a lot of **mud** on the truck. I have a lot of **stuff**.
	any	This isn't any **fun**. I don't smell any **smoke**. Do you want any **rice**?
	much	This isn't much **fun**. That man has so much **hair**! Don't give me too much **jelly**.
	some	I want some **water**. Please pass me some **mustard**.
	a little	This popcorn needs a little **salt**. Please give me a little **pasta**.
	less	I'd like less **meat**.
• Cannot be preceded by the quantity adjectives **many** and **a few**		NOT: I have many stuff. She has a few cash.

Verb Form and Function (Units 4, 5, 7, 8, 10, 11, 15, and 16)

Form	Function
Adding the suffix **-s** to most verbs …	makes the verbs **third person singular**, **present tense**.
• sit + s = sits • skid + s = skids • pack + s = packs	• The rabbit **sits** in the grass. • The cab **skids** on the ramp. • She **packs** her bags for the trip.
Adding the suffix **-es** to verbs ending in **s**, **z**, **x**, **ch**, **sh**, or **tch**	makes the verbs **third person singular**, **present tense**.
• press + es = presses • buzz + es = buzzes • wax + es = waxes • switch + es = switches • wish + es = wishes • pitch + es = pitches	• He **presses** the button to open the door. • The bee **buzzes** around the room. • John **waxes** his car once a month. • She **switches** on the radio. • Jamal **wishes** he had a wagon. • Monica **pitches** her trash into the can.
Adding the suffix **-ed** to regular verbs	makes the **past tense**.
• jump + ed = jumped • smell + ed = smelled • end + ed = ended	• She **jumped**. • Stuart **smelled** the roses. • The class **ended** well.
Adding **will** before main verbs	makes the **future tense**.
• will + nap = will nap • will + send = will send • will + use = will use	• The baby **will nap** after lunch. • They **will send** it later. • Ron **will use** blue paint.

Verb Form and Function (*continued*)

Form	Function
Adding the suffix **-ing** to main verbs with the helping verb **am, is,** or **are**	makes the **present progressive**.
• go + ing = going • come + ing = coming • drop + ing = dropping	• I **am going** to the circus. • She **is coming** over to visit. • Leaves **are dropping** from the tree.
Adding the suffix -**ing** to main verbs with helping verbs **was** or **were**	makes the **past progressive**.
• push + ing = pushing • dump + ing = dumping • run + ing = running	• He **was pushing** the cart. • They **were dumping** sand into the water. • She **was running** down the street.
Adding the suffix -**ing** to main verbs with helping verbs **will be**	makes the **future progressive**.
• act + ing = acting • bring + ing = bringing • swim + ing = swimming	• I **will be acting** in the play. • She **will be bringing** her list. • They **will be swimming** at 6:00.
Adding the suffix -**ing** to verbs	forms a **present participle**, which can also act as an **adjective**.
• skid + ing = skidding • cry + ing = crying • migrate + ing = migrating	• The **skidding** car crashed into the tree. • I picked up the **crying** baby. • The **migrating** birds were high in the sky.

Form	Function
Adding the suffix **-ed** or **-en** to a verb	forms a **past participle**, which can also act as an **adjective**.
• hurry + ed = hurried • drive + en = driven	• The **hurried** effort did not help. • The **driven** athlete set new records.
Adding the suffix **-ed** to regular main verbs with the helping verb **have** or **has**	makes the **present perfect**.
• walk + ed = walked • wait + ed = waited	• I **have walked** there many times. • She **has waited** for an hour.
Adding the suffix **-ed** to regular main verbs with helping verb **had**	makes the **past perfect**.
• call + ed = called • live + ed = lived	• He **had called** his friend before he left. • You **had lived** across town before you moved here.
Adding the suffix **-ed** to regular main verbs with helping verbs **will have**	makes the **future perfect**.
• solve + ed = solved • obtain + ed = obtained	• By bedtime, she **will have solved** the problem. • I **will have obtained** my degree by next summer.

Subject and Object Pronouns (Units 4, 6)

Person	Singular		Plural	
	Subject	Object	Subject	Object
First Person	I	me	we	us
Second Person	you	you	you	you
Third Person	he, she, it	him, her, it	they	them

Verb Forms (Units 4, 5, 7, 9, 10, and 11)

The Present Tense (Unit 4)

Person	Singular	Plural
First Person	I pass.	We pass.
Second Person	You pass.	You pass.
Third Person	He, she, it passes.	They pass.

The Past Tense (Unit 7)

Person	Singular	Plural
First Person	I passed.	We passed.
Second Person	You passed.	You passed.
Third Person	He, she, it passed.	They passed.

The Future Tense (Unit 10)

Person	Singular	Plural
First Person	I will pass.	We will pass.
Second Person	You will pass.	You will pass.
Third Person	He, she, it will pass.	They will pass.

Verb Forms (*continued*)

The Present Progressive (Unit 5)

Person	Singular	Plural
First Person	I am sitting.	We are sitting.
Second Person	You are sitting.	You are sitting.
Third Person	He, she, it is sitting.	They are sitting.

The Past Progressive (Unit 9)

Person	Singular	Plural
First Person	I was passing.	We were passing.
Second Person	You were passing.	You were passing.
Third Person	He, she, it was passing.	They were passing.

The Future Progressive (Unit 11)

Person	Singular	Plural
First Person	I will be passing.	We will be passing.
Second Person	You will be passing.	You will be passing.
Third Person	He, she, it will be passing.	They will be passing.

Verb Forms (*continued*)

The Present Perfect (Unit 28)

Person	Singular	Plural
First Person	I have walked.	We have walked.
Second Person	You have walked.	You have walked.
Third Person	He, she, it has walked.	They have walked.

The Past Perfect (Unit 29)

Person	Singular	Plural
First Person	I had walked.	We had walked.
Second Person	You had walked.	You had walked.
Third Person	He, she, it had walked.	They had walked.

The Future Perfect (Unit 30)

Person	Singular	Plural
First Person	I will have walked.	We will have walked.
Second Person	You will have walked.	You will have walked.
Third Person	He, she, it will have walked.	They will have walked.

Forms of *Be*, *Have*, and *Do* (Units 13, 15, and 16)

Be	Present		Past		Future	
Person	Singular	Plural	Singular	Plural	Singular	Plural
First Person	I **am**	we **are**	I **was**	we **were**	I **will be**	we **will be**
Second Person	you **are**	you **are**	you **were**	you **were**	you **will be**	you **will be**
Third Person	he, she, it **is**	they **are**	he, she, it **was**	they **were**	he, she, it **will be**	they **will be**

Have	Present		Past		Future	
Person	Singular	Plural	Singular	Plural	Singular	Plural
First Person	I **have**	we **have**	I **had**	we **had**	I **will have**	we **will have**
Second Person	you **have**	you **have**	you **had**	you **had**	you **will have**	you **will have**
Third Person	he, she, it **has**	they **have**	he, she, it **had**	they **had**	he, she, it **will have**	they **will have**

Do	Present		Past		Future	
Person	Singular	Plural	Singular	Plural	Singular	Plural
First Person	I **do**	we **do**	I **did**	we **did**	I **will do**	we **will do**
Second Person	you **do**	you **do**	you **did**	you **did**	you **will do**	you **will do**
Third Person	he, she, it **does**	they **do**	he, she, it **did**	they **did**	he, she, it **will do**	they **will do**

Irregular Verbs (Units 1–30)

Base Verb	Past Tense	Past Participle
be (am, is, are)	was/were	been
beat	beat	beaten
become	became	become
begin	began	begun
bend	bent	bent
bleed	bled	bled
blow	blew	blown
break	broke	broken
breed	bred	bred
bring	brought	brought
buy	bought	bought
catch	caught	caught
choose	chose	chosen
come	came	come
cost	cost	cost
creep	crept	crept
cut	cut	cut
deal	dealt	dealt
dive	dove	dived
do	did	done
drink	drank	drunk
drive	drove	driven
eat	ate	eaten
feed	fed	fed
feel	felt	felt
fit	fit	fit
flee	fled	fled
fly	flew	flown
forbid	forbade	forbidden
forget	forgot	forgotten
forgive	forgave	forgiven
freeze	froze	frozen
get	got	gotten

Base Verb	Past Tense	Past Participle
give	gave	given
go	went	gone
grow	grew	grown
have	had	had
hide	hid	hidden
hit	hit	hit
keep	kept	kept
know	knew	known
lay (= put)	laid	laid
lead	led	led
leave	left	left
lend	lent	lent
let	let	let
lie (= recline)	lay	lain
make	made	made
mean	meant	meant
meet	met	met
mistake	mistook	mistaken
overcome	overcame	overcome
overtake	overtook	overtaken
pay	paid	paid
put	put	put
read	read	read
ride	rode	ridden
ring	rang	rung
rise	rose	risen
run	ran	run
say	said	said
see	saw	seen
seek	sought	sought
sell	sold	sold
send	sent	sent
shake	shook	shaken

Irregular Verbs (*continued*)

Base Verb	Past Tense	Past Participle
shine	shone	shone
shoot	shot	shot
show	showed	shown
sing	sang	sung
sit	sat	sat
sleep	slept	slept
speak	spoke	spoken
speed	sped	sped
spend	spent	spent
spread	spread	spread
spring	sprang	sprung
stand	stood	stood
steal	stole	stolen
stick	stuck	stuck
strike	struck	struck
string	strung	strung
sweep	swept	swept
swim	swam	swum
swing	swung	swung
take	took	taken
teach	taught	taught
think	thought	thought
throw	threw	thrown
thrust	thrust	thrust
understand	understood	understood
wake	woke	woken
weave	wove/weaved	woven/weaved
weep	wept	wept
win	won	won
withstand	withstood	withstood
write	wrote	written

Spelling Rules (Units 5, 6, 10, 15, 17, and 22)

Rule	Examples
Words Ending With Double Letters	
At the end of one-syllable words, after a short vowel, / s /, / f /, / l /, and / z / are usually represented by double letters **-ss**, **-ff**, **-ll**, **-zz**.	• pa**ss** • blu**ff** • wi**ll** • ja**zz**
Doubling Rule	
Double the final consonant in a word before adding a suffix beginning with a vowel when: • The word is one syllable. • The word has one vowel. • The word ends in one consonant.	• sip + ing = si**pp**ing • skid + ed = ski**dd**ed
Drop e Rule	
When adding a suffix that begins with a **vowel** to a **final silent e** word, drop the **e** from the base word. When adding a suffix that begins with a **consonant** to a **final silent e** word, do not drop the **e** from the base word.	• hope + ing = **hoping** • hope + ful = **hopeful**

Spelling Rules (*continued*)

Rule	Examples
Words Ending in <u>o</u>	
When a word ends in a consonant followed by <u>o</u>, form plural nouns and third person singular, present tense verbs by adding -**es**. Adding -**es** keeps the sound for <u>o</u> long. When a word ends in a vowel followed by <u>o</u>, form the plural noun by adding -**s**.	• hero**es** • zero**es** • go**es** • video**s**
Change <u>y</u> Rule	
When a base word ends in **y** preceded by a consonant, change **y** to **i** before adding a suffix, except for -**ing**.	• try + ed = tr**i**ed • try + ing = try**ing** • happy + est = happ**i**est • happy + ness = happ**i**ness
Advanced Doubling Rule	
Double the final consonant in a word before adding a suffix beginning with a vowel when: • The word is more than one syllable. • The final syllable is stressed. • The final syllable has one vowel followed by one consonant.	• begin + ing = begi**nn**ing • regret + able = regre**tt**able

Adjectives (Units 14, 15, and 17)

Adjective	Comparative
Adding the suffix **-er** to an adjective	compares one person, thing, or group to another person, thing, or group. The suffix **-er** means "more."
• fast + er = faster • small + er = smaller • big + er = bigger	• She is a **faster** runner than Sam. • Her backpack is **smaller** than my backpack. • That group of boys is **bigger** than this group of boys.

Adjective	Superlative
Adding the suffix **-est** to an adjective	compares one person, thing, or group to two or more persons, things, or groups. The suffix **-est** means "most."
• fast + est = fastest • small + est = smallest • big + est = biggest	• She is the **fastest** runner in school. • I got the **smallest** slice of pizza. • That gym has the **biggest** swimming pool of all.

Articles With Proper Nouns

Category	Type of Name	the	Ø Article (No Article)	Examples
People	**Plural names of people**	X		the Johnsons the Garcias the Beatles the Yankees
	People with titles		X	President Kennedy Queen Elizabeth Prime Minister Indira Gandhi Senator Clinton Dr. Rodriguez
	Formal names of people with titles	X		the President of the United States the Queen of England the Prime Minister of India
Places	**Streets, roads, avenues, boulevards, and lanes**		X	First Street Peachtree Road Fifth Avenue General MacArthur Boulevard Apple Valley Lane
	Universities, colleges, and schools		X	UCLA Georgia State University Agnes Scott College Jefferson High School
	Exception: Use **the** if *of* is part of the name of the university or college	X		the University of Texas the College of Music
	Continents		X	Africa Anarctica Asia Australia Europe North America South America
	Countries		X	Brazil Japan Korea

Category	Type of Name	the	Ø Article (No Article)	Examples
Places	*Exception:* Use **the** with countries beginning with the word **United** or **Kingdom**, or containing the word **Republic**	X		the United States of America the Kingdom of Saudi Arabia the People's Republic of China the Republic of the Congo the Dominican Republic
	Hotels, motels, theaters, and museums	X		the Peabody Hotel the Standard Motel the Fox Theater the Museum of Modern Art
	Shopping malls, stadiums, and parks		X	Northpoint Mall Yankee Stadium Central Park
	Bridges, zoos, and gardens	X		the Golden Gate Bridge the Central Park Zoo the Botanical Gardens
	Oceans	X		the Arctic Ocean the Atlantic Ocean the Indian Ocean the Pacific Ocean the Southern Ocean
	Seas and gulfs	X		the Mediterranean Sea the Sea of Japan the Persian Gulf the Gulf of Mexico
	Rivers and canals	X		the Mississippi River the Yangtze River the Suez Canal
	Deserts, forests, and canyons	X		the Sahara Desert the Black Forest the Grand Canyon
	Single **lakes, mountains, and islands**		X	Lake Ontario Copper Mountain Oahu
	Plural **lakes, mountains, and islands**	X		the Great Lakes the Rocky Mountains the Hawaiian Islands

Articles With Proper Nouns (*continued*)

Category	Type of Name	the	Ø Article (No Article)	Examples
Places	**Cities**		X	Atlanta Los Angeles New York
	Exception: Use **the** when using the formal name of the city	X		the City of Los Angeles the City of New Orleans
	States		X	California New York Texas
	Exception: Use **the** when using the formal name of the state	X		the State of California the State of New York the State of Texas
Languages	Referred to in the *general* sense		X	English Mandarin Spanish
	Referred to in the *specific* sense	X		the English language the Mandarin language the Spanish language
Religions	Referred to in the *general* sense		X	Buddhism Catholicism Hinduism Islam Judaism
	Referred to in the *specific* sense	X		the Buddhist religion the Catholic religion the Hindu religion the Islamic religion the Jewish religion

Prepositions (Units 4–30)

about	before	during	on	unlike
above	behind	except	onto	until
across	below	for	outside	up
after	beneath	from	over	upon
against	beside	in	past	with
along	besides	inside	since	within
amid	between	into	than	without
among	beyond	like	through	
around	by	near	to	
as	despite	of	toward	
at	down	off	under	

Conjunctions (Units 7, 11, 14, 26, and 27)

Coordinating Conjunctions

and	but	or		

Subordinating Conjunctions

although	how	than	when	why
as	if	unless	where	
because	since	until	while	

Confusing Word Pairs

Pair	Meanings	Example Sentences	Unit
precede	Means "to come before in time or order." (*verb*)	Announcements usually **precede** the class.	25
proceed	Means "to communicate, to move on." (*verb*)	After the interruption, we **proceeded** to finish the test.	
device	Means "a plan, procedure, or technique." (*noun*)	The student invented a **device** for doing homework.	25
devise	Means "to invent or imagine." (*verb*)	The students will **devise** a plan to complete their work.	

Confusing Word Pairs (*continued*)

Pair	Meanings	Example Sentences	Unit
advice	Means "a recommendation regarding a decision or course of conduct." (*noun*)	The counselor gave **advice** about the test.	25
advise	Means "to counsel, recommend, or inform." (*verb*)	The counselor will **advise** students about their schedules.	
lie	Means "to recline." (*verb*, can never take a direct object)	The children **lie** in bed.	26
lay	Means "to put or place." (*verb*, must take a direct object)	The girls **lay** the chess pieces on the table.	
gone	Means "go." (*verb*, past participle)	He had **gone** to meet his mother.	26
went	Means "go." (*verb*, past tense)	They **went** to many competitions.	
then	Indicates time, order of events, or a summary of what was said. (*adverb*)	First, he washed the dishes. **Then**, he had to dry them.	27
than	Links two parts of a comparision. (*preposition* or *conjunction*)	Her homework in high school was much harder **than** her homework in middle school.	
like	Means "similar to." (*preposition*, can introduce a prepositional phrase, but not a clause)	I am lucky to have a caring friend **like** you.	27
as	Means "similar to." (usually a *subordinating conjunction* introducing an adverbial clause)	We treated the children **as** we would treat any younger people.	
less	Means "not as great in amount or quantity." (*adjective* expressing uncountable amounts and used with singular nouns)	There was **less** light than needed for the photograph.	28
fewer	Means "a smaller number of things or people." (*adjective* expressing countable amounts and used with plural nouns)	**Fewer** people came to see the paintings than were expected.	

Pair	Meanings	Example Sentences	Unit
bring	Means "to carry something from a distant place to a closer place." (*verb*)	She will **bring** a puppet from Europe to our local theater.	28
take	Means "to carry something from a nearby place to a place that is farther away." (*verb*)	Later, someone will **take** the puppet back to Europe.	
already	Means "by this time or previously." (*adverb*)	The movie has **already** started.	29
all ready	Means "prepared or available for action." (phrase acting as an *adjective*)	The team was **all ready** to leave when the call came.	
who	Refers to people. (*relative pronoun*)	The advertisers, **who** target young people, are very persuasive.	29
which	Refers to things. (*relative pronoun*)	Advertisements, **which** are everywhere, come in many forms.	
your	Indicates ownership. (*possessive adjective*)	Is this **your** book?	30
you're	Means "you are." (*contraction*)	**You're** late for class.	
there	Means "in that place." (*adverb*)	Place the book **there**.	30
their	Indicates ownership. (*possessive adjective*)	My brothers would not share **their** videos.	
they're	Means "they are." (*contraction*)	**They're** very thirsty.	

Phrasal Verbs (Units 22 and 23)

Phrasal Verb	Meanings
blow up	destroy by using an explosive
catch on	learn, understand
do over	repeat, redo
dream up	devise, invent
dust off	brush
eat out	dine in a restaurant
fill out	complete
fill up	fill to capacity
find out	discover
get by	survive
give away	give something to someone else for free
give back	return
go on	continue
hand in	submit
leave out	omit
look into	investigate
look up	search for
make up	invent
pass down	teach or give something to someone who will be alive after you have died
pick out	choose
point out	show, indicate
put off	postpone
put on	put clothing on
put out	extinguish
puzzle out	identify
puzzle over	ponder
run across	find by chance
run into	meet someone unexpectedly

Phrasal Verbs (*continued*)

Phrasal Verb	Meanings
set up	arrange
show up	arrive
switch off	turn off
take after	resemble
take down	write, lower
throw away	discard
try on	test the fit
turn down	lower, reject
wake up	arise from sleep

Idioms

Idioms (Units 1–30)

Idiom	Meaning
at the drop of a hat	immediately and without urging
be a fly in the ointment	be a detrimental detail; a drawback
be a fly on the wall	be somewhere secretly to see and hear what happens
be a horse of a different color	be another matter entirely; something else
be a live wire	be a vivacious, alert, or energetic person
be a piece of cake	be very easy to do
be a thorn in your side	be a constant annoyance or pain to you
be a tough act to follow	be so good it is not likely that anyone or anything else that comes after will be as good
be a tough nut to crack	be a difficult problem to solve
be all thumbs	be awkward, especially with your hands
be all wet	be entirely mistaken
be at sixes and sevens	be in a state of confusion or disorder
be at the end of your rope	be at the limit of one's patience, endurance, or resources
be beside yourself	be very concerned or worried
be down to the wire	be the very end, as in a race or contest
be fishy	cause doubt or suspicion
be fit as a fiddle	be in good health
be head and shoulders above the rest	be much better than other similar people or things
be in a pickle	be in trouble or out of luck; be in a difficult situation with little hope of getting out of it
be in full swing	be at the highest level of activity
be in hot water	be in serious trouble or in an embarrassing situation with someone in authority
be in on the act	be included in an activity
be in the cards	be likely or certain to happen
be in the doghouse	be in great disfavor or trouble

Idiom	Meaning
be in the public eye	be frequently seen in public or in the media; be well-known
be in the red	be operating at a loss; in debt
be in the swim	active in the general current of affairs
be in the wind	likely to occur; in the offing
be just the tip of the iceberg	be a very small part of a larger problem
be like a fish out of water	appear completely out of place
be off the hook	be released from blame or obligation
be on call	be available when summoned for service
be on pins and needles	be in a state of tense anticipation
be on the blink	be out of working order
be on the button	be exactly; precisely accurate
be on the move	be busily moving about; active; making progress; advancing
be on the rack	be under great stress
be on to	be aware of or have information about
be on your last leg	be unable to continue
be one in a million	be a very special person because of good qualities
be out at the elbows	be poorly dressed; lacking money
be out of line	be uncalled for; improper; out of control
be out of the woods	be safe from trouble or danger
be out of your hands	be no longer within your responsibility or in your care
be out to lunch	not be in touch with the real world
be over the hill	be past the prime of life; be slowing down
be over the hump	be past the worst or most difficult part or stage
be penny wise and pound foolish	be careful in small matters, but careless about important things
be the bottom line	be the final result or most crucial factor

Idiom	Meaning
be under the wire	be at the finish line; just in the nick of time; at the last moment
be up a creek	be in a difficult situation
be up to speed	perform at an acceptable level
be water over the dam	be something that is past and cannot be changed
be within an inch of	be almost to the point of
be your own worst enemy	believe things that prevent you from becoming successful
bite the bullet	face a painful situation bravely and stoically
bite the dust	fall dead, especially in combat; be defeated; come to an end
bite the hand that feeds you	repay generosity or kindness with ingratitude and injury
blow a gasket	explode with anger
blow the whistle on someone or something	expose a wrongdoing in the hope of bringing it to a halt
break a leg	used to wish someone success in a performance
break new ground	do or discover something new
break the mould	be new and different
bring down the house	get overwhelming audience applause
bring home the bacon	support a family by working; earn a living
burn the candle at both ends	work from early in the morning until late at night and so get very little rest
call into question	raise doubt about
call it a day	stop whatever you have been doing for the rest of the day
call it quits	stop working or trying
call the shots	exercise authority; be in charge
call your bluff	challenge another with a display of strength or confidence
catch red-handed	catch someone in the act of doing something wrong
catch you in the act	catch you doing something illegal or private
catch you later	see or speak to you at a later time
come apart at the seams	become so upset that you lose all self-control

Idiom	Meaning
come full circle	after changing a lot, come back to the same opinion or place you were in the beginning
come over to our side	join our group; take another position on the issue
come straight from the horse's mouth	came from the person who has direct personal knowledge of the matter
come to life	become excited
come up smelling like a rose	result favorably or successfully
cook your goose	ruin your chances
cost an arm and a leg	be high priced, though possibly not worth the cost
cover your tracks	hide evidence in order to dodge pursuers
cry uncle	show a willingness to give up a fight
cry your eyes out	weep inconsolably for a long time
cut off your nose to spite your face	make a situation worse for yourself when you are angry with someone
cut the mustard	perform up to expectations or to a standard
do the trick	bring about the desired result
don't bug me	leave me alone
draw a blank	be unable to remember something
draw a veil over	hide or avoid something unpleasant
draw straws	decide by lottery with straws of unequal lengths
drive you crazy	make you angry, confused, or frustrated
drop you like a hot potato	get rid of someone or something as quickly as possible
eat your words	retract something you have said
face the music	accept the unpleasant consequences of your own actions
fall through the cracks	pass unnoticed, neglected, or unchecked
feed you a line	deceive you
fill the bill	serve a particular purpose
fly the coop	make a getaway; escape
get down to brass tacks	begin talking about important things; get down to business
get it off your chest	let go of your pent-up feelings

Idiom	Meaning
get off your back	have someone stop bothering you
get on the stick	begin to work
get on your nerves	irritate or exasperate you
get ripped off	be taken advantage of
get the ax	get fired
get the short end of the stick	get the worst of an unequal deal
get this show on the road	get started with an act or project
get up on the wrong side of bed	be in a really bad mood
give it your best shot	try as hard as you can to accomplish something
give me a ring	phone me
give someone the shirt off your back	be extremely generous
go along for the ride	join an activity for no particular reason
go bananas	go crazy
go down the tubes	fall into a state of failure or ruin
go fly a kite	go away or stop annoying someone (usually said in anger)
go to bat for	give help to; defend
go to the dogs	decline, come to a bad end
go up in flames	be utterly destroyed
go up in smoke	be totally destroyed
have a bone to pick	have grounds for a complaint or dispute
have a chip on your shoulder	have a belligerent attitude or grievance
have a domino effect	have a cumulative effect produced when one event sets off a chain of related events
have a grandstand view	be in a position where you can see something very well
have a leg to stand on	have a good defense for your opinions or actions
have a memory like an elephant	be able to remember things easily and for a long period of time

Idiom	Meaning
have a skeleton in your closet	have a source of shame or disgrace that is kept secret
have a sweet tooth	like sweet foods
have an iron in the fire	have an undertaking or project in progress
have butterflies in your stomach	have a feeling of unease or nausea caused by fearful anticipation
have cabin fever	feel uneasiness or distress because of being in an enclosed space
have egg on your face	be embarrassed or humiliated for something foolish that you did or said
have you in stitches	have you laughing uncontrollably
have your fingers crossed	hope for a successful or advantageous outcome
have your head in the clouds	be unaware of the facts of a situation
hit a raw nerve	upset someone by talking about a particular subject
hit close to home	affect your feelings or interests
hit the books	study; prepare carefully for class
hit the ceiling	lose your temper suddenly; become angry
hit the deck	get out of bed; fall or drop to a prone position; prepare for action
hit the jackpot	win; have success
hit the roof	lose your temper; become violently angry
hit the sack	go to bed
hit the spot	be exactly right; be refreshing
hold your horses	slow down; wait a minute; be patient
keep body and soul together	be barely able to pay for things that you need to survive
keep it under your hat	keep something a secret
keep your ear to the ground	pay attention to everything that is happening around you and to what people are saying
keep your fingers crossed	hope for a successful or advantageous outcome

Idiom	Meaning
keep your shirt on	don't get angry; be patient
kick the habit	free oneself from an addiction, such as cigarettes
lay your cards on the table	discuss the issue honestly
lend a hand	help someone
let sleeping dogs lie	don't make someone angry by stirring up trouble or talking about something that has caused problems in the past
let the cat out of the bag	let a secret be known
live in a dream world	have unrealistic goals or expectations
look a gift horse in the mouth	be critical or suspicious of something you have received as a gift or for free
look down your nose at	regard with contempt or condescension
look up to	admire
make a beeline	go straight toward something
make a dent in	get started with a series of chores
make a drop in the bucket	make an insufficient or inconsequential amount in comparison to what is required
make a mountain out of a molehill	exaggerate a minor problem
make no bones about	be forthright and candid about; acknowledge freely
make the grade	measure up to a given standard
make tracks	move or leave in a hurry
make waves	cause a disturbance or controversy
make your skin crawl	make you feel afraid or digusted
make your toes curl	make you feel very embarrassed for someone; frighten or shock someone
miss the boat	arrive too late and miss out on something
move mountains	achieve something that is very difficult
not have the stomach for something	not feel brave or determined enough to do something unpleasant
open a can of worms	set unpleasant events in motion

Idiom	Meaning
open your eyes	become aware of the truth of a situation
paint the town red	go on a spree; go out and have a good time
pass the buck	shift responsibility or blame to another person
pass the hat	take up a collection of money
pat on the back	congratulate; encourage someone
play into the hands of	act or behave so as to give an advantage to (an opponent)
play possum	pretend to be sleeping or dead
play the game	behave according to the accepted customs
play with fire	take part in a dangerous or risky activity
point you in the right direction of something	suggest that you do or buy a particular thing
pound the pavement	travel the streets on foot, especially in search of work
prey on your mind	worry constantly about something
pull a fast one	play a trick or carry out a fraud
pull the rug out from under you	remove all support and help from you; ruin your plans, hopes, or dreams
pull your leg	kid, fool, or trick you
push your luck	expect continued good fortune
put all your eggs in one basket	risk everything all at once
put the cart before the horse	do things out of order; not do things logically
put to bed	make final preparations for completing a project
put two and two together	draw the proper conclusions from existing evidence or indications
put your finger on something	point out or describe exactly; find something
put your house in order	organize your affairs in a sensible, logical way
put your shoulder to the wheel	work hard at something; make a concentrated effort
ring a bell	arouse an indistinct memory

Idiom	Meaning
rock the boat	make trouble; risk spoiling a plan
rub your nose in it	remind you of something unfortunate that has happened
run in the family	be characterized by something common to many members of the same family
run like clockwork	operate with machinelike regularity and precision; perfectly
run out of gas	exhaust your energy or enthusiasm
saved by the bell	rescued from a difficult situation just in time
see eye-to-eye	be in agreement
see the writing on the wall	see the dark side of the cvourse of future events
seize the day	take advantage of present opportunities
send someone packing	dismiss someone abruptly
set the scene	describe a situation where something is going to happen soon
shake a leg	hurry
shoot the breeze	talk idly; have a trivial conversation
sink or swim	fail or succeed on your own
skate on thin ice	take a big chance; risk danger
snap out of it	go back to your normal condition from depression, grief, or self-pity
stack the deck	order things against someone
steal the scene	be the most popular or the best part of an event or situation
step on your toes	offend or hurt someone's feelings
stick to your ribs	be substantial or filling (used with food)
stick your neck out	take a risk
straddle the fence	to be undecided or uncommitted
stretch the rules	do something or allow someone to do something which is not usually allowed
stretch your legs	walk
strike a chord	remember something because it is similar to what you are talking about

Idiom	Meaning
strike it rich	gain sudden financial success
stuck in a rut	staying in a way of living that never changes
take a dim view of	disapprove of something
take a hike	leave because your presence is unwanted
take a rain check	ask to do something at a later date
take a shot in the dark	take a wild guess; an attempt that has little chance of succeeding
take a stand	take an active role in demonstrating your belief in something
take an eye for an eye	permit an offender to suffer what a victim has suffered
take at your word	be convinced of your sincerity and act in accord with what you say
take five	take a short rest or break, as of five or ten minutes
take it from the top	start from the beginning
take the bull by the horns	deal with a problem directly and resolutely
take the cake	be the most outrageous or disappointing; win the prize; be outstanding
take the rough with the smooth	accept the unpleasant parts of a situation as well as the pleasant parts
the sky is the limit	have no limit to what you can spend, how far you can go, or what you can achieve
throw a curve ball	surprise someone with something that is difficult or unpleasant to deal with
throw caution to the wind	take a huge risk; be very daring; act recklessly and hastily
throw the baby out with the bath water	throw out something valuable along with something useless
tilt at windmills	confront and engage in conflict with an imagined opponent or threat
turn over a new leaf	make a new start; abandon your faults
turn your back on	deny; reject; abandon; foresake
wait for the other shoe to drop	wait for an event that seems likely to happen

Idiom	Meaning
waste your breath	accomplish nothing after talking to someone
weave a tangled web	be involved in a complicated decision
(when) push comes to shove	(when) the situation becomes more difficult or matters escalate
whistle in the dark	attempt to keep up your courage
win by a landslide	get the most of the votes in an election
wing it	go through a situation or process without any plan
work like a dog	work very hard
work like a dream	work very well
work your fingers to the bone	labor extremely hard; toil
wouldn't dream of doing something	never do something because you think it is wrong or silly

Glossary of Terms

Books A, B, C, D, and E include these terms. Unit numbers following each definition indicate where these terms first appear.

Adjective. A word used to describe a noun. An adjective tells which one, how many, or what kind. A prepositional phrase may also be used as an adjective. Example: *The **quick** team **from the school** won the game.* (Unit 6)

Adjective, possessive. A word that comes before a noun and is used to describe the noun in terms of possession. Examples: *my, your, his, her, its, our, their. **My** desk is messy.* (Unit 7)

Adverb. A word used to describe a verb, an adjective, or another adverb. An adverb answers the questions *when, where,* or *how.* A prepositional phrase may also be used as an adverb. Examples: *He ran **yesterday**. She hopped **in the grass**. He batted **quickly**.* (Unit 4)

Antonym. A word that means the opposite of another word. Examples: *good/bad; fast/slow; happy/sad.* (Unit 2)

Apostrophe. A punctuation mark used in possessive singular and plural nouns. Examples: *Fran's hat, the boys' cards.* It is also used in contractions. Examples: *isn't, can't.* (Units 2, 7)

Assimilation. The change in the last letter of a prefix to sound the same as or more similar to the first letter of the base word or root to which it is attached. This change makes pronunciation easier. Examples: *in + legal = illegal; con + bine = combine.* (Unit 21)

Attribute. A characteristic or quality, such as size, part, color, or function. Examples: *She lost the **big** stamp. Fish have **gills**. He has a **green** truck. A clock **tells time**.* (Unit 5)

Autobiography. A special type of biography in which writers tell of their own lives, rather than someone else's. Example: *"Savion Glover: The Man Can Move"* is an autobiography. (Unit 26)

Base verb. The form of a verb without any suffixes; the infinitive form without *to.* Examples: *be, help, spell.* (Unit 7)

Biography. A type of literature that tells the story of someone's life. Example: *"Leonardo da Vinci: The Inventor"* is a biography. (Unit 13)

Clause, adjectival. A dependent clause that functions as an adjective, usually beginning with a relative pronoun. Example: *The boys, **who were best friends,** fought each other in the boxing competition.* (Unit 28)

Clause, adverbial. A dependent clause that functions as an adverb. It expands the predicate part of the sentence and usually begins with a subordinating conjunction.

Example: *I lived in the old house **while I dreamed of a new one**.* (Unit 26)

Clause, dependent. A group of words that cannot stand by itself and combines with an independent clause to create meaning. Example: *. . . while I dreamed of a new one.* (Unit 26)

Clause, independent. A group of words that has one subject and one predicate, representing a complete thought. Examples: *The poet wrote quickly. The poem rhymes.* (Unit 25)

Climax. A sequential point in narrative literature. It is the turning point in a story, the point at which tension drops and the falling action begins. (Unit 27)

Colon. A punctuation mark used to follow the greeting in a business letter, introduce a list following an independent clause, or separate the hour from minutes when writing time. Examples: Dear Mr. Wilson: *. . . We had many pets: cats, dogs, and rabbits. 11:30 a.m.* (Unit 26)

Comma. A punctuation mark used to signal a pause when reading or writing to clarify meaning. Example: *Due to snow**,** school was cancelled.* (Unit 5)

Command. A sentence that makes a request. Example: *Show the parts of the invention.* (Unit 13)

Compare and contrast. A type of paragraph or composition that tells how two or more things are alike and how they are different. (Unit 25)

Compound word. A word made up of two or more smaller words. Examples: *backdrop, hilltop.* (Unit 3)

Conclusion. How a story ends. (Unit 27)

Conflict. The major problem faced by the main characters in a story, also called rising action. (Unit 27)

Conjunction, coordinating. A function word that joins words, phrases, or clauses in a sentence or across two sentences. Examples: *and, but, or.* (Unit 7)

Conjunction, subordinating. A word that establishes the relationship between a dependent clause and the rest of the sentence. Examples: *because, if, while.* (Unit 26)

Consonant. A closed speech sound in which the airflow is restricted or closed by the lips, teeth, or tongue. Letters represent consonant sounds. Examples: <u>m</u>, <u>r</u>, <u>g</u>, <u>w</u>, <u>q</u>. (Unit 1)

Consonant blend. Consonant sound pair in the same syllable. The consonants are not separated by vowels. Initial blends are letter combinations that represent two different consonant sounds at the beginning of a word. Examples: **bl**ack, **br**im, **sk**ill, **tw**in. Final blends are letter pairs that represent two different consonant sounds at the end of a word. Examples: bu**mp**, se**nd**, la**st**. (Unit 11)

Consonant cluster. Three or more consecutive consonants in the same syllable. Examples: <u>scr</u>, <u>spl</u>. (Unit 11)

Contraction. Two words combined into one word. Some letters are left out and are replaced by an apostrophe. Examples: *isn't, can't, I'd.* (Unit 7)

Digraph, consonant. Two-letter grapheme that represents one consonant sound. Examples: <u>ch</u> (chop), <u>sh</u> (dish), <u>th</u> (thin). (Unit 8)

Digraph, vowel. Two-letter grapheme that represents one vowel sound. Examples: <u>ai</u> (rain), <u>ee</u> (see), <u>oa</u> (boat). (Unit 19)

Direct object. A noun or pronoun that receives the action of the main verb in the predicate. It answers the question: Who or what received the action? Examples: *Casey hit the **ball**. She dropped the **mitt**.* (Unit 3)

Direct object, compound. Two direct objects joined by a conjunction in a sentence. Example: *The bugs infest **crops and animals**.* (Unit 9)

Doubling rule. A spelling rule in English that doubles a final consonant before adding a suffix beginning with a vowel when 1) a one-syllable word 2) with one vowel 3) ends in one consonant. Examples: *hopping, robbed.* (Unit 6)

Drama. A story, such as a play, musical, or opera, written for characters to act out. Example: *"These Shoes of Mine."* (Unit 15)

Expository text. Text that provides information and includes a topic. Facts and examples support the topic. Example: *"What Is Jazz?"* (Unit 5)

Expression. A common way of saying something. An expression is similar to an **idiom**. Example: *all wet* means "mistaken; on the wrong track." (Unit 7)

Fable. A literary genre whose main characters are usually animals. A fable teaches a moral lesson. Example: *"The Tortoise and the Hare"* is an example of a fable. (Unit 19)

Fiction. A literary genre that includes stories that are not true. Fiction is sometimes based on real people, places, or events. *"Raymond's Run"* is an example of fiction. (Unit 19)

Figurative language. Language that is not literally true. It includes literary devices such as simile, metaphor, personification, and symbol. (Unit 29)

First-person account. A type of writing, either fiction or nonfiction, in which the narrator recalls personal experiences. Example: *"A. H. Gardiner's Account"* in *"King Tut: Egyptian Pharaoh."* (Unit 17)

First person point of view. A narrative told from the perspective of the storyteller. Examples: *To come. To come. To come.* (Unit 27)

Folktale. A literary genre consisting of an old story, told over many generations, about a hero or nature. Early folktales were told orally and often changed as they were retold. Example: "*A Collection of Puzzling Tales.*" (Unit 22)

Form. The element of poetry that defines the poem's actual structure. Examples of poetic forms include quatrain, sonnet, and free verse. (Unit 25)

Future perfect. A verb form that expresses an action that will be completed in the future before another future action. The future perfect is formed with **will have** plus the past participle. Example: *By next Friday,* **I will have finished** *Anne Frank's diary.* (Unit 21)

Genre. A literary category. Examples of genres include: biography, fiction, folktale, nonfiction, science fiction, and short story. (Unit 13)

Homophones. Words that sound the same but have different meanings. Examples: *son/sun; some/sum; one/won.* (Unit 7)

Idiom. A common phrase that cannot be understood by the meanings of its separate words— only by the entire phrase. Example: *be in the wind* means "likely to occur." (Unit 4)

Imagery. The element of poetry which refers to the creation of mental pictures, or images, for the reader. Metaphor, simile, and personification are examples of techniques that poets use to create imagery. (Unit 25)

Indirect object. A noun or pronoun often placed between the main verb and the direct object. It tells to whom or for whom the action was done. Example: *The king offered his* **son** *a gift.* (Unit 17)

Loan words. Words borrowed by English from other languages. Examples: *atrium, enchilada, suede.* (Unit 27)

Melody. The element of poetry which is created by a poet's use of sound. Examples of melody include alliteration, rhyme, assonance, consonance, and onomatopoeia. (Unit 25)

Metaphor. A figure of speech that compares people, places, things, or feelings without using the words *like* or *as.* Examples: *He is a* **prince**. *Her* **sunny** *smile.* (Unit 14)

Meter. Patterns of stressed and unstressed syllables create meter or poetic rhythm. (Unit 25)

Mood. A literary device in a text or poem that conveys a general emotion of a work or an author. Example: "*The First Transcontinental Railroad*" uses mood as a literary device. (Unit 18)

Mystery. A literary genre in which the author creates suspense around an unknown and provides clues for the reader, who tries to predict the unknown. Example: *"The Disappearing Man."* (Unit 22)

Myth. An anonymous tale based on the traditional beliefs of a culture that often includes supernatural beings and heroes. Example: *"Legendary Superheroes."* (Unit 15)

Narrative text. Text that tells a story. A story has characters, settings, events, conflict, and a resolution. Example: *"Atlas: The Book of Maps."* (Unit 2)

Noun. A word that names a person, place, thing, or idea. Examples: *teacher, city, bat, peace.* (Unit 1)

Noun, abstract. A word that names an idea or a thought that we cannot see or touch. Examples: *love, Saturday, sports, democracy.* (Unit 3)

Noun, common. A word that names a general person, place, or thing. Examples: *man, city, statue.* (Unit 3)

Noun, concrete. A word that names a person, place, or thing that we can see or touch. Examples: *teacher, city, pencil.* (Unit 3)

Noun, proper. A word that names a specific person, place, or thing. Examples: *Mr. West, Boston, Statue of Liberty.* (Unit 3)

Onomatopoeia. A literary device created when a word's sound suggests its meaning. Examples: *crash, bang, zip.* (Unit 16)

Open syllable. A syllable ending with a vowel sound. Examples: *go, be, pay.* (Unit 15)

Participial phrase. A phrase that begins with a participle and is followed by a word (or group of words) that modifies it or receives its action. It functions as an adjective. Examples: *The tsunami, **crashing on the shore**, caused devastation. He stood on the bridge, **watching the people go by**.* (Unit 26)

Past participle. The **-ed** or **-en** form of a verb after the helping verbs **have**, **has**, **had**, or **will have**. It can also act as an adjective to describe a noun. Examples: *Traffic clogged the **divided** highway. The **driven** athlete set new records.* (Unit 16)

Past perfect. A verb form that shows that one action in the past happened before another action in the past. The past perfect is formed with **had** and the past participle of the main verb. Example: *Anne Frank **had received** a diary before she went into hiding.* (Unit 21)

Perfect. A verb form used to place the time of one action relative to the time of another action. (Unit 21)

Personification. Figurative language that assigns human characteristics to an animal, idea, or a thing. Example: *"Roberto Clemente: The Heart of the Diamond."* (Unit 16)

Persuasive essay. A form of writing designed to influence the reader. Specific components include a statement of position, reasons and supporting facts or examples, anticipated objections, and a call for action. (Unit 29)

Phonogram. A set of letters that consistently represents a set of sounds. Example: *qua* for / kwŏ / as in **quad**. (Unit 29)

Phrasal verb. A verb that usually consists of two parts. The first part is the verb and the second part is a word that looks like a preposition but does not function like a preposition. Instead, it is part of the meaning of the phrasal verb. The meaning of a phrasal verb is usually different from the meanings of its individual words. Example: *She **tried on** her new dress.* (Unit 22)

Phrase. A group of words that does the same job as a single word. Examples: *at lunch, in the park, to stay in shape.* (Unit 4)

Plot. A literary term referring to the pattern of events in a narrative or drama. Example: *"The Marble Champ."* (Unit 20)

Plural. A term that means "more than one." In English, nouns are made plural by adding **-s** or **-es**. Examples: *figs, backpacks, dresses.* (Unit 1)

Poetry. A type of literature that includes some or all of these six elements: thought, imagery, mood, melody, meter, and form. Poetry selections are included in *"Circle Poems Take Many Forms."* (Unit 25)

Predicate. One of two main parts of an English sentence. It includes the main verb of the sentence. Examples: *He **digs**. She **lost the big stamp**.* (Unit 2)

Predicate adjective. An adjective that follows a linking verb and describes the subject. Example: *Kokopelli's music is **beautiful**.* (Unit 20)

Predicate, complete. The verb and all of its modifiers in a sentence. Example: *The class **clapped during the song**.* (Unit 8)

Predicate, compound. Two or more verbs joined by a conjunction. Example: *The class **sang and clapped**.* (Unit 8)

Predicate nominative. A noun that follows a linking verb and renames, or tells more about, the subject. Example: *The girl is a **runner**.* (Unit 19)

Predicate, simple. The verb in a sentence. Example: *The class **clapped** during the song.* (Unit 8)

Prefix. A morpheme added to the beginning of a word to modify its meaning. Examples: ***mis**interpret, **non**stop, **un**plug.* (Unit 13)

Preposition. A function word that begins a prepositional phrase. Examples: *at, from, in.* (Unit 4)

Prepositional phrase. A phrase that begins with a preposition and ends with a noun or a pronoun. A prepositional phrase is used either as an adjective or as an adverb. Examples: *at the track, from the old map, in traffic.* (Unit 4)

Present participle. The -**ing** verb form that expresses present action. It follows a helping verb, such as *am, is, are.* The -**ing** forms of verbs can also act as adjectives to describe nouns Examples: *She is coming to the picnic. The running water spilled on the floor.* (Units 5, 15)

Present perfect. A verb form that shows a connection between the past and the present. The present perfect is formed with **have** or **has** and the past participle of the main verb. Examples: *I have been here for two years. She has been here for four years.* (Unit 21)

Progressive. A verb form that indicates ongoing action in time. Examples: *I am going* (present); *I was going* (past); *I will be going* (future). (Units 5, 9, 11)

Pronoun. A function word used in place of a noun. Pronouns can be subject, object, or possessive. (Units 4, 6, 7)

Pronoun, indefinite. A pronoun that refers to an unspecified or unknown person or thing. Examples: *anyone, nobody, something.* (Unit 23)

Pronoun, object. A pronoun that takes the place of the object in a sentence. Example: *Jason threw it.* (Unit 7)

Pronoun, possessive. A pronoun that shows possession. Examples: *mine, yours, his, hers, ours, theirs. Mary's desk is neat. Mine is messy.* (Unit 7)

Pronoun, relative. A pronoun that relates back to a noun or pronoun that has already been mentioned in the independent clause. Examples: *that, which, who, whom, whose.* (Unit 28)

Pronoun, subject. A pronoun that takes the place of the subject in a sentence. Also called a nominative pronoun. Example: *He ran down the street.* (Unit 7)

R-controlled syllable. A syllable that contains a vowel followed by **r**. Examples: *her, far, sport.* (Unit 14)

Resolution. The part of the story after the turning point, or climax. Also called falling action. (Unit 27)

Root. The basic meaning part of a word. It carries the most important part of the word's meaning. A root usually needs a prefix or suffix to make it into a word. Roots of

English words often come from other languages, especially Latin. Example: *ex* + **tract** = *extract*. (Unit 20)

Schwa. A vowel phoneme in an unstressed syllable that has reduced value or emphasis. The symbol for schwa is ə. Example: *lesson (lĕs'ən)*. (Unit 13)

Science fiction. A type of literature that features a setting and people that are futuristic or fantastic. Example: *"Podway Bound: A Science Fiction Story."* (Unit 13)

Semicolon. A punctuation mark used to join two related independent clauses. Example: *The poet's meanings are clear; I understood the poem.* (Unit 25)

Sentence. A group of words that has at least one subject and one predicate and conveys a complete thought. Examples: *She ran. The map is in the cab.* (Unit 1)

Sentence, complex. A sentence with one independent clause and one or more dependent clauses. Example: *The boys, who were best friends, fought each other in the competition.* (Unit 28)

Sentence, compound. Two independent clauses joined by the conjunction **and**, **or**, or **but** (Unit 10) or by a semicolon (Unit 25). Examples: *Nguyen swims **and** his brother drives. The poet's meanings are clear; I understood the poem.*

Sentence, declarative. A sentence which states a fact or opinion and ends with a period. Examples: *Their car was parked at the curb. The joke was funny.* (Unit 25)

Sentence, exclamatory. A sentence which expresses strong emotion and ends with an exclamation point. Examples: *We won! What a great day!* (Unit 25)

Sentence, imperative. A sentence which gives a command and ends in a period. Examples: *Speak more slowly, please. Watch your step.* (Unit 25)

Sentence, interrogative. A sentence which asks a question and ends with a question mark. Examples: *Have you memorized your speech? Do you play chess?* (Unit 25)

Sentence, simple. A group of words that has one subject and one predicate and conveys a complete thought. Example: *The man ran fast.* (Unit 2)

Simile. A figure of speech that makes a comparison. A simile always uses the words "like" or "as." Examples: *He runs **like the wind**. Her dreams are **as** big **as the ocean**.* (Unit 14)

Statement. A sentence that presents a fact or opinion. Examples: *The map is flat. The twins are remarkable.* (Unit 2)

Story. An account of related events. A story has characters, setting, events, a conflict, and a resolution. Example: *"Floki, Sailor Without a Map."* (Unit 2)

Stress. The emphasis that a syllable has in a word. Examples: *atlas* (at'ləs), *lesson (lĕs'ən).* (Unit 13)

Subject. One of two main parts of an English sentence. The subject names the person, place, thing, or idea that the sentence is about. Examples: ***She*** raps. ***Boston*** *digs.* (Unit 2)

Subject, complete. A subject (noun or pronoun) and all of its modifiers. Example: ***The blue egg*** *fell from the nest.* (Unit 7)

Subject, compound. A subject that consists of two or more nouns or pronouns joined by a conjunction. Example: ***Ellen and her class*** *passed.* (Unit 7)

Subject, simple. The noun or pronoun that is the subject of a sentence. Example: *The **bird** sings. The blue **egg** fell from the nest.* (Unit 7)

Suffix. A word ending that modifies a word's meaning. Examples: ***-ing***, ***-ed, -ly, -ment****.* (Unit 17)

Syllable. A word or word part that has one vowel sound. Examples: *bat, dig, tox-ic, pic-nic.* (Unit 3)

Symbol. An image, figure, or object that represents a different thing or idea. Example: *In ancient Egypt, a pyramid is a **symbol** of the creation mound.* (Unit 17)

Synonym. A word that has the same or a similar meaning to another word. Examples: *big/huge, quick/fast, fix/repair.* (Unit 3)

Tense. Changes in the form of a verb that show changes in time: present, past, or future. Examples: *act, acted, will act.* (Units 4, 7, 10)

Thought. The element of poetry that contains the poem's message. One component of thought is the theme, which is often stated as a universal truth—unlimited by time or space. Example: *Time is a great equalizer.* (Unit 25)

Transition phrase. A group of words which introduces events, creates rising action, or signals a climax in a story. Example: *Things were going well until . . .* (Unit 27)

Trigraph. A three-letter grapheme that represents one sound. Example: **-tch** (wa**tch**). (Unit 8)

Verb. A word that describes an action (*run, make*) or a state of being (*is, were*) and shows time. Examples: *acts* (present tense, happening now); *is dropping* (present progressive, ongoing action); *acted* (past tense, happened in the past); *will act* (future tense, will happen in the future). (Units 4, 5, 7, 10)

Verb, helping. An auxiliary verb that precedes the main verb in a sentence. Helping verbs include forms of *be, do,* and *have.* (Unit 11)

Verb, linking. A verb that connects, or links, the subject of the sentence to a word in the predicate. Forms of **be** can act as linking verbs. Example: *The girl **is** a runner.* (Unit 19)

Verb phrase. A group of words that does the job of a verb, conveys tense, and has two parts, which are the helping verb and the main verb. Example: *The bus **is stopping**.* (Unit 9)

Vowel. A speech sound in which the airflow is open. Letters represent vowel sounds. Examples: <u>**a**</u>, <u>**e**</u>, <u>**i**</u>, <u>**o**</u>, <u>**u**</u>, and sometimes <u>**y**</u>. (Unit 1)

Vowel diphthong. A speech sound that moves from one vowel position to another, producing a gliding sound. The two vowel diphthongs each have two letter combinations: <u>**oi**</u>/<u>**oy**</u> and <u>**ou**</u>/<u>**ow**</u>. Examples: *oil, boy, out, cow.* (Unit 23)

Unit 25

Stonehenge: Secrets of an Ancient Circle

Britannia. 2005. "Stonehenge," from the Web site http://britannia.com/history/h7.html (accessed March 1, 2005).

English Heritage. 2005. "Information on Stonehenge," from the Web site http://www.english-heritage.org.uk/stonehenge (accessed March 1, 2005).

Burl, Aubrey. 1999. *Great Stone Circles: Fables, Fictions, Facts*. New Haven, CT: Yale University Press.

Chippindale, Christopher. 1983. *Stonehenge Complete*. Ithaca, NY: Cornell University Press.

Circle Poems Take Many Forms

Neihardt, John G. 1961. *Black Elk Speaks: Being the Life Story of a Holy Man of the Oglala Sioux*. Lincoln, NE: University of Nebraska Press. Copyright © 1932, 1959, 1972 by John G. Neihardt. Copyright © 1961 by the John G. Neihardt Trust. Copyright © 2000 by the University of Nebraska Press. Used by permission of the University of Nebraska Press.

Prelutsky, Jack. 1994. "I Was Walking in a Circle," from *A Pizza the Size of the Sun*. New York, N.Y.: Greenwillow Books. Text copyright © 1996 by Jack Prelutsky. Used by permission of HarperCollins Publishers.

Wright, Richard. 1998. "716," *Haiku: This Other World*. New York, N.Y.: Arcade Publishing. Used by permission. Copyright © 1998 by Ellen Wright. Reprinted from *Haiku: This Other World* by Richard Wright, published by Arcade Publishing, New York, New York.

Wright, Richard. 1998. "745," *Haiku: This Other World*. New York, N.Y.: Arcade Publishing. Used by permission. Copyright © 1998 by Ellen Wright. Reprinted from *Haiku: This Other World* by Richard Wright, published by Arcade Publishing, New York, New York.

Circles in Nature

Cummings, E.E. 1994. "who knows if the moon's," from G.J. Firmage (Ed.), *E.E. Cummings Complete Poems 1904–1962*. New York: Liveright. Copyright 1923, 1925, 1951, 1953, © 1991 by the Trustees for the E.E. Cummings Trust. Copyright © 1976 by George James Firmage. Used by permission of Liveright Publishing Corporation.

Esbensen, Barbara J. 1996. "circles," from *Echoes for the Eye: Poems to Celebrate Patterns in Nature*. New York: HarperCollins Publishers. Text copyright © 1996 by Barbara Juster Esbensen. Used by permission of HarperCollins Publishers.

Markham, Edwin. 1913/1915. "Outwitted," from *The Shoes of Happiness and Other Poems*. Garden City, N.Y.: Doubleday, Page & Company.

Living in a Circle

The Buckminster Fuller Institute. 2005. "Who is Buckminster Fuller?" from The Buckminster Fuller Institute Web site. http://www.bfi.org/introduction_to_bmf.htm (accessed March 1, 2005).

The Buckminster Fuller Institute. 2005. "Domes," from The Buckminster Fuller Institute Web site. http://www.bfi.org/ (accessed February 3, 2005).

Welcome to Puerto Rico. 2005. "Taino Indians Culture," from the Welcome to Puerto Rico Web site. http://welcome.topuertorico.org/reference/taino.shtml (accessed February 3, 2005).

_____. 2005. "Indiana Convention Center & RCA Dome," from the Web site http://iccrd.com/dome/generalinfo_specs.asp (accessed February 3, 2005).

_____. 2005. "Hogan: Dine (Navajo) Traditional House," from the Web site http://www.kstrom.net/isk/maps/houses/hogan.html (accessed February 3, 2005).

_____. 2005. "Building a Hogan," from the Web site http://waltonfeed.com/peoples/navajo/hogan.html (accessed February 3, 2005).

_____. 2005. "The Hogan," from the Web site http://www.vanderbilt.edu/snap/culture.html (accessed February 3, 2005).

Eltsosie, Suzanne. 2005. "The Navajo Hogan," from the American Indian Social Studies Curricula Web site. http://www.marquette.edu/library/neh/eltsosie/resource/hogan.htm (accessed February 3, 2005).

Beelitz, Paul F. 1985. "The Kazakhs and Their Yurts," from *Faces*, vol. 1, no. 6. Carus Publishing, 315 Fifth St., Peru, IL 61354. All rights reserved. Adapted with permission.

Bledsoe, Helen Wieman. 1985. "Snug Arctic Houses," from *Cobblestone*, vol. 6, no. 11. Carus Publishing, 315 Fifth St., Peru, IL 61354. All rights reserved.

Bruce, Melba. 1989. "At Home With Willie Peshlakai," from *Cobblestone*, vol. 10, no. 7. Carus Publishing, 315 Fifth St., Peru, IL 61354. All rights reserved.

Cavanaugh, Laurie A. 2002. "Domes Dominate," from *Odyssey*, vol. 11, no. 6. Carus Publishing, 315 Fifth St., Peru, IL 61354. All rights reserved.

D'Alto, Nick. 2002. "Built on Thin Air!" from *Odyssey*, vol. 11, no. 6. Carus Publishing, 315 Fifth St., Peru, IL 61354. All rights reserved.

Frank, Nancy Cooper. 2003. "A Movable House: The Mongolian Ger," from *Faces*, vol. 20, no. 2. Carus Publishing, 315 Fifth St., Peru, IL 61354. All rights reserved.

Kavasch, E. Barrie. 1985. "Plains Indian Tipis," from *Faces*, vol. 1, no. 6. Carus Publishing, 315 Fifth St., Peru, IL 61354. All rights reserved.

Kavasch, E. Barrie. 1985. "Painted Tipis of the Plains Indians," from *Faces*, vol. 1, no. 6. Carus Publishing, 315 Fifth St., Peru, IL 61354. All rights reserved.

Magee, Bernice E. 1999. "The Tainos," from *Faces*, vol. 15, no. 6. Carus Publishing, 315 Fifth St., Peru, IL 61354. All rights reserved. Adapted with permission.

Miller, Brandon Marie. 1988. "Native American Architecture," from *Cobblestone*, vol. 9, no. 8. Carus Publishing, 315 Fifth St., Peru, IL 61354. All rights reserved.

The Circle of Life

Royal Shakespeare Company. 2005. "Shakespeare: Life and Times," from the Web site http://www.rsc.org.uk/shakespeare/87.asp (accessed March 1, 2005).

Shakespeare, William. 1895. *As You Like It*. Boston: Heath.

Unit 26

Tsunamis

National Oceanic and Atmospheric Administration. 2005. "Tsunamis," from the NOAA Web site. http://www.noaa.gov/tsunamis.html (accessed March 10, 2005).

Owen, James. 2005. "Tsunami Family Saved by Schoolgirl's Geography Lesson," from *National Geographic News* (January 18, 2005) from the National Geographic Web site. http://news.nationalgeographic.com/news/2005/01/0118_050118_tsunami_geography_lesson.html (accessed March 10, 2005).

_____. 2005. "Girl, 10, used geography lesson to save lives," from *Telegraph*, from the Web site http://www.telegraph.co.uk/news/main.jhtml?xml=/news/2005/01/01/ugeog.xml&sSheet=/portal/2005/01/01/ixportaltop.html (accessed March 10, 2005).

Wiseman, Paul. 2005. "Politics Enters Plan for Tsunami Warning System," from *USA Today*, from the *USA Today* Web site. http://www.usatoday.com/news/world/2005-03-02-tsunami-warning-system_x.htm (accessed March 10, 2005).

_____. 2005. "Tsunami risk areas being mapped," from *Phuket Gazette*, from the *Phuket Gazette* Web site. http://www.phuketgazette.net/news/index.asp?id=4075 (accessed March 10, 2005).

National Geographic News. 2004. "The Deadliest Tsunami in History?" from the National Geographic Web site. http://news.nationalgeographic.com/news/2004/12/1227_041226_tsunami.html (accessed March 10, 2005).

Pendick, Daniel. 2005. "A Deadly Force," from PBS Online. http://www.pbs.org/wnet/savageearth/tsunami/index.html (accessed March 10, 2005).

The Museum of Unnatural Mystery. 2005. "Tsunami: Deadly Waves," from the Web site http://www.unmuseum.org/tsunami.htm (accessed March 10, 2005).

The House on Mango Street

Cisneros, Sandra. 1994. *The House on Mango Street*. New York: Alfred A. Knopf. Used by permission of Susan Bergholz Literary Services.

Rules of the Game

Tan, Amy. 1989. "Rules of the Game," from *The Joy Luck Club*. Copyright © 1989 by Amy Tan. Used by permission of G.P. Putnam's Sons, a division of Penguin Group (USA), Inc.

Tan, Amy. 1989. *The Joy Luck Club*. Copyright © 1989 by Amy Tan. Excerpt digitalized by permission of the author and the Sandra Dijkstra Agency.

Savion Glover: The Man Can Move

Gold, Sylviane. 2005. "Bring In da Bach, Bring In da Mendelssohn," from *The New York Times* (January 2). Copyright © 2005 by The New York Times Co. Reprinted with permission.

Glover, Savion. 1999. *Savion!: My Life in Tap*. New York: N.Y.: William Morrow and Company/HarperCollins Publishers. Copyright © 1999 by Savion Glover. Used by permission of HarperCollins Publishers.

The Women's Suffrage Movement

Anthony Center for Women's Leadership. 2005. "The Susan B. Anthony Legacy Race," from the Web site http://www.rochester.edu/sba (accessed March 7, 2005).

National Park Service. 2005. "Women's Rights: National Historical Park, New York," from the Web site http://www.nps.gov/wori (accessed March 7, 2005).

Grolier's Encyclopedia Americana. 2005. "History of Women's Suffrage: Women's Suffrage," from the Scholastic Web site. http://teacher/scholastic.com/activities/suffrage/history.htm (accessed March 7, 2005).

The Reader's Companion to American History. 2005. "Seneca Falls Convention," from the Houghton Mifflin Web site. http://college.hmco.com/history/readerscomp/rcah/html/ah_078100_senecafallsc.htm (accessed March 7, 2005).

WayBack Stand Up For Your Rights. 2005."Alice Paul's Fight for Suffrage," from the PBS Web site. http://pbskids.org/wayback/civilrights/features_suffrage.html (accessed March 7, 2005).

Unit 27

Wolf Society

_____. 2005. "Eastern Timberwolf, Canis lupus lycaon, Connecticut Pack," from the Web site http://www.clcookphoto.com/grrsnap.htm (accessed March 17, 2005).

_____. 2004. "Pack Life," from the Wolf Guide Web site. http://www.

aboutwolves.org/thewolf/packlife.htm (accessed March 17, 2005).

_____. 2005. "Communication and Social Order Within a Wolf Pack: Howling," from the Web site http://canidae.ca/WCOMM.HTM (accessed March 15, 2005).

_____. 2005. "Alpha Status, Dominance, and Division of Labor in Wolf Packs: Results and Discussion," from the USGS: Northern Prairie Wildlife Research Center Web site. http://www.npwrc.usgs.gov/resource.mammals.alstat/alpst.htm (accessed March 15, 2005).

_____. 2005. "Social Organization," from the Web site http://www.bio.davidson.edu/people.vecase/Behavior/Spring2004/porter/Social%20Organization.htm (accessed March 15, 2005).

_____. 2005. "Wolf Families," from the International Wolf Center Web site. http://www.wolf.org/wolves/learn/justkids.kids_wolf_families.asp (accessed March 15, 2005).

_____. 2004. "About the Wolf," from The Wolf Society of Great Britain Web site. http://www.wolfsociety.org.uk/education.general/about-the-wolf.htm (accessed March 15, 2005).

_____. 1998. "Wolf Wisdom: Packs," from the WERC Web site. http://www.wolfcenter.org.Hertel/html/Packs.html (accessed March 15, 2005).

Mech, L. David. 1987. "At Home with the Arctic Wolf," from *National Geographic* (May), vol. 171, no. 5.

Mech, L. David. 1977. "Where Can the Wolf Survive?" from *National Geographic* (October), vol. 152, no. 4.

David Copperfield

Dickens, Charles. 1849. "Chapter 11: I Begin Life on My Own Account, and Don't Like It," from *The Complete Works of Charles Dickens* Web site. http://www.dickens-literature.com (accessed March 30, 2005).

Youth Activists Work for Social Change

Keedle, Jayne. 2003. "Taking a Shot at Stopping Gun Violence," from the *Newsweek*: Learning With *Newsweek* Web site. http://msnbc.msn.com/id/3069558/ (accessed March 24, 2005).

_____. 2005. "Leadership Stories: Niko and Theo Milonopoulous," from the Leadership Online Web site. http://www.leadershiponlinewkkf.org/stories/niko_theo.asp (accessed March 17, 2005).

Williams, Erica. 2005. "Kids campaign against gun violence in L.A.," from the Web site http://www.4children.org/pdf/502gs.pdf (accessed March 17, 2005).

_____. 2002. "Niko and Theo Milonopoulous Named Join Together Heroes," from the Join Together Online Web site. http://www.jointogether.org/gv/news/features/print/0,2060,552411,00 (accessed March 17, 2005).

Church, Gail. 1997. "Success Stories: Tree Musketeers," from the Smart Communities Network: Creating Energy Smart Communities Web site. http://www.sustainable.doe.gov/success/tree_musketeers.shtml (accessed March 22, 2005).

Stand Alone or Join the Crowd

Thurber, James. 1940. "The Fairly Intelligent Fly," from *Fables for Our Time and Famous Poems Illustrated*. New York & Evanston: Harper & Row. Used by permission of The Barbara Hogenson Agency, Inc. All rights reserved.

Bode, Janet. 1989. "Sook," from *New Kids on the Block: Oral Histories of Immigrant Teens*. New York, London, Toronto, Sydney: Children's Press/Franklin Watts. Copyright © 1989 by Franklin Watts. Reprinted by permission of Franklin Watts, an imprint of Scholastic Library Publishing, Inc.

Unit 28

A View of the Eye

Allison, Linda. 1987. "Eye See: Experiments With Seeing," from *Brown Paper School Book: Blood and Guts* by The Yolla Bolly Press. Copyright © 1976 by The Yolla Bolly Press. By permission of Little, Brown and Co., Inc.

_____. "How the Eye Works," from the Web site http://www.bausch.com/us/vision/concerns/eyeworks.jsp (accessed April 13, 2005).

My First View of Ellis Island

Corsi, Edward. 1935. "The First Time I Saw Ellis Island," from *In the Shadow of Liberty, American Quilt Teacher's Theme Guide*. New York: Scholastic, Inc. Copyright © 1993 by Instructional Publishing Group. Used by permission of Ayer Company Publishers.

Lazarus, Emma. 1883. "The New Colossus," from *Emma Lazarus, The New Colossus (1883)*, from the Web site http://wroads.virginia.edu/~CAP/LIBERTY/lazarus.html (accessed April 1, 2005).

Amigo Brothers

Thomas, Piri. 2002. "Amigo Brothers," adapted from *Stories From El Barrio*. Copyright © 1978 by Piri Thomas. Reprinted by permission of the author. All rights reserved.

Ansel Adams: View Through a Lens

Alinder, Mary Street (ed.). 1985. "Monolith," from *Ansel Adams: An Autobiography*. Boston: Little, Brown and Company. Copyright © 1985 by the Trustees of the Ansel Adams Publishing Rights Trust. Used by permission of Time Warner Trade Publishing.

View Through a Window

Jackson, Marjorie. 2003. "Through the Window in Art," from *Cricket Magazine* (June), vol. 30, no. 10. Cricket Magazine Group, 315 Fifth Street, Peru, IL 61354-0300. Copyright © 2003 by Marjorie Jackson.

_____. 2005. "Tilly Willis: Painter," from the Web site http://www.tillywillis.com/biography.htm (accessed April 25, 2005).

_____. 2005. "Biography: Ann Hamilton," from the PBS Web site. http://www.pbs.org/art21/artists/hamilton/ (accessed April 2, 2005).

_____. 2005. "Ann Hamilton," from the Albright-Knox Art Gallery Web site. http://www.albrightknox.org/acquisitions/acq_2002/Hamilton.html (accessed April 25, 2005).

Unit 29

Advertisements: It's Your Call

_____. 2005. "Cell Phones Catering To Kids," from the CBS News Web site. http://www.cbsnews.com/stories/2005/03/31/earlyshow/series.main684359.shtml (accessed April 21, 2005).

Smith, Hedrick. 2005. "National Statistics: Snapshots of Work and Family in America," from Juggling Work and Family on the PBS Web site. http://www.pbs.org/workfamily/discussion_snapshots.html (accessed April 21, 2005).

Gaudin, Sharon. 2001. "Cell phone facts and statistics," from the NetworkWorldFusion Web site. http://www.nwfusion.com/research/2001/0702featside.html (accessed April 21, 2005).

A Call to Poetry

Rodriguez, Luis J. 1989. "The Calling," from *Poems Across the Pavement*. San Fernando, CA: Tia Chucha Press. Reprinted by permission of Luis J. Rodriguez. All rights reserved.

Silko, Leslie Marmon. 1981. "Story From Bear Country," from *Storyteller*. Copyright © 1981 by Leslie Marmon Silko. Reprinted from *Storyteller* by Leslie Marmon Silko.

New York, N.Y.: Seaver Books. Used by permission of Seaver Books.

Nye, Naomi Shihab. 2002. "Postscript," from *19 Varieties of Gazelle: Poems of the Middle East*. Text copyright © 2002 by Naomi Shihab Nye. New York, N.Y.: Greenwillow Books, an imprint of HarperCollins Publishers. Used by permission of HarperCollins Publishers.

The Call of the Wild

London, Jack. 1903. "The Sounding of the Call," adapted from *The Call of the Wild*. New York, N. Y.: The Library of America, Literary Classics of the United States, Inc.

Unit 30

The Eighteenth Camel

Schmidhauser, Thelma. "The Eighteenth Camel," from *Cricket Magazine* (November), vol. 30, no. 13. Cricket Magazine Group, 315 Fifth Street, Peru, IL 61354-0300. Copyright © 2002 by Thlema Schmidhauser. Reprinted by permission.

The Pig: An Individual Dilemma

Kimenye, Barbara. 1965. "The Pig," from *Kalasanda Revisited*. Copyright © 1965 by Barbara Kimenye. Published by Oxford University Press, Eastern Africa. Used by permission of Barbara Kimenye.

A Remarkable Individual

Weihenmayer, Erik. 2001. "Zero, Zero," as adapted from *Touch the Top of the World*. Copyright © 2002 by Erik Weihenmayer. Used by permission of Dutton, a division of Penguin Group (USA), Inc.

Hike High

Arguello, Jorge, and Janan Young. 2005. "Hike High," from the Web site *Poems, Photographs & Music*, Arguello Arts & Music. http://www.majical.com/lyrics. html (accessed May 25, 2005). Used by permission of the authors.

Word History

American Heritage Dictionary of the English Language (Fourth ed.). 2000. Boston: Houghton Mifflin. http://www. yourdictionary.com/ahd/c/c/0368100.html (accessed April 4, 2005).

The Columbia Encyclopedia (Sixth ed.). 2001. Columbia University Press. http:// www.bartleby.com/65/ci/circus.html (accessed April 7, 2005).

Photo and Illustration Credits

Cover

Illustration

© Martin French/Morgan Gaynin Inc.

Unit 25

Photographs

1: © Digital Vision/Fotosearch. 16: *top.* © Royalty-Free/Corbis. 16: *bottom.* © Richard Mudhar, www.megalithia.com. 17: © Richard Mudhar, www.megalithia.com. 29: © Eyewire. 31: © PhotoDisc. 32: © Royalty-Free/Corbis. 34: © Jupiter Images.

Illustrations

18–28, 34, 37–38: Ryan Burke.

Unit 26

Photographs

54: © Yuriko Nakao/Reuters/Corbis. 56: *left.* © Jupiter Images. 56: *center.* © Eyewire (Photodisc). 56: *right.* © Jupiter Images. 58: © Jupiter Images. 60: © Jupiter Images. 64: *top.* © Corel. 64: *center.* © Frank Capri/Contributor/Corbis. 65: © Royalty-Free/Corbis. 67: © George Simhoni/Masterfile. 68: © Photodisc Blue/Getty Images. 72: © Taxi/Getty Images. 79: © Michael Walls/Corbis Outline. 80: © New York Times. 81: © Michael Walls/Corbis Outline. 83: © Michael Walls/Corbis Outline. 85: ©Bettmann/Corbis. 86: © Bettmann/Corbis. 89: © Bettmann/Corbis. 90: *bottom.* © Corbis. 90: *small.* © Corbis.

Illustrations

39: © Martin French/Morgan Gaynin Inc. 55: Steve Clark. 64–76: Ryan Burke. 79–83: Steve Clark.

Unit 27

Photographs

91: © Jeff Greenberg/Indexstock. 106–107: © Layne Kennedy/Corbis. 108–122: © Jupiter Images. 123: *left boy.* © Punchstock. 123: *left girl.* © Jupiter Images. 123: *two central boys.* © Punchstock. 123: *right girl.* © Jupiter Images. 125: Courtesy of Tree Musketeers. 127: © Joseph Mehling/Dartmouth College Photographer. 129: © Jupiter Images. 131: *girl.* © Jupiter Images. 131: *boy.* © Punchstock. 132: © PhotoDisc.

Illustrations

107: Steve Clark.

Unit 28

Photographs

133: © Veer. 148: © Jupiter Images. 150: *statue.* © Jupiter Images. 150: *ticket.* © PhotoDisc. 150: *boats in water.* © Corbis. 150: *kids at railing.* © Lucien Aigner/Corbis. 152: *ship.* © Bettmann/Corbis. 152: *Ellis island.* © Underwood & Underwood/Corbis. 167: © Ansel Adams Publishing Rights Trust/Corbis. 168: © Artville. 171:*left.* Through the Window, 1992 (oil on canvas), Willis, Tilly (Contemporary Artist)/Private Collection/Bridgeman Art Library. 171: *right.* The Red Cape (Madame Monet) c.1870 (oil on canvas), Monet, Claude (1840-1926)/Cleveland Museum of Art, OH, USA, Lauros/Giraudon/Bridgeman Art Library. 172: *left.* Marc Chagall, Paris Through the Window (Paris par la fenetre). 1913. Oil on Canvas. 135.8 x 141.4 cm (53.5 x 55.75 inches). The Solomon R. Gugenheim Museum, New York. Gift, Solomon R. Gugenheim, 1937. 37.438/ © 2005 Artists Rights Society (ARS), New York / ADAGP. Paris. 172: *right.* © The Human Condition, 1933 (oil on canvas), Magritte,

Rene (1898-1967)/National Gallery of Art, Washington DC, USA, Lauros/Giraudon /Bridgeman Art Library/ © 2005 C. Herscovici, Brussels/Artists Rights Society (ARS), New York 173: © Barbara McCann. 174: Ann Hamilton, reflection (12:15), 1999-2000, Iris print on Arches watercolor paper, edition of 10, paper: 47 x 34 inches, image: 24 x 24 inches, Courtesy: Sean Kelly Gallery, New York.

Illustrations

149: Peg Gerrity. 153–165: Ryan Burke.

Unit 29

Photographs

175: © Digital Vision/Veer. 190: *billboard, salesman.* © Punchstock. 190: *phone.* © Jupiter Images. 191: © Jupiter Images. 192: © Jupiter Images. 193: © Jupiter Images. 201: © Punchstock. 203–214: © Jupiter Images.

Illustrations

195–200: Ryan Burke. 204: Ryan Burke. 211–212: Ryan Burke.

Unit 30

Photographs

215: © Punchstock. 232-235: © Jupiter Images. 236: © Getty Images. 238–240: © Jupiter Images. 242: *left.* © Oscar White/Corbis. 242: *top.* © 2005 Jamie Bloomquist. 242: *right.* © Jupiter Images. 243: © 2005 Jamie Bloomquist. 244: © Jupiter Images. 245: © 2005 Jamie Bloomquist. 247: © 2005 Jamie Bloomquist. 248: © 2005 Jamie Bloomquist. 249: © Jupiter Images. 251: *left.* © Jupiter Images. 251: *top.* © 2005 Jamie Bloomquist. 253: © Jupiter Images. 254: © Jupiter Images.

Illustrations

231: Reprinted by permission of *Cricket Magazine* (November 2002), vol. 30, no.3. Copyright © 2002 by Carus Publishing Company.